THE SEDUCTION OF CHRISTIANITY

SPIRITUAL DISCERNMENT IN THE LAST DAYS

D0030444

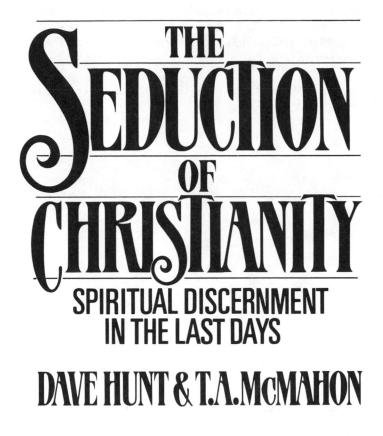

THE SEDUCTION OF CHRISTIANITY

SPIRITUAL DISCERNMENT IN THE LAST DAYS

DAVE HUNT & T.A. McMAHON

HARVEST HOUSE PUBLISHERS
Eugene, Oregon 97402

Except where otherwise indicated, all Scripture quotations in this book are taken from the New American Standard Bible, © The Lockman Foundation 1960, 1962, 1963, 1968, 1971, 1972, 1973, 1975, 1977. Used by permission.

Verses marked KJV are taken from the King James Version of the Bible.

Cover design: Terry Dugan Design

THE SEDUCTION OF CHRISTIANITY

Copyright © 1985 Dave Hunt and T.A. McMahon
Published by Harvest House Publishers
Eugene, Oregon 97402

Library of Congress Catalog Card Number 84-81211
Trade edition ISBN 0-89081-441-4
Cloth edition ISBN 0-89081-539-9

All rights reserved. No portion of this book may be reproduced in any form without the written permission of the Publisher.

Printed in the United States of America.

CONTENTS

THE SPREADING DELUSION

We have written this book reluctantly, yet knowing it had to be done. We have no desire to cause controversy or division; our sole purpose is to expose a seduction that is gathering momentum and is no respecter of persons. All of us are being affected, from the average Christian to mature and respected leaders. It is our desire to rescue rather than to condemn.

Most Christians are now in agreement that something was terribly wrong with Jim Jones; yet until the mass suicide in Jonestown almost no one recognized that fact. Even those who had suspicions were unwilling to probe deeply enough to be certain. We now know that this attitude was an unfortunate mistake. It took the deaths of nearly a thousand well-meaning people to awaken consciences to the dangers of cults and cult leaders. There is now general agreement that "cultism" is dangerous, though definitions still differ.

We are in danger of making "cultism" the measure of evil and being blind to anything else that doesn't fit a particular definition of "cultism." The church needs to recognize that cults are only part of a much larger and more seductive deception known as the New Age movement. This is a broad coalition of networking groups all working for world unity based upon religious experiences and beliefs that have their roots in Eastern mysticism. Yet many Christian leaders have expressed the same reluctance about becoming "overly negative" toward the New Age movement as they once did about the cults.

In the following pages, whenever we use the term "New Age" we are referring to the "great delusion" that the Bible warns will sweep the world in the "last days" and cause humanity to worship the Antichrist. We are also warned in Scripture

7

that many people who call themselves Christians will succumb to this deception and that a great apostasy will occur prior to the return of Jesus Christ; the delusion will sweep through the professing church as well as secular society. So it should be no surprise to find increasing controversy within the church concerning the New Age movement.

This has already begun, and the reason is fairly obvious: Christians are quite comfortable in discussing cults existing outside the traditional church, such as the Mormons, Jehovah's Witnesses, Christian Science, or Hare Krishnas. The New Age movement, however, involves things that are firmly entrenched within the church, such as psychotherapy, visualization, meditation, biofeedback, Positive Confession, Positive or Possibility Thinking, hypnosis, Holistic medicine, and a whole spectrum of self-improvement and success/motivation techniques. To criticize any of these supposedly "scientific" methodologies is to offend large numbers of Christians, including many church leaders who sincerely practice and promote these techniques.

It is a tragedy of our time that the average Christian is either too easily persuaded or cannot be persuaded at all. Too few seem willing to take the time to think the issues through and check the Scriptures for themselves. Those who would escape the growing seduction must get back to the Bible and know what they believe and why, rather than succumbing to the temptation of accepting facile answers provided by "experts." During the prophesied apostasy, even church leaders will be led astray (Matthew 7:22,23), and those who follow their teachings will suffer the same tragedy. We must be certain that we are following the Lord and not men. Jesus said:

> I am the good shepherd; and I know My own, and My own know Me. . . . And a stranger they simply will not follow, but will flee from him, because they do not know the voice of strangers. . . .
>
> My sheep hear My voice, and I know them, and they follow Me; and I give eternal life to them, and they shall never perish; and no one shall snatch them out of My hand (John 10:14,5,27,28).

To avoid the seduction that is at the heart of apostasy, we must be able to distinguish the voice of Christ through His Word from the confusing mixture of truth and error that is spoken in His name. To help make that distinction, we have conducted an extensive investigation of today's popular teachings. Some readers will find it difficult to accept the evidence because it may implicate some prominent Christian leaders. Yet the evidence will speak for itself.

In the following pages we quote from the books and sermons as well as the radio, television, and seminar talks of a number of influential Christian leaders, both men and women, past and present. Many are sincere and dedicated servants of the Lord whose lives and ministries influence millions. We cannot state too emphatically that we consider even the leaders referred to in the following pages to be among the *victims*, which we all are to some extent.

It should be clearly understood that we are not making a blanket condemnation of anyone, nor are we questioning motives. Only God can judge men's hearts, and we must leave that to Him. It is every Christian's responsibility, however, to judge teachings and fruit and to accept and follow only that which is clearly according to the Word of God. That is as true of this book as it is of any other.

It should also be understood that those whom we name are not always the worst offenders, nor are they the only examples that could be given. Even those named are mentioned only to provide documentation and to show the extensiveness of the seduction. We would caution readers not to judge specific individuals, but rather the teachings and practices that are being pointed out.

This is not a hairsplitting theological treatise but a handbook for spiritual survival. It is our deep conviction, based upon years of research and mountains of evidence, that the secular world is in the late stages of succumbing to the very deception that Jesus and the apostles predicted would immediately precede the Second Coming. We are gravely concerned that millions of Christians are falling victim to the same delusion.

1

Success and Sorcery

See to it that no one takes you captive through philosophy and empty deception, according to the tradition of men, according to the elementary principles of the world rather than according to Christ.

Colossians 2:8

When the Son of Man comes, will He find the faith on the earth?

Luke 18:8

Christianity may well be facing the greatest challenge in its history: a series of powerful and growing seductions that are subtly changing biblical interpretations and undermining the faith of millions of people. Most Christians are scarcely aware of what is happening, and much less do they understand the issues involved.

The seduction is surprisingly easy. It does not take place as an obvious frontal assault from rival religious beliefs. That would be vigorously resisted. Instead, it comes to some Christians in the guise of faith-producing techniques for gaining spiritual power and experiencing miracles and to others as self-improvement psychologies for fully realizing human potential that are seen as scientific aids to successful Christian living. Or it may take other forms. Charles Colson has written:

I have spoken of the frontal assaults and the sneak attacks. There is something worse. . . . The enemy is

11

in our midst. He has so infiltrated our camp that many simply no longer can tell an enemy from a friend, truth from heresy.[1]

A Trojan Horse Inside the Church?

Even the leading cult-watchers have generally failed to recognize the Trojan horse that has penetrated both the church and their own ranks and is seducing from within.

Strangely enough, most of today's Christian leaders who rightly cry so mightily against so many evils are saying little if anything about the revival of *sorcery* that is sweeping both the secular world and the church. In many cases it reflects a lack of awareness or naivete, and in some cases an unwillingness to admit their own involvement. Why is this? It is because most Christians are so uninformed about occultism that they wouldn't recognize it except in its most blatant forms. Nor do very many Christians seem to understand the passages in the Bible forbidding occult practices, so they cannot recognize sorcery on that basis either. In the following pages we will document the sobering fact that not only liberals but conservatives as well are being seduced in overwhelming numbers. The extent to which antiChristian and even occult beliefs and methodologies have been integrated into Christianity within the last few years is staggering, and this trend is now accelerating at an alarming rate.

The bait on the pagan hook has always been the promise of godhood that the Serpent offered to Eve. The attempt to realize this godhood has involved the human race in numerous forms of occultism throughout its history. One word that is often used to encompass all pagan/occult practices is "sorcery." In the following pages, when we use that word our intended meaning will be: any attempt to manipulate reality (internal, external, past, present, or future) by various mind-over-matter techniques that run the gamut from alchemy and astrology to positive/possibility thinking.

Sorcery: The Unrecognized Enemy

Ancient sorcery's mind-over-matter techniques often seem to

work and are radically changing our world—from science and medicine to psychology and education. Nobel laureate Roger Sperry recently said, "Current concepts of the mind-brain relation involve a direct break with the long-established materialist and behaviorist doctrine that has dominated neuroscience for many decades."[2] Physicist George Stanciu, coauthor of *The New Story of Science*, states: "Physics, neuroscience and now psychology are throwing off 19th century materialism."[3] Physics is becoming metaphysics once again as science turns to mysticism. Developed behind the Iron Curtain by Bulgarian Georgi Lozanov and catching on rapidly in the West, "Superlearning" is one example:

> Drawing from yoga, music, hypnosis, autogenics, parapsychology, and drama, Lozanov put together what he called *suggestology*, which applied altered states of consciousness to learning, healing and development.[4]

What the secular world calls "mind power" many Christians confuse for "faith." Likewise, the impersonal "Force" that occultists also refer to as Universal Mind or Nature is naively accepted by large numbers of both Christians and non-Christians as just another way of referring to God, when in fact it is a substitute for Him. Consequently, what often passes for "the power of the Spirit" in the church can scarcely be distinguished from the alleged "mind-powers" of psychics. Parapsychologists have been conducting scientific experiments with psychics for years, and the idea of "psychic power" is gaining credibility.

Professional psychics are no longer as unique as they were only a few years ago, but now number in the hundreds and are being taken seriously by a large segment of society. Moreover, similar "mind powers" are being developed by the general populace through a smorgasbord of psychological methodologies. These are not only taught by well-known mind-over-matter cults such as Scientology, the Forum (formerly est—Erhard Seminars Training), Lifespring, and Silva Mind Control, but are the standard fare at today's PMA (Positive Mental Attitude) motivational and success seminars. The ability to exert "mind over matter" is no longer considered to be something weird or occult, but is now thought to be part of a natural, normal, yet *infinite* human potential that can be experienced by anyone who follows certain alleged "laws of success."

These New Age techniques are not new at all, however, but are the same old sorcery under new labels. Many modern practitioners, including leading Christians, seem unaware of the true nature of the dangerous mind-game they are playing. Sorcery called by any other name is still sorcery, and it is everywhere in today's space-age society, seeking to hide its true identity behind scientific or psychological terminology and success/motivation and self-development labels.

An occultist himself and one of the world's leading occult authorities and historians, Manly P. Hall has declared:

> . . . there is abundant evidence that in many forms
> of modern thought—especially the so-called "pros-
> perity" psychology, "will-power building" metaphysics
> and systems of "high-pressure" salesmanship—black
> magic has merely passed through a metamorphosis, and
> although its name may be changed, its nature remains
> the same.[5]

Success Is the Name of the Game

Success is the name of the game today, not only out there in the world, but inside the church as well. Humility is out and self-esteem is in, even though we are urged in Scripture, "Let each esteem others better than themselves" (Philippians 2:3 KJV). It used to be common knowledge that the besetting sin of the human race was pride. Now, however, we are being told that our problem is not that we think too highly of ourselves, but too lowly, that we all have a bad self-image, and that our greatest need is to build up our self-esteem. Though Peter wrote, "Humble yourselves, therefore, under the mighty hand of God, that He may exalt you at the proper time" (1 Peter 5:6), we are being urged to "visualize" ourselves into success. Paul's inspired declaration that Christ "emptied Himself, taking the form of a bondservant . . . [and] humbled Himself by becoming obedient to . . . death on a cross'' (Philippians 2:7,8) is now explained by Robert Schuller, in the context of today's success-oriented world, to mean:

> Jesus knew his worth, his success fed his self-esteem. . . . He suffered the cross to sanctify his self-esteem. And he bore the cross to sanctify your self-esteem.
>
> And *the cross will sanctify the ego trip* [emphasis in the original]![6]

Success and self-esteem have become so important in the church that they seem to overshadow everything else. Robert Schuller states: "A person is in hell when he has lost his self-esteem."[7] As Christianity's "number one TV preacher,"[8] he is watched on nearly 200 TV stations each Sunday by an audience of nearly 3 million.[9] A prolific author, his books are frequently on *The New York Times* best-seller list. According to *Christianity Today*, "Schuller is now reaching more non-Christians than any other religious leader in America."[10] Schuller's influence is enormous, and his "Gospel of Success"[11] is being accepted and preached by increasing numbers of Christian leaders. What does Schuller find wrong with the old gospel? Although Paul wrote that "Christ Jesus came into the world to save sinners" (1 Timothy 1:15), and Christ Himself said that He came to call "sinners to repentance" (Luke 5:32), Robert Schuller writes:

> I don't think anything has been done in the name of Christ and under the banner of Christianity that has proven more destructive to human personality and, hence, counterproductive to the evangelism enterprise than the often crude, uncouth, and unchristian strategy of attempting to make people aware of their lost and sinful condition.[12]

If Moses lived today, it would not be said of him that he chose to "suffer affliction with the people of God" (Hebrews 11:25 KJV) but that he chose to "suffer wealth, success, and popularity with the people of God." It used to be said, "All who desire to live godly in Christ Jesus will be persecuted" (2 Timothy 3:12), but today it is said, "Those who live godly lives will be honored and successful in this world.'' Not just individual Christians, but churches also now pursue success, and the larger the church the more successful it is considered to be. On that basis, by far the most successful pastor in the world is Paul Yonggi Cho, who heads the world's largest church, with about 400,000 members. Cho teaches that positive thinking, positive speaking, and positive visualizing are the keys to success. *Anyone* can literally ''incubate'' and give birth to physical reality by creating a vivid image in his or her mind and focusing upon it. In the foreword to Yonggi Cho's book, *The Fourth Dimension*, Robert Schuller writes:

> I discovered the reality of that dynamic dimension in prayer that comes through visualizing. . . .
> Don't try to understand it. Just start to enjoy it! It's true. It works. I tried it.[13]

Christian colleges, seminaries, missions, and relief organizations are also in the success game, and most of them look to the techniques of big business for running their own affairs. If it works for the University of California, why not for a Christian college? If it works for General Motors, why not for a Christian relief organization? This is no doubt true when it comes to certain things such as accounting and management. However, sorcery is rampant in the business world and enters the church in the form of success/motivation and PMA techniques and the latest psychotherapies baptized with Christian terminology.

Think and Grow Rich

Most of the masters of business success/motivation and PMA techniques have been seduced into sorcery, and are seducing millions of other people as well. Most of the basic ideas and techniques behind self-improvement courses that literally permeate society today can be traced back to one man, Napoleon Hill. Something of the scope of Hill's influence is indicated in the following remarks by Earl Nightingale, who is one of today's most popular and influential success/motivation leaders, in a Success Motivation Institute (SMI) tape. He is discussing only one of Hill's books, *Think and Grow Rich*, which Nightingale declares to be "one of the most amazing books ever written":

> Without question, this single book has had a greater influence on the lives, accomplishments and fortunes of more individuals than any other work of its kind.
>
> All over the free world there are literally thousands of successful men in all lines of work who are where they are today because they once...bought a copy of *Think and Grow Rich*, and they'll be quick to tell you so....
>
> I've sat in richly-paneled, carpeted executive offices and listened to world-famous business leaders, some of them old enough to be my father, tell me that everything worked out fine after they had read *Think and Grow Rich*....
>
> Why has this book out of all the thousands of self-help books remained the one towering giant?... When the last page of *Think and Grow Rich* was read, the hand which put the book down on the table was a different hand. The man who then stood and walked out into the world was a different, a changed man.... The man was now the possessor of the unique, unseen talent for turning dreams into reality, thoughts into things...he who had been the passenger was now suddenly the captain.[14]

Supersalesman and top motivational speaker Og Mandino, whose books have sold more than 7 million copies, lists *Think and Grow Rich* as one of the twelve greatest self-help books of all time.[15] Napoleon Hill's books are offered at Christian bookstores across the country and recommended by numerous Christian leaders. In *Making the Most of Your Mind*, coauthors Stephen B. Douglass and Lee Roddy state:

> In recent years, a number of secular books have related success to the power of the mind. The authors of these books have begun to plumb the depths of the reservoir of potential God has placed in the human mind.

Napoleon Hill was one such secular writer.... After 20 years of research he wrote an eight-volume omnibus called *The Law of Success*, parts of which are condensed in his best-selling book, *Think and Grow Rich*.... [He] probably did the most useful research in history....[16] (*See note at end of chapter.)

The Subtle Deception

The large following that Napoleon Hill has both among successful businessmen and Christian leaders is difficult to reconcile with his open advocacy of sorcery. Hill's books contain consistently throughout their pages some of the most blatant occult teachings one could find anywhere. Yet Christians who recommend his writings, if they offer a word of caution, do so only concerning Hill's emphasis upon wealth. After quoting extensively, repeatedly, and favorably from three of Hill's books, Douglass and Roddy caution that they have quoted from *Think and Grow Rich* "because of the focus on the activities and attitudes of the mind, not the discussion of the development of wealth."[17]

Yet it is Hill's teachings *about the mind* that are far more dangerous than his emphasis on wealth. The whole point in mentioning Douglass and Roddy is that they are fine, sincere servants of the Lord who would not for a moment endorse Hill's occultism. Yet they recommend him and his books highly, which contain occultism that they apparently overlooked, and which could seduce those who, upon endorsement, read Hill's books for themselves. Hill explains in some detail that he learned the mind-power techniques contained in his books from disembodied spirit entities. Demons masquerading as Ascended Masters used Hill to deceive the millions who have adopted the "success" techniques they gave him. Hill declares:

Now and again I have had evidence that unseen friends hover about me, unknowable to the ordinary senses. In my studies I discovered there is a group of strange beings who maintain a school of wisdom....

The School has Masters who can disembody themselves and travel instantly to any place they choose...to
give knowledge directly, by voice....

Now I knew that one of these Masters had come
across thousands of miles, through the night, into my
study....

I shall not set down every word he said...much of
what he said already has been presented to you in the
chapters of this book and will follow in other chapters.

"You have earned the right to reveal a Supreme
Secret to others," said the vibrant voice. "You have
been under the guidance of the Great School.... Now
you must give the world a blueprint...."[18]

The "Supreme Secret": A Counterfeit Faith

The secrets of success that form the foundation for most
success/motivation books and seminars were given to Hill by
demons posing as "Masters who can disembody themselves and
travel instantly to any place they choose." The "Supreme Secret"
they authorized Hill to "reveal" to the world has been preserved
in occult tradition for thousands of years and reminds one of
the serpent's offer of godhood to Eve: *"Anything the human
mind can believe, the human mind can achieve."* [emphasis in
the original].[19] This seductive idea lies behind the Human Potential movement, which is another name for the New Age movement. If it is indeed true that we can achieve *anything* we conceive,
then we must be gods. This "secret of the ages" is also called
by Hill "The Magic Power of Belief."[20] Its basic premise is that
the human mind has mysterious inherent powers that are capable
of creating one's own reality: "Truly, deeply believe you will have
great wealth, and you will have it."[21] This is the sorcerer's
counterfeit "faith" and is the basis for what the secular world
calls PMA (Positive Mental Attitude). The "PMA Science of
Success"[22] was made famous by Napoleon Hill in *Success
Through A Positive Mental Attitude*, which he co-authored with
W. Clement Stone as a guide for tapping into "the great universal storehouse of Infinite Intelligence, wherein is stored all

knowledge and all facts, and which may be contacted through the subconscious...."[23] PMA is still the very heart of most success methods today. It was Hill who laid the foundation, and he explains:

> PMA is a catalyst, which makes any combination of success principles work.... PMA attracts good luck. Success is achieved and maintained by those who try and keep on trying with PMA.
> This is a universal law...that we translate into physical reality the thoughts and attitudes we hold in our minds, no matter what they are.[24]

Far from having the gracious and loving but sovereign God as its object of trust, this "power of belief" enables those who have been initiated into its secrets to *command* forces to obey their thoughts. If *anyone* can "make a miracle happen," then it isn't a genuine miracle from God, but sorcery, and man is now playing God.

Nor is it only the liberals who are falling into this trap. Presbyterian pastor Ben Patterson of Irvine, California, has observed:

> Of late, evangelicals have out-liberaled the liberals, with self-help books, positive-thinking preaching, and success gospels.[25]

Anyone who imagines that because he thinks certain thoughts or speaks certain words God *must* respond in a certain way, has slipped into sorcery, and, if not playing God, is at the very least attempting to manipulate God. Charles Capps, one of the leaders in the Positive Confession movement, says, "This is not theory. It is fact. It is spiritual law. It works every time it is applied correctly.... You set them [spiritual laws] in motion by the words of your mouth...everything you say—will come to pass."[26] Yonggi Cho declares:

> By the spoken word we create our universe of circumstances....[27]
> You create the presence of Jesus with your mouth....
> He is bound by your lips and by your words....[28]

The similarities between what these Christian leaders teach and the "Supreme Secret" given to Hill by demonic beings to share with the world is at the least highly disturbing. It is also disturbing that Christian leaders would quote favorably from Hill's writings, when it is obvious that sorcery is the very heart and substance of the success method he teaches.

We are not condemning everything else a Christian leader writes or speaks simply because he quotes Napoleon Hill. Yet it is because Hill is mixed in with so much good that his concepts are accepted. This is why we must contend for the purity of the Word of God without addition of the deadly deceptions that slide in unless we are on our guard.

Contending for the Faith

Jude wrote that we must "contend earnestly for the faith which was once for all delivered to the saints" (Jude 3). It is impossible to always be "positive" while contending for truth. H.A. Ironside, longtime pastor of Moody Memorial Church in Chicago, declared: "The faith means the whole body of revealed truth, and to contend for all of God's truth necessitates some negative teaching.... Any error, or any truth-and-error mixture, calls for definite exposure and repudiation. To condone such is to be unfaithful to God and His Word, and treacherous to imperiled souls for whom Christ died."[29] Dave Wilkerson, a pastor, best-selling author, and founder of Teen Challenge, has said:

> There is an evil wind...blowing into God's house, deceiving multitudes of God's chosen people.... It is a scriptural take-off on Napoleon Hill's book, *Think and Grow Rich*.
>
> This perverted gospel seeks to make gods of people. They are told, "Your destiny is in the power of your mind. Whatever you can conceive is yours. Speak it into being. Create it by a positive mind set. Success, happiness, perfect health is all yours—if you will only use your mind creatively. Turn your dreams into reality by using mind power."

Let it be known once and for all, God will not abdicate His lordship to the power of our minds, negative or positive. We are to seek only the mind of Christ, and His mind is not materialistic; it is not focused on success or wealth. Christ's mind is focused only on the glory of God and obedience to His Word.

No other teaching so ignores the Cross and the corruption of the human mind. It bypasses the evil of our ruined Adam nature, and it takes the Christian's eye off Christ's gospel of eternal redemption and focuses it on earthly gain.

Saints of God, flee from this...![30]

---

* As a result of the publication of *The Seduction of Christianity*, Douglass and Roddy have removed all reference to Napoleon Hill from *Making the Most of Your Mind*.

2

Paganism in Modern Dress

O God, the nations [pagans] have invaded Thine inheritance.... Help us, O God of our salvation.
                                                    Psalm 79:1,9

The things which the Gentiles [pagans] sacrifice they sacrifice to demons, and not to God; and I do not want you to become sharers in demons.
                                                    1 Corinthians 10:20

Mind Science: Linking Christianity and Sorcery

Ernest Holmes founded the Church of Religious Science, also known as Science of the Mind, upon the "Supreme Secret" that the "Masters of Wisdom" revealed to Napoleon Hill. It is closely related to the Positive Thinking of Norman Vincent Peale and the Possibility Thinking of Robert Schuller. In fact, Peale credits Holmes with making him into a positive thinker.[1] In 1958 Holmes prophesied, "We have launched a Movement which, in the next 100 years, will be the great new religious impulsion of modern times...[destined] to envelop the world...."[2] Here is the way Holmes explained this "Supreme Secret":

SCIENCE OF MIND teaches that the originating, supreme, creative Power of the Universe, the source of all substance, the Life in all living things, is a cosmic Reality Principle which is present throughout the Universe and in every one of us.

SCIENCE OF MIND teaches that Man controls the course of his life. . . by mental processes which function according to a Universal Law. . . that we are all creating our own day-to-day experiences. . . by the form and procession of our thoughts.[3]

Man, by thinking, can bring into his experience whatsoever he desires. . . [emphasis in original].[4]

This most basic idea of ancient sorcery has taken firm hold in our modern world. It is the cornerstone of the human potential movement and the essential ingredient in success/motivation/ PMA seminars. It has also become the major link between sorcery and Christianity. Though expressed in slightly different phrases, it is the common language of all those who have, wittingly or unwittingly, replaced faith in God with a self-serving faith in some mysterious Force that can be used by our minds to get what we want. Norman Vincent Peale is, of course, one of the most successful evangelists of the power of the mind. He explains it like this:

. . .Your unconscious mind. . .[has a] power that turns wishes into realities when the wishes are strong enough.[5]

Is God a Placebo?

Robert Schuller's *possibility thinking* is the same product as Peale's *positive thinking* marketed under a different brand name. Schuller declares: "Now—Believe and You Will Achieve."[6] Paul Meyer, the president of Success Motivation Institute, expresses it this way: "Vividly imagine, sincerely believe, ardently desire, enthusiastically act and it must inevitably come to pass."[7]

Paul Yonggi Cho declares: "Through visualization and dreaming you can incubate your future and hatch the results."[8] Such teaching has confused sincere Christians into imagining that "faith" is a force that makes things happen because they *believe*. Thus faith is not placed *in* God but is a power directed *at* God, which forces Him to do for us what we have *believed* He will do. When Jesus said on several occasions, "Your faith has saved [healed] you," He did not mean that there is some magic power triggered by believing, but that faith had opened the door for Him to heal them. If a person is healed *merely because he believes he will be healed*, then the power is in his mind and God is merely a placebo to activate his belief. If everything works according to the "laws of success," then God is irrelevant and grace obsolete. All one needs to do is to exercise Hill's "power of belief." On an Amway motivational tape, Robert Schuller sums it up:

> You don't know what power you have within you!... You make the world into anything you choose. Yes, you can make your world into whatever you want it to be.[9]

Such ideas are accepted in the world as sound PMA principles, and are becoming increasingly popular within the church. For example, in March 1985 the large and evangelical Prestonwood Baptist Church in North Dallas, Texas, hosted the first Annual Christian Leadership Conference. The featured speaker was Paul Yonggi Cho, who almost always presents excellent biblical teaching sometimes unfortunately mixed with occult ideas of visualization and mind-power. Sharing the platform with him on March 18 was Mary Kay Ash, founder of Mary Kay Cosmetics. In her talk she indicated that she had learned some powerful success principles from a book by Claude Bristol. In fact it is a classic example of basic occultism being passed off as mind-power, accepted under that guise by Christians and confused for faith. Mrs. Ash said:

> Claude Bristol wrote a book called *The Magic of Believing*, and in that book he said, "Is there something, a Force, a factor or a power, call it what you will, which a few people understand and use to overcome their difficulties, then to achieve outstanding success?"...
> He [Bristol] said, "Gradually I discovered that there is a golden thread that makes life work. That

thread can be named in a single word: belief.''

Now I know that Bristol was not too concerned with *what* people believed, he simply saw in action the *power of belief,* and he recorded what he saw.[10]

Faith in God or Faith in Faith?

Many sincere Christians have been influenced by the sorcerer's gospel to imagine that faith has some power in itself. Once again, to them faith is not placed *in* God but is a power directed *at* God, which forces Him to do for us what we have *believed* He will do. At the very least this makes God subject to alleged ''laws'' that we can activate by ''faith''; at worst it eliminates God from the process altogether, putting everything in our own hands and thus turning us into gods who can make anything happen by our ''power of belief.'' If everything works according to such ''law,'' then God is no longer sovereign and there is no place for grace. All one needs to do is to exercise this ''power of belief.'' That is the basic idea behind sorcery.

In contrast, Jesus said, ''Have faith *in God*'' (Mark 11:22). Faith must have an object: It is unreserved and absolute trust *in God*. There is no one and nothing in the universe that can be trusted totally except God. True faith grows out of an obedient relationship with Him. God answers prayer on the basis of His sovereignty, wisdom, mercy, and grace, not because some ''law'' compels Him to act. He cannot be manipulated by man or angels through mental processes, spoken words, or any other device.

The Sorcerers' Goal: Masters of Our Fate

If we can make God or some cosmic Force do our bidding by the thoughts we think or words we speak, then we have achieved the sorcerer's goal: We have become masters of our own fate and can make anything happen that we want to happen simply by *believing* that it will happen. The power is in our *belief,* and God Himself must do what we *believe* He will do, because whatever we *believe* must come to pass! Rampant among

Christians today, this seductive idea is exactly what these "Masters" taught Hill and exactly what he came to believe and teach—that he could become a "Master" too:

> Know your own mind—live your own life. You can make your life what you want it to be.... Self-confident faith in yourself is an indispensable ingredient for good living....
>
> A healthy ego makes you more receptive to the influences which guide you from a region beyond the power of our five senses to know.... Unseen, silent forces influence us constantly...there are unseen watchers....
>
> I can find faith which vastly enlarges my powers... always I know I am the master of my fate, I am the Captain of my soul....[11]

That was the attractive bait on the hook, and it led Napoleon Hill ever deeper into sorcery. He rejected the God of the Bible and the Christian faith that his father crudely tried to force into him when he was a boy,[12] and instead opted for an impersonal Force or Universal Mind,[13] which he called "God." What Hill embraced was basic Hindu/Buddhist occultism, including reincarnation,[14] spirit mediumship,[15] and automatic writing.[16] The promotion of sorcery is not hidden in an obscure sentence here or there, but is plainly declared as the major theme woven throughout his books.

How the Seduction Enters the Church

How then could Christian leaders read, apparently enjoy, and recommend to others Napoleon Hill's heretical and deeply occult books? Part of it is due to the fact that psychology or business success techniques are considered to be "neutral" and therefore not threatening to Christianity. The concepts of unlimited human potential and miraculous mind-powers that presumably reside in that 90 percent of the brain we allegedly don't use are growing in popularity in the world and creating confusion in the church. Douglass and Roddy state:

> . . . God placed an incredible principle in the human mind, and. . . if we are confident and positive and assured, God can use. . . all of the chemistry that positiveness conjures up within us to help us accomplish whatever it is that we are seeking to do.[17]

This is a mixture of truth and error that sincere Christian leaders are bringing into the church. Douglass and Roddy make it very clear that they are not "endorsing the idea that a person ought to substitute positiveness for trusting in God."[18] Having said that, there is a sense of being on safe ground, and it is easy to fail to see the real danger. *Substitution* is not the big problem, since almost everyone would easily recognize and reject such obvious error. *Confusion* is the problem. There is not a word of caution to indicate that the major experts they quote for support are occultists. Napoleon Hill and W. Clement Stone, for example, talk about "God" in the books that Douglass and Roddy recommend, but their "God" is a metaphysical "Divine Power"[19] that can be tapped into through mind-power techniques. Hill and Stone don't *substitute* PMA for faith, but promote an even more dangerous idea: that PMA and faith are *one and the same*, that believing in the power of the mind is somehow the same as believing in God; that the human mind is some kind of magic talisman that wields a metaphysical force[20] with infinite potential because somehow it is part of what they call Infinite Intelligence.[21] This is the "God" of the mind-science cults and of the New Age.

An Ideal Vehicle for the Seduction

It would be impossible to understand our modern world without taking into consideration the way it has been shaped and molded by psychology. Nothing else even comes close to matching its influence upon the beliefs and lifestyles of contemporary society. Almost all of this has taken place since World War II, which according to *Life* magazine created the "greatest upsurge" of interest in psychology in history.[22] In 1946 the U.S. Congress passed the National Mental Health Act, establishing a national program with federal funds. As a result, psychology courses exploded in universities across the country and spread rapidly from there to the seminaries. Prior to the war, "few theological schools had even bothered to teach counseling courses" involving psychology, but "by the 1950s, almost all of them did [and] over 80 percent were offering additional courses in psychology...."[23] Today some of the biggest names on the psychological scene have come out of seminaries. Paul Vitz, who is a psychology professor at New York University, has written:

> Psychology as religion exists...in great strength throughout the United States.... [It] is deeply anti-Christian...[yet] is extensively supported by schools, universities, and social programs financed by taxes collected from Christians.... But for the first time, the destructive logic of this secular religion is beginning to be understood....[24]

Already in 1951 Carl Rogers could boast that "professional interest in psychotherapy" was "in all likelihood the most rapidly growing area in the social sciences today."[25] And now in the 1980s, psychology has attained the status of a guru whose "scientific standards of behavior" are relieving consciences of obedience to God's moral laws. In this way, as well as through its introduction of sorcery as science, psychology is the major change agent in transforming society. As investigative journalist Martin L. Gross has so well said:

> Psychology sits at the very center of contemporary society as an international colossus whose ranks number in the hundreds of thousands....
>
> Its experimental animals are an obliging, even grateful human race. We live in a civilization in which, as never before, man is preoccupied with self....
>
> As the Protestant ethic has weakened in Western society, the confused citizen has turned to the only alternative he knows: the psychological expert who claims there is a new scientific standard of behavior to replace fading traditions....
>
> Mouthing the holy name of science, the psychological expert claims to know all. This new truth

is fed to us continuously from birth to the grave.[26]

Humanistic and transpersonal psychologies have now embraced the entire spectrum of sorcery. For example, the 22nd Annual Meeting of the Association for Humanistic Psychology held in Boston August 21-26, 1984, was heavily flavored with Hindu/Buddhist occultism. The official daily schedule included "Early morning; Yoga, Tai Chi, Meditation." About half of the "Pre-Conference/Post-Conference Institutes" involved blatant sorcery, with such subjects as "Visualization and Healing...Trance States and Healing...operations of alchemy...guided imagery... Shamanic (witchcraft) Ecstasy and Transformation...Being the Wizard We Are."

The extent to which psychology and education have embraced the pagan/occult traditions of the past is favorably summed up in this statement by the late Dr. Beverly Galyean, consultant to the Los Angeles school system, in an article by her in *The Journal of Humanistic Psychology*:

> The ancients of all cultures filled their folkloric epics with tales of visions, dreams, intuitive insights, and internal dialogues with higher beings whom they saw as the sources of ultimate wisdom and knowledge.
>
> By accepting as true the narratives of spiritual seekers from all cultures, we now have evidence of various levels of consciousness possible to human beings....
>
> Human potential is inexhaustible and is realized through new modes of exploration (i.e. meditation, guided imagery, dream work, yoga, body movement, sensory awareness, energy transfer (healing), reincarnation therapy, and esoteric studies)....
>
> Meditation and guided imagery activities are the core of the [confluent/holistic education] curriculum.[27]

Variations of such psychology have infiltrated the church, Christian schools and seminaries, because pastors and other leaders have accepted the claim that it is scientific and neutral. Most Christians have failed to recognize the fact that Christianity and psychotherapy are actually two rival and irreconcilable religious systems. Their union as "Christian psychology" creates an unequal yoke that brings into the church the seductive influence of secular psychology. And now with the leading psychologists and psychiatrists so heavily involved in selfism and sorcery, Christian psychology inevitably succumbs to some of the same delusions and brings them into the church. A good example is the "Training in Spiritual Direction" seminars that began in a Protestant church in Austin, Texas. The brochure reads in part:

> The experiential focus utilizes relaxation, guided fantasy...inner dialogue, gestalt and dream work... founded on the principles of spiritual direction...[in] the Old and New Testaments...within the mystical/ascetical tradition of the Roman Catholic Church.
>
> The conceptual material is biblically sound and makes use of the perspectives of contemporary psychology, especially transpersonal. The dominant schools of psychology included are analytical (Jung) and Psychosynthesis (Assigioli). Significant use is made of psychoanalytic (Horney, Erikson, Berne etc.) and humanistic (Fromm, Perls, Maslow etc.) thought.[28]

Paganism in Modern Dress

Feminist leader Gloria Steinem has declared:

> By the year 2000 we will, I hope, raise our children to believe in human potential, not God....[29]

Today's psychologists are trying to plumb the mysterious depths of what many people now think is *unlimited* human potential through fantasy and role-playing in order to develop the "power of the imagination." Napoleon Hill's technique of visualizing "guides," which has been used by witch doctors and other occultists for thousands of years, is now one of the most exciting and widely used methods of "transformation" being promoted by many psychologists. Jean Houston, for example, co-founder of the Foundation for Mind Research where LSD was first licensed by the government to be used in researching hidden depths of the mind,[30] uses many techniques from ancient sorcery,[31] among them the visualization and even *materialization* of what she calls "the Group Spirit" that manifests in seemingly real form.[32]

Demons don't even have to hide their activity anymore. Their existence would not be admitted by most psychologists and many clergymen no matter how hard they tried to prove themselves to be real. Whatever happens is considered to be the product of one's allegedly unlimited *imagination*. Napoleon Hill was convinced that his nine "Counselors," though so real that they frightened him at first, were only imaginary. Hill wrote:

> These nine men [from the past] were Emerson, Paine, Edison, Darwin, Lincoln, Burbank, Napoleon, Ford and Carnegie. Every night...I held an imaginary council meeting with this group whom I called my "Invisible Counselors."
>
> In these imaginary council meetings I called on my cabinet members for the knowledge I wished each to contribute, addressing myself to each member....
>
> After some months of this nightly procedure, I was astounded by the discovery that these imaginary figures became apparently *real*. Each of these nine men developed individual characteristics, which surprised me....
>
> These meetings became so realistic that I became fearful of their consequences, and discontinued them for several months. The experiences were so uncanny, I was afraid if I continued them I would lose sight of the fact that the meetings were purely *experiences of my imagination*.
>
> This is the first time that I have had the courage to mention this.... I still regard my cabinet meetings as being purely imaginary, but...they have led me into glorious paths of adventure...[and] I have been miraculously guided past [scores] of difficulties....
>
> I now go to my imaginary counselors with every difficult problem which confronts me and my clients. The results are often astonishing... [emphasis in the original].[33]

The Power of the Imagination?

So it is with today's psychologists who use the same basic sorcerer's technique: The often-remarkable results these mysterious entities produce, though inexplicable to science, are nevertheless credited to the power of the imagination. In seminars called "The Power of The Imagination" sponsored by Marquette University, psychologists have trained thousands of persons across America to visualize "inner guides" similar to Hill's and with equally astonishing results. Though it can easily be proved that the imagination is *not* unlimited (who can visualize a new prime color, for example?) this deceptive belief has gained a strong foothold within the church. The power of the imagination is becoming confused with *inspiration* and power of the Holy Spirit.

Korean pastor Paul Yonggi Cho declares that it was through the power of the "imagination" that God created the world, and that because man is a "fourth-dimension" spirit-being like God, he too, whether occultist or Christian, can create his own world through the power of his imagination.[34]

Occultists have long known that the most powerful way to tap into the spirit dimension is through *visualization*, about which we will have much more to say later. Norman Vincent Peale calls this *Positive imaging*, which he says is a word "derived from *imagination*"[35] and is "positive thinking carried one step further."[36] Peale has said:

> There is a powerful and mysterious force in human nature...a kind of mental engineering...a powerful new-old idea....
> The concept is a form of mental activity called imaging....
> It consists of vividly picturing, in your conscious mind, a desired goal or objective, and holding that image until it sinks into your unconscious mind, where it releases great untapped energies....
> When the imaging concept is applied steadily and systematically, it solves problems, strengthens personalities, improves health, and greatly enhances the chances for success in any kind of endeavor.

> The idea of imaging has been around for a long time,
> and it has been implicit in all the speaking and writing
> I have done in the past.[37]

If it strutted or danced down church aisles in its authentic paint and feathers as the antibiblical religion it is, paganism would be promptly rejected by Christians. But when dressed in a business suit, clerical collar, or robe and introduced to the congregation as the latest innovation in theology, psychology, medicine, business success, and self-improvement techniques for developing human potential, seductive sorcery is warmly embraced as a true friend and supporter of Christianity.

What we will be documenting in subsequent chapters is far more than isolated pockets of error. Not only is its extent staggering, but sorcery within the church follows a pattern that fits precisely the biblical warnings from Jesus and His disciples concerning a great deception that would sweep the world in the last days. Therefore it is necessary first of all to understand the prophetic context in which the seduction is taking place.

3

Signs of the Times?

> When you see a south wind blowing, you say, "It will be a hot day," and it turns out that way. You hypocrites! You know how to analyze the appearance of the earth and the sky, but why do you not analyze this present time?
>
> Luke 12:55,56

This book is not a hairsplitting theological treatise, but a handbook for spiritual survival. Numerous prophecies, including those from Jesus Himself, warn that the worldwide spiritual deception just prior to His return will be so seductive that it will "mislead, if possible, even the elect" (Matthew 24:24). It is only reasonable to assume that those warnings have been given to help us to recognize this deception when it comes.

The Bible contains many accounts that would lead us to believe that those living upon earth at the time prophecy is fulfilled are expected to recognize events transpiring in their day as the fulfillment of what the prophets have foretold. For example, referring in his Pentecost sermon to what was happening on that historic day, Peter declared: "*This* is what was spoken of through the prophet Joel" (Acts 2:16). The view Jesus had of prophecy was equally practical. He called the two disciples on the road to Emmaus "fools" for not correlating Old Testament prophecies with events that had happened to Him (Luke 24:25,26). And in the verses quoted at the beginning of this chapter, He called the Jews of His day "hypocrites" for not recognizing, on the basis of what their own prophets had said, the signs indicating the unique time in which they lived.

Would Jesus also call us fools and hypocrites for not recognizing that we are living in the "last days" on the basis of the signs we have been given? Could we be deceived if we don't take heed to these warnings? And how can we take heed unless at some point in time we relate what we have been warned about with what is happening in the world?

Why Does the Bible Describe the Last Days?

We cannot escape the fact that the Bible repeatedly and purposefully addresses the subject of the "last days" and gives numerous signs by which those living at the time are to recognize them. Jesus specified a number of definite signs as though He intended that those living in the last days, though unable to tell the exact "day or hour" of His coming (Matthew 24:36) would be able to recognize when His second coming was very near. Apparently it will be extremely important to be able to do so. Referring to the future events He had prophetically described, Jesus said:

> Now learn a parable from the fig tree: when its branch has already become tender, and puts forth its leaves, you know that summer is near; even so you too, when you see all these things, recognize that He is near, right at the door (Matthew 24:32, 33).

There can be no reasonable doubt that the Bible describes the "last days" with the obvious intent that *some generation at some time* will be able to "recognize that He is near, right at the door." It is our responsibility to determine whether we are that generation or not. We must make this determination not on the basis of "new revelation," personal bias, or a desire to be always "positive," but by taking Bible prophecies at face value and then examining the evidence. Jesus and His apostles placed great emphasis upon certain signs and warned us not to be asleep and thus fail to recognize them and be caught by surprise. Paul wrote that Christians are "not in darkness, that the day should overtake you like a thief" (1 Thessalonians 5:4).

Some Persuasive Evidence

Critics argue that some of the signs Jesus gave—wars, rumors of wars, earthquakes, famines, pestilence—have been happening in cycles down through history. Therefore the mere fact that they are occurring today, even though with greater frequency and intensity, does not in itself prove that we are in the "last days." We shall see that it is not necessary to argue that point. There are other very significant signs of the "last days" for which that argument is meaningless. These generally overlooked signs not only indicate that Christ's return is very near but carry grave consequences for every person on planet Earth. We ignore them at our peril.

There can be no doubt that our generation has seen unique historic developments that are necessary preliminary events leading up to Armageddon. Yet impressive as these indications are, there is much more.

For the *first time* in global history, humanity now has in its hands the terrifying weapons that make it possible to destroy all life on planet Earth. Without such weapons the biblical prophecies about Christ intervening to save the human race from extinction would be meaningless. We also have, for the *first time* in history, the mass-communication and data-processing systems necessary for controlling the entire world economically, politically, and militarily. Thus for the *first time* there exists the means for the practical fulfillment of the prophecies in Revelation 13 concerning the Antichrist's control of the world. Moreover, this comes at the precise time that all the other necessary ingredients for Armageddon are in place.

The First Sign Jesus Gave: A Warning

Clearly, the worn-out objection of skeptics that every generation has thought it was living in the last days on the basis of prophesied signs is absurd. Previous generations may have thought so, but none prior to ours has had the evidence to support that view. *No* generation from the 70 A.D. exile until 1948 saw Israel return to its homeland, much less the other specific developments mentioned above. Ours is the *first* generation in history that has seen *all* of the necessary ingredients come together in its day for fulfilling end-time prophecies. Yet there are other prophesied signs that are even more significant.

Though extremely important, all of the impressive evidence we could give or that has been mentioned so far would not tell us how near we may be to the second coming of Jesus Christ without certain further essential confirmation. There are several other signs of a nature different from any we have yet listed that are usually overlooked altogether or given only passing reference by experts in biblical prophecy. Yet these are the most significant signs of all, and they give us good cause for believing that "He is near, right at the door."

After His disciples asked Jesus, "What will be the sign of Your coming and of the end of the age?" the very first thing He said was, "See to it that no one misleads you" (Matthew 24:3,4). He went on to warn them that the last days immediately prior to His return would be characterized by the greatest deception the world has ever seen. He indicated that this would be *religious* deception and that it would involve three specifics: 1) false prophets, 2) false messiahs, and 3) false miracles.

Religious deception is the first major sign that Jesus gave to indicate that His second coming is near. It is also the most important. Christ and His apostles emphasized it the most, and with good reason. The consequences of being deceived by false prophets and false messiahs are far worse than being victimized by famine, disease, or war. Here is how Jesus summarized His solemn warning:

> For false Christs and false prophets will arise and show great signs and wonders, so as to mislead, if possible, even the elect. Behold, I have told you in advance (Matthew 24:24,25).

False Prophets

Down through history there have always been a few false prophets. Jesus warned that in the last days there would be *many* and that they would deceive *many* people. For that to come true, there would have to be a worldwide interest and belief in predicting the future. Even 20 years ago that would have seemed an unlikely possibility for an age of science; yet this prophecy made by Christ nearly 2000 years ago is being fulfilled in today's space age. Ridiculed as superstition by science not many years ago, prophecy is today being experimented with and verified in laboratory research, where it is now called "precognition."

That term reflects the materialistic desire to deny anything supernatural and instead to explain the ability to foretell the future as a purely *natural* power arising out of an allegedly infinite human potential. On the one hand, that approach denies biblical prophecy, which comes as a revelation from God. The door is thus opened wide for demonic entities to deceive modern man. (Since their very existence is denied nothing they do would be attributed to them.) Moreover, there would be no such thing as *false* prophecy if precognition is a *natural* process. Nature is neither false nor true. As a result, the *false prophets* that Jesus warned about are more free to deceive in the space age than ever before in human history. And the growing eagerness among some Christians to accept "new revelation" in spite of its conflict with the Bible makes the church increasingly vulnerable to false prophets as well.

Louisa Rhine, wife of Duke University's J. B. Rhine (the father of American parapsychology), has documented numerous convincing cases of "precognition."[1] In their "remote-viewing" experiments, in which psychics were asked to describe distant sites from latitude/longitude coordinates picked at random by computer, SRI scientists Harold Puthoff and Russell Targ discovered that certain psychics, such as Hella Hammid, could describe the site even before the computer designated it![2] Former astronaut Edgar Mitchell, sixth man to walk on the moon and commander of Apollo 14, founded the Institute of Noetic Sciences to explore what he calls "the most promising frontier of all: *the human mind.*" According to Mitchell, "Interest in the potential of the mind has grown at a phenomenal rate among scientists in widely differing fields."[3] He considers precognition to be an important part of that "potential." Mitchell has said:

> ...prominent men and women from such unlikely fields as neurophysiology, theoretical physics, and anthropology have been looking seriously into such matters as...the always perplexing yet well documented capabilities of some people for mental activities ranging from telepathy and clairvoyance to precognition and telekinesis.
>
> What sort of scientists are daring to pursue these once "taboo" subject areas? Dr. Herbert Benson, Harvard University; Dr. Elmer Green, Menninger Clinic; Dr. Charles Tart, University of California; Dr. Stanley Krippner, President of the Saybrook Institute; Dr. Dan Goleman, Senior Editor, *Psychology Today*; and Dr. Hal Puthoff, Stanford Research Institute, to name just a few.[4]

The growing acceptance of "precognition" by science is encouraging the average citizen to put increasing faith in the predictions of a mushrooming pantheon of psychic seers. Not long ago Edgar Cayce and Jeane Dixon were regarded skeptically by most people. Today there are hundreds of professional psychic prophets with large followings. Dozens of varieties of courses for developing psychic "mind-powers," from Alpha Level Training to Mind Dynamics, turn out thousands of amateurs who can do everything Cayce did and more. Graduates of Silva Mind Control, for example, are given their money back if they cannot accurately diagnose persons whose names they have been given but whom they have never heard of, much less seen or met. Some of the world's top business and political leaders wouldn't make a move without consulting their astrologer or psychic. The ingredients for fulfilling Christ's prophecy that *many* false prophets would deceive *many* followers are now present as never before in modern history.

It is interesting to observe that many of the predictions made by today's modern seers speak of coming disasters similar to those found in Bible prophecies, with an added "positive" note of hope that sounds suspiciously like certain kinds of "positive thinking" being taught in the church today. Andrija Puharich is one of today's most brilliant medical scientists, with about 60 patents to his credit. The following excerpts from a talk to fellow scientists by Puharich give some indication of the type of deception that even the most intelligent will accept even though it is in clear conflict with the Bible:

> I'm a scribe, the information...was given to me by some extraterrestrial source...you know that person as Jehovah in the Christian Bible....
>
> That name is the title of the leader of a civilization... called Hoova...52,000 light ages away....
>
> I put on record...in meticulous detail everything that will happen through the year 2,000...[including] this period of devastation, of cataclysm, of destruction....
>
> It's going to be difficult [to survive] but I want you to know that those who want to will survive...my colleagues [and I] saw that you could do healings without [medicine]...you just had to use your mind properly....[5]

False Christs

The Lord's prophecy about *many* false Christs appearing in the last days is also coming to pass. While there have always been some pretenders, today's world is flooded with those who claim to be Christ. Jim Jones and Charles Manson were two among many. Most of the Eastern gurus who have invaded the West in the last 20 years make the same claim. That a full-page ad could appear in major newspapers around the world announcing "The Christ Is Now Here," as happened in April 1982, is just one more indication that this is an idea whose time may have come. Those behind it have clearly stated what the ad implied: "The Christ" is *not* Jesus. The biblical test of the spirit of Antichrist is: "Who is a liar but he that denieth that Jesus is the Christ? He is antichrist..." (1 John 2:22 KJV).

Within the past 20 years, tens of millions of people in the West have been converted to a basic tenet of Eastern mysticism that we believe will play a key role in the acceptance of the Antichrist. That concept is *reincarnation*, which is gradually superseding the once-dominant Western belief in resurrection. It is almost inevitable that anyone dabbling in occultism will eventually, like Napoleon Hill and many of his readers, embrace reincarnation. Shirley MacLaine is a good example, and her recent best-selling autobiography has convinced many readers.[6] One cannot believe in both resurrection and reincarnation; the two are mutually contradictory. Jesus was *resurrected*, not *reincarnated*, and the difference between the two is both obvious and important.

Reincarnation is based upon a belief in the "law of karma," which allegedly requires that subsequent lives be lived in order to pay in kind for the deeds done in prior lives. A husband who beats his wife in this life, for example, must return in a subsequent life as a wife who is beaten by her husband. Thus karma cannot solve the problem of evil, but can only perpetuate it, for the person who commits a crime must become the victim of the same crime. This in turn requires that someone else commit the crime, who must then become a future victim, ad infinitum. Going back in the other direction, the experiences of this life are the result of karma from a past life, which resulted from a yet prior life, and so on endlessly into the past. Where did it all begin? The Hindu speaks of the time when the three *gunas* (qualities) of the godhead were in perfect balance and there was only the void. Something caused an imbalance in the godhead, which began the *prakriti* (manifestation) and has been going on ever since. Thus everyone is reaping the bad karma that began in the godhead and is built into the very fabric of the universe.

In spite of the fact that this philosophy is absolutely hopeless, senseless, and immoral, many leading psychiatrists have become believers in reincarnation. This is because some of their patients, while being "regressed" into the past under hypnosis, have recited details from alleged prior lives, including all kinds of verifiable factual data that they could not have fabricated on their own.[7]

Psychiatrist Helen Walmbach, for example, has "regressed" more than 5000 patients into prior lives, and her careful analysis of their recorded "memories" is very convincing.[8] We will deal with the deception involved in hypnotic trances and other forms of altered states of consciousness later.

The importance of reincarnation in preparing the world to accept the Antichrist is clear. No would-be "Christ" could claim to be the biblical Messiah without the physical proof of the nailprints in his hands and feet and a spear wound in his side. However, if the world is not looking for the *resurrected Jesus* but for the latest *reincarnation* of the "Christ spirit," then no nailprints or spear wound would be necessary. Antichrist can claim to be the Christ and be believed if he has sufficient psychic powers to seemingly work the "miracles" that are expected of Christ when He returns. That could well be how he "proves" who he is.

Paul warned that Antichrist's "coming is in accord with the activity of Satan, with all power and signs and false wonders, and with all the deception of wickedness..." (2 Thessalonians 2:9,10). This puts in a very vulnerable position those Christians who accept anything that seems to be miraculous as coming from God. Although miracles are important, we must beware of placing greater emphasis upon them than Scripture supports. Jesus Himself said of John the Baptist that there was no greater prophet born of women (Luke 7:28), and yet we are told that John "did no miracle" (John 10:41 KJV). And of Jesus it is said, though He did so many miracles, yet the Jews still did not believe on Him (John 12:37). The Bible does not teach that the great need today is for a miracle ministry, as is so heavily emphasized on much Christian television. Rather, it warns us that we need discernment to know the difference between what is of God and what is of Satan.

False Miracles

Having rejected biblical miracles, today's science is accepting the false miracles of Satan—not for what they are, but as alleged natural powers of the mind, which we call "psychic phenomena."

It is through the new acceptance of psychic powers (psi) that our generation is being prepared in the third way that Christ said spiritual deception would seduce those on earth in the last days. Science fiction has made superhuman powers believable, because so much presented by this genre has already become reality. Almost anything is believable now—not as a miracle from God but as the result of tapping into some alleged universal Force.

Although there are still many skeptics, psychic research has come into its own in the past few years. A high percentage of not only ordinary people but top scientists as well are now convinced that human potential includes incredible powers of the mind such as precognition, telepathy, clairvoyance, and telekinesis. These powers are allegedly available to anyone who knows how to tap into the Force through reaching the right state of consciousness.

Though materialists, the Soviets are as deeply involved in psychic research as are the Americans. Of course they try their best to maintain strictly materialistic explanations, such as designating telepathy "biological radio" in spite of the fact that no brain waves can be detected emanating more than a few inches from the skull, whereas telepathy experiments have been successfully conducted over vast distances and even between earth and orbiting cosmonauts. Numerous books have appeared documenting psi research, such as *Frames of Meaning: The Social Construction of Extraordinary Science; Parapsychology and the Experimental Methods; Psychic Discoveries Behind the Iron Curtain*; and *Brain, Mind, and Parapsychology*; and many others. As Marilyn Ferguson has said:

> Historically, many great scientists have been drawn to psi. Among the first officers of the Society for Psychical Research in Britain were three Nobel laureates: the discoverer of the electron, J.J. Thompson; the discoverer of argon, Lord Rayleigh; and Charles Richet.
>
> William James, usually described as the father of American psychology, co-founded the American Society for Psychical Research. Among the Nobel laureates specifically interested in psi were Alexis

Carrel, Max Planck, the Curies, Schrodinger, Charles Sherrington, and Einstein....

Carl Jung and Wolfgang Pauli, a Nobel physicist, coauthored a theory about synchronicity. Pierre Janet, a great French scientist of the nineteenth century, actively investigated psi. Luther Burbank and Thomas Edison had a strong interest in the field.[9]

There can be little doubt that our generation, as none before it in modern history, is beginning to be greatly influenced by the largely overlooked major sign that Jesus gave of the last days—religious deception involving false prophets, false Christs, and false miracles. In view of the many other signs converging in our day, it seems at least probable that the world is being set up for Antichrist as never before in its history. There is, however, yet more evidence that is even more intriguing and convincing.

4

An Official World Religion?

> . . . who opposes and exalts himself above every so-called god or object of worship, so that he takes his seat in the temple of God, displaying himself as being God.
>
> 2 Thessalonians 2:4

> All who dwell on the earth will worship him.
>
> Revelation 13:8

Many people think of prophecy as an intriguing subject that involves the latest rumors concerning an alleged Trilateralist plot, the newest developments in the Middle East, or recent maneuvers by the Soviets and Arabs in their continuing campaign against Israel. Interesting as that may be, there is something far more important. Whether one has a year's supply of food in case of famine or a suitable shelter for surviving a nuclear attack may be important, but it affects one's temporal condition only. However, to be deluded into believing "the lie" that we are warned will seduce the entire world into accepting the Antichrist will affect one's eternal destiny (2 Thessalonians 2:11,12).

We have been in the midst of a cult/occult explosion for the last 25 years—an explosion that began with the drug movement and turned into a mystical trip mainly oriented to Hindu/Buddhist practices. The counterculture that began as a largely political movement protesting the Vietnam war and evils of a materialistic society became a *spiritual* movement through the influence of drugs and Eastern mysticism. The failure of

47

materialistic science to answer ultimate questions (but instead bringing us to the brink of a nuclear holocaust and ecological collapse) has caused modern man to turn to the realm of the spirit for the answers he seeks. This is preparing humanity for the coming world religion of Antichrist, and the prophetic warnings in the Bible concerning it deserve to be taken seriously.

The Cashless Controlled Society

Biblical prophecies also have a good deal to say about political, military, and economic developments in the last days. As "negative" as it sounds, Antichrist will rule the earth. The Bible declares in unequivocal language:

> And he causes all, the small and the great, the rich and the poor...to be given a mark on their right hand, or on their forehead, and he provides that no one should be able to buy or to sell, except the one who has the mark (Revelation 13:16,17).

In our modern world, 1900 years after these words were written by John under the inspiration of the Holy Spirit, they at last make sense. Today's credit card system has brought the fulfillment of this ancient prophecy closer than almost anyone would have guessed 50 years ago. Nor is it any secret that we are heading for a completely cashless society, which will be one more step toward this prophecy's fulfillment. There are about 600 million credit cards now in use in the United States alone. In 1983 the reported fraudulent credit card transactions were about 200 million dollars. The possibility of counterfeiting cards is being eliminated by new devices such as those developed by Light Signatures, Inc., of Los Angeles.[1] However, this does not solve the problem of lost or stolen cards. The only real solution is to do away entirely with cards as well as with cash.

The logical manner for accomplishing this is exactly what the Bible prophesied 1900 years ago: There will eventually be an irremovable identification number on the hand or forehead of every person on the planet. We now have the technology not just to impregnate a *number* but to implant a *micro chip* with considerable data that would be invisible except to electronic scanning devices. This is the next logical step for banking and commerce, but it could also allow surveillance from satellite of the movements of every person on earth.

This may be why "the mark of the beast" will only be put into operation by Antichrist himself. Speculation about what that mark will be and the meaning of "666" has filled volumes. The most important thing is to realize that receiving it will be an act of submission to Antichrist, causing all who take this mark to forfeit the possibility of salvation. Those who do not accept it will lose the privilege of buying or selling. The choice will be between time and eternity.

The Coming World Government

It is no longer a question of *whether* but *when* humanity will be united both economically and politically under a one-world government. Lists of the many top leaders and organizations working openly toward this goal can be obtained by anyone who is interested. Books on the subject are legion, from James P. Warburg's *The West In Crisis* ("We are living in a perilous period of transition from the era of the fully sovereign nation-state to the era of world government")[2] to *Between Two Ages,* by Assistant to the President for National Security Affairs Zbigniew Brezenski, in which he openly advocates a one world government as a necessity. The United States has officially made statements favorable of a new world order, such as the following addressed to the Secretary-General of the United Nations: "[It] would be hard to imagine that the American people would not respond very positively to an agreed and safeguarded program to substitute an international rule of law and order...."[3] Of the Carter administration, the *Washington Post* said:

> If you like conspiracy theories about secret plots to take over the world, you are going to love the administration of President-elect Jimmy Carter. At last count 13 Trilateralists had gone into top positions... extraordinary when you consider that the Trilateral Commission only has about 65 American members.[4]

Even Ronald Reagan, who was supposedly an outsider bringing
new faces into government, immediately following his victory in
1979 appointed "a 'transition team' which would later select,
screen and recommend appointees for major administration
posts...of the fifty-nine...[on] that team, twenty-eight were
members of the CFR, ten belonged to the secret and elite Bilder-
berg group, and no less than ten were Trilaterals."[5] The coming
world government has been dealt with in countless books and
sermons. Yet the most important part of what the Bible tells us
about the Antichrist is seldom mentioned.

It would be fruitless to speculate further about global conspiracy theories involving the Trilateralists, Masons, Illuminati,
or New Age networks. These organizations are only pawns in
the real game. No one is going to take over the world by con-
spiring to do so. Far more important than knowing the individuals
and groups involved is understanding the common lie that deceives
them all. The mastermind behind the scenes is Satan himself, and
the world takeover is his move. Even so, that can only come when
God allows it, and it will be made possible through some startling
developments. A very probable scenario is presented in *Peace,
Prosperity, and the Coming Holocaust*, so we won't take further
time to discuss that here. Regardless of how it is going to come
about, however, the Bible declares that it *will* happen:

> And the whole earth was amazed and followed after
> the beast [Antichrist]...saying, "Who is able to wage
> war with him?"
> ...and authority over every tribe and people and
> tongue and nation was given to him (Revelation
> 13:3,4,7).

In attempting to understand these prophecies, we must not
forget that Antichrist will be far more than a military/political
dictator: He will also be the revered and *worshiped* head of an
unprecedented official world religion. The world's loyalty to him
will be of a *religious* nature. His takeover of the world is above
all a *spiritual* event toward which Satan has plotted since the
Garden of Eden. Those who overlook that fact miss the real
significance of Antichrist and are more likely to fall prey to the

deception by which the world will be seduced into worshiping him. When we finally see prophecy in its religious context, it takes on new meaning and urgency.

What Secret to His Power?

In language that cannot be misinterpreted, the Bible foretells that Antichrist will declare himself to be God and that the whole world—Marxists, Maoists, Muslims, Hindus, Buddhists, atheists, professing Christians, *everyone*—will believe this astonishing claim and *worship* him. This seems so fantastic that many sincere Christians have tried to interpret this prophecy to mean only that Western Europe (the revived Roman Empire) and possibly also the remainder of the Western world will be under the Antichrist. However, the words used in Revelation 13 to describe Antichrist's dominion, whether political or religious, are unequivocal: "the whole earth," "every tribe and people and tongue and nation," "all who dwell on the earth," and "the earth and those who dwell in it."

There can be no doubt as to the meaning intended: that the entire human race (except for those few who will resist and pay for it with their lives) will *worship* a mere man as God. Earth's inhabitants at that time will not recognize this claim as the outrageous lie of a diabolical counterfeit. It will seem to be the sincere revelation of truth from the very Savior the world desperately needs. Here is what the Bible says:

> And for this reason God will send upon them a deluding influence so that they might believe the lie....
>
> And the whole earth...worshiped the dragon, because he gave his authority to the beast; and they worshiped the beast....
>
> And all who dwell on the earth will worship him, everyone whose name has not been written...in the book of life of the Lamb who has been slain (2 Thessalonians 2:11; Revelation 13:3,4,8).

Surely the Soviets, Chinese, Arabs, Western Europeans, Americans, and *everyone* upon planet Earth would never surrender absolute control to Antichrist without fighting to the finish, if he were merely an aspiring world dictator. Even assuming that he had conquered or blackmailed the world through some secret superweapon, it would certainly be necessary for him to disarm the Soviets, Chinese, and all those he had conquered in order to keep them in subjection. Yet the Bible indicates that at Armageddon the armies of all nations will gather against Jerusalem, which means they will still have their weapons.

The logical secret to Antichrist's mysterious power over humanity lies in the astonishing fact that the entire world will *worship* him as *God*. Worship brings reverence and obedience. Military power is hardly necessary to force the members of a religion to obey the "God" they worship. His bold claim that he is God, however, is not made by Antichrist as a ploy to gain control. There is something much deeper behind it.

The new world religion of Antichrist will be thought of as scientific. This new religious science will promise to lead humanity into the experience of its own divinity, that each of us is "God." This basic lie of the serpent in the Garden of Eden will seem to be validated by the godlike psychic powers the Antichrist will manifest and the whole world will pursue. It will be a religion of self-love and self-worship, centered in man himself and oriented to man's personal success rather than to the glory of the true God.

It is already clear that we are heading rapidly in this very direction. The evidence is there for all to see in the New Age movement, which is a blend of science and Eastern religions.

The New "Spiritual" Science

Another name for the New Age movement is the Holistic movement, about which we will have much more to say later. Under this influence, science, medicine, psychology, sociology, and education have all taken a sharp turn to the "spiritual," but not in a biblical sense. Instead, they have turned to the occult, and Christians need to be aware of the seduction that they face in every area of today's society. Parents especially need to awaken to the fact that their children are being seduced by occultism taught now as science in our public schools under the move to

"Holistic education." The world is being conditioned to accept the coming satanic religion of Antichrist as a scientific mind-technology.

The turn to a new "religious science" has been apparent for some years in the field of psychology, but is now accelerating. Both humanistic and transpersonal psychologies are heavily involved in what they call "spiritual" therapies and concerns, which are simply a revival of occultism under psychological labels, as we will document later. Past president of the Association for Humanistic Psychology, Jean Houston, is called the "Prophet of the Possible"[6] (upon whom Margaret Mead's mantle has presumably fallen). Known as "a dazzling visionary, scholar, and teacher in the human potential movement"[7] and a leading spokesperson for the coming "transformation into the New Age," Houston declared in an interview:

> I predict that in our lifetime we will see the rise of essentially a New World Religion. . . . I believe a new spiritual system will emerge. . . .[8]

Increasing numbers of influential world leaders are expressing in New Age terms the growing belief that the predicted world government must be founded upon a new world religion. Five months before his death in Los Angeles, Buckminster Fuller, designer of the geodesic dome and the world's most honored architect, declared that man's future on "Spaceship Earth depends entirely" upon his cooperation with the "Divine Mind always present in each individual."[9] The belief that we can tune into this inner "Divine Mind" to experience "peace through [Eastern] meditation [Yoga]"[10] was the major premise of a recent prestigious "Universal Peace Conference." The conference was held in India at the World Spiritual University, headquarters of the Brahma Kumris Raja Yoga society, a United Nations affiliate. Among the 3000 delegates from 42 countries were such notables as Tibet's Dalai Lama, Stanford University professor and SRI scientist Willis Harmon, and United Nations Assistant Secretary-General Robert Muller. In his keynote speech to the delegates, Muller said:

> The time has come to obtain peace on this planet. . .
> the United Nations Charter has to be supplemented by

a charter of spiritual laws....

I think that what is wrong...we have forgotten that...we have a cosmic evolution and [spiritual] destiny....[11]

Gurus and Godhood

The prophecy quoted at the beginning of this chapter that "he takes his seat in the temple of God, displaying himself as being God" (2 Thessalonians 2:4) will have its primary fulfillment in a particular man, Antichrist, and the temple yet to be rebuilt in Jerusalem. There is an obvious secondary application. The human body is supposed to be the temple of God. God intends that we should open our hearts to receive Jesus Christ as Savior and Lord and be indwelt by His Spirit. Paul wrote to the Christians at Corinth: "You are a temple of God...the spirit of God dwells in you" (1 Corinthians 3:16). The teaching of Eastern religions, however, is that the *self* is God, but we just don't realize it. The spirit of Antichrist causes humans to look within themselves in that temple of the heart where the spirit of God ought to dwell, and to declare their own deity.

The goal of Yoga is "self-realization"—to look deeply within what ought to be the temple of the one true God and there to discover the alleged "true Self" or "higher Self" and declare self to be God. This is the religion of Antichrist; and for the first time in history it is being widely practiced throughout the Western world as Transcendental Meditation and other forms of Yoga that are now taught in nearly every YWCA or YMCA, in public and private schools from kindergarten to graduate level, and in many churches. Humanity is being conditioned to accept a coming world ruler who will have the psychic powers from Satan to "prove" that he has indeed "realized" his own "godhood."

The many gurus who have invaded the West are actively converting millions to this satanic religion of Antichrist with a missionary zeal and success that is a new phenomenon for Eastern religions. Each claiming to be God himself, the gurus have opened the Western world to the belief and practice of worshiping a man as God, and to the idea that each person can realize his own godhood through following his guru. It will not seem strange, therefore, when Antichrist claims to be God; and the millions who have been worshiping gurus such as Rajneesh and Muktananda will easily worship Antichrist.

The hundreds of Eastern gurus are preparing us for the ultimate Guru; the many false Christs are paving the way for the Antichrist. San Diego psychiatrist Samuel H. Sandweiss is one example of the millions of Westerners who have been converted by one guru or another. The following are excerpts from a letter he wrote to his wife in May 1972 from India, where he had gone to investigate a miracle-working guru known as Sai Baba, who has about 20 million devoted followers:

> There is no doubt in my mind that Sai Baba is divine. I astound myself. . .a rational, scientific man, to say such a thing.
>
> I believe Baba to be an incarnation of God. . . . How strange, when just a few days ago I was such a skeptic. Yesterday I experienced more miracles. . .Baba is allowing me to see this wonderful power close-up. . . .
>
> I am witnessing in live color and in the flesh an experience a million times more astonishing than the fairy-tale stories I have been telling my four sweet children. . .after witnessing Baba's greatness, I can do nothing but accept fully what he says.
>
> Yesterday. . .a very well known nuclear physicist with an international reputation came here. . . . I saw this man lie face-down at Baba's feet. . . .[12]

The Seductive Appeal of Self-Deification

It is true that people join cults for a variety of reasons: to find love, security, community, their own identity, or God. However, the goal of "cosmic evolution" and the "destiny" of humanity to realize its inherent godhood referred to by U.N.'s Robert Muller is the predominant theme running through most of the cults now popular in the West. For example, Joseph Smith's Mormonism, Ernest Holmes' Church of Religious Science, and Herbert W. Armstrong's Worldwide Church of God all teach it. Raised a fundamentalist and now one of the most influential New Age leaders, David Spangler lays it all out, including cosmic evolution of the self to godhood and the key role played by Lucifer (Satan):

> When man entered upon the pathway of self, he entered into a great creative adventure...of learning the meaning of divinity by accepting to himself the responsibility of a microcosmic world unto whom he is the god.... There he can say, "I have fully and absolutely accepted the responsibility of who and what I am"....
>
> The being that helps man to reach this point is Lucifer...the angel of man's evolution...the spirit of light in the microcosmic world.[13]

Werner Erhard, founder of est (Erhard Seminars Training), declares, "You're god in your universe."[14] Creme's Maitreya states, "Man is an emerging God.... My plan and My Duty is to reveal to you a new way...which will permit the divine in man to shine forth."[15] Maharishi Mahesh Yogi, founder of the TM cult, perverts the Bible by saying, "Be still and know that you are God...."[16] Sun Myung Moon has written, "God and man are one. Man is incarnate God."[17] Echoing the same lie from Eden's serpent, Ernest Holmes, founder of the Church of Religious Science, declared, "All men are spiritually evolving until...each will fully express his divinity...."[18] As the Master who traveled the astral plane to communicate in an audible voice to Napoleon Hill declared (concerning the person who fully followed the teachings of the Temple of Wisdom):

> He will not only understand the true purpose of life, but also he will have at his command the power to fulfill that purpose *without having to experience another incarnation on this earthly plane* [emphasis in original].
>
> And the Masters of the Great School, on this earthly plane and all other planes, will rejoice at his triumph and will bid him godspeed toward his own Mastership.[19]

That this message of self-deification is gaining credibility and acceptability at an accelerating rate around the world is another convincing sign that the coming of Christ must be drawing near. There can be no doubt that this belief will play a major role in causing the world to accept the Antichrist and his world religion, as the Bible foretells. That the world would follow such teachings comes as no surprise. But there is cause for alarm when we realize how closely related the deification of self is to the entire Human Potential movement, and how this movement has penetrated the evangelical church and is subtly seducing overwhelming numbers of Christians. Self is the predominant theme of a large percentage of Christian books and sermons. Former Episcopal priest Alan Watts turned Zen Buddhist Master is a good example of where this seduction leads "Christians" who succumb to it. Watts declared:

> The appeal of Zen, as of other forms of Eastern philosophy, is that it unveils...a vast region...where at last the self is indistinguishable from God.[20]

Man-God

The world will be convinced that this godhood which the cults and gurus offer has apparently been realized by Antichrist. Satan will give him supernatural powers to back up his claim that he is the first human to have achieved the full potential of our alleged inherent godhood. That this amazing world ruler is a self-realized Master in the fullest sense of Eastern tradition will be "proved" through the demonstration of supernatural powers that seemingly rival the miracles of Jesus Christ described in the Bible. This will give credence to the hope that everyone else in the world can also reach the goal of "self-realization." It will seem to be the exciting dawning of a New Age for humanity and planet Earth!

It is important to understand that Antichrist will not claim to be God in the classical biblical sense, but *a man who has achieved godhood*. In fact Antichrist will deny the existence of God as a personal Being who has created out of nothing all that exists. The respectability and broad popularity that this belief has achieved is exemplified in John Denver. Like Marsha Mason and many other popular celebrities, Denver was a follower of Swami Muktananda before the latter's death.

Muktananda's advice to his disciples was: "Kneel to your own self. Honor and worship your own being. God dwells within you as You." Of Werner Erhard and Muktananda, Denver declared, "They're gods and they know it...they're running the universe."[21] Inspired by this insight, Denver expressed the goal that millions of Westerners now hold as the result of the influence of the gurus: "One of these days I'll be so complete I won't be a human. I'll be a god."[22] This concept that seemed so incredible to almost everyone in the West just a few years ago is now accepted as a liberating new truth by those who *experience* it. Increasing numbers of celebrities, such as Shirley MacLaine, are testifying to the transforming power of mystical experiences. In her best-seller *Out On a Limb*, MacLaine explains that she now accepts what she once considered "science fiction or...the occult" because "it happened to me."[23]

The power of mystical experience (a form of *initiation*) is expressed eloquently by Robert Schuller's good friend and repeat guest on his "Hour of Power" TV program, Gerald Jampolsky. This famous psychiatrist and best-selling author/lecturer tells of his meeting with Swami Muktananda:

> He touched me with peacock feathers. I began to have the impression that our minds were joined. He touched me again on the head with his hand.
>
> After this, beautiful colors appeared all around me, and it seemed as though I had stepped out of my body and was looking down on it. I saw colors whose depth and brilliance were beyond anything I had ever imagined.
>
> I began to talk in tongues. A beautiful beam of light came into the room and I decided at that moment to stop evaluating what was happening and simply be one with the experience, to join it completely.... For the next three months, my energy level was heightened and I required very little sleep. I was filled with an awareness of love unlike anything I had known before.[24]

Within this context the otherwise-incredible Antichrist prophecies become believable. It is no longer difficult to imagine that *everyone will worship him*. If initiation by gurus such as Muktananda has such a transforming power, what will it be like to be initiated into Antichrist's New Age kingdom? Moreover, Antichrist will symbolize the Godhood they all hope to achieve. It is important to remember that everyone will know that they are not worshiping the God of the Bible. They would not worship the true God, because to acknowledge His existence would be to admit their own inferiority and total dependence upon Him. To acknowledge Antichrist as God, however, is to reaffirm their own claim to godhood. He has simply "realized" ahead of others what all hope to achieve; and the fact that he has reached this goal is proof that all can reach it. Everyone will want to sit at his feet and submit to his power in order to learn the secret he has acquired.

The Luciferic Initiation

Whatever the exact nature of the "mark" which the Antichrist will require to be implanted upon hand or forehead, it will have more than political/economic significance. Not only will it give the possessor the right to buy and sell, but it will identify those who are in Antichrist's kingdom—his loyal followers who worship him as God. Thus the implantation of this mark will be an initiation into the official world religion. This will involve the entire world in Satan worship: "The whole earth...worshiped the dragon [Satan]" (Revelation 13:3,4).

This seems impossible to believe, because most people think of Satan-worshipers as weird fanatics performing bizarre rituals under a full moon at midnight in a cemetery. On the contrary, this will all be very scientific and respectable. Few if any will be aware that they are worshiping *Satan*. And those who are, like David Spangler, will call him Lucifer, who is allegedly "an agent of God's love acting through evolution."[25] Spangler is not alone in honoring Lucifer; and such ideas repeated often enough exert a subtle influence even upon Christians. This is especially true of children and teenagers. Christians had better awaken to what is happening to their children.

Take the recently popular movie *2010*, for example. In the film, a new sun suddenly appeared in the sky and brought peace to earth just as the Americans and Soviets were about to engage in nuclear war. What the film did not explain, Arthur C. Clarke did in his book: the sun was named *Lucifer*, no doubt in honor of the power that brought it into existence. Spangler further explains the relationship of Antichrist to Lucifer and why Lucifer will be worshiped:

> Christ is the same force as Lucifer....[26] Lucifer prepares man for the experience of Christhood...[he is] the great initiator.... Lucifer works within each of us to bring us to wholeness, and as we move into a new age...each of us in some way is brought to that point which I term the Luciferic initiation...that many people now, and in the days ahead, will be facing, for it is an initiation into the New Age.[27]

The Great Delusion

So the world will undergo a Luciferic initiation into Satan worship, and it will be considered the latest advance of science. This would have seemed impossible even 50 years ago, but today it is right in line with growing trends. Already we can see the beginning stages of what the Bible prophesies. An incredible worldwide delusion is gathering momentum. Every person on earth during these last days prior to Christ's return must face it and choose God's truth or Satan's lie. So compelling will be the seduction that Jesus warned that "even the elect" would be deceived "if it were possible." Such language ought to put every Christian on his guard.

What is most important for us to understand is that the glue that will hold Antichrist's empire together is the universal acceptance of what the Bible calls "the lie" that man is God. The consequences ought to be obvious: If we claim that we are God, we have demeaned the very concept of God. We haven't lifted ourselves up to God's level, but have dragged God down to our level.

If everything is God, as Hinduism teaches, then nothing is God, because the very word "God" has lost its meaning. Thus the declaration that man is God is religious atheism. That kind of heavy delusion doesn't happen in a moment; it requires considerable preparation. That it will indeed happen, however, is clearly stated. This is not pessimism but realism. It should not cause us to become fatalistic, but to work even more diligently to rescue as many as we possibly can before it is too late.

The Bible plainly declares that Christ died for the entire world (John 3:16, etc.), and that God "desires all men to be saved and to come to the knowledge of the truth" (1 Timothy 2:4). Therefore, in spite of prophecies about coming delusion and the Antichrist's takeover, we must attempt to convert all people for Christ. That is a worthy goal, and the love of Christ would compel us, for God is not willing that any should perish. However, there must be genuine repentance and conversion. The Bible repeatedly makes it clear that the issue is *truth*, and Paul warns that all those who "did not receive the love of the truth so as to be saved" would be given from God Himself "a deluding influence so that they might believe *the lie*" (2 Thessalonians 2:10,11).

Clearly we must take great care that the message we preach to the world is indeed *the truth*. Unfortunately, as we will see in the following pages, *the lie* has come into the church, and those who claim to be Christians are joining the world in the worship of self with its alleged unlimited powers of the mind. Though it may seem "negative," we dare not ignore the solemn fact that the Bible warns of a coming apostasy—not as a possibility, but as a certainty. In fact we are told quite clearly that many in the church *will* be seduced before the second coming of Christ takes place.

5

The Coming Apostasy

With regard to the coming of our Lord Jesus Christ, and our gathering together to Him...let no one in any way deceive you, for it [the day of the Lord] will not come unless the apostasy comes first, and the man of lawlessness is revealed.

2 Thessalonians 2:1,3

Be on guard...[lest] that day come on you suddenly like a trap; for it will come upon all those who dwell on the face of all the earth.

Luke 21:34,35

The above Scriptures, as well as many others like them, present a very grim picture of the future. A day of judgment is coming suddenly that will be "like a trap" snapping shut on everyone "on the face of all the earth." Under a strong delusion, *everyone* who did not "receive the love of the truth so as to be saved" (2 Thessalonians 2:10) and whose name therefore "has not been written...in the book of life of the Lamb" (Revelation 13:8) will believe *the lie*, will be initiated into Satan's kingdom, and will worship him and the Antichrist.

What Will Happen to the Christians?

The large numbers of Christians in the world (perhaps several hundred million) would certainly be an obstacle in the way of Antichrist. The idea that Christians will prevent Antichrist from

63

gaining control by converting the world is becoming increasingly popular, though it hardly seems to fit Scripture. From the many prophecies which state that "the whole world" will worship Antichrist, it seems clear that Christians will either change their convictions or be removed. One possible interpretation of 2 Thessalonians 2:6,7 is that the Holy Spirit indwelling true believers exercises a restraining influence "until he is taken out of the way." Certainly this restraint and the obstacle Christians present would be "taken out of the way" by their sudden removal through Christ catching them up into heaven in an event called "the rapture." This seems to be the promise of Scripture:

> In my Father's house are many dwelling places; . . . I go to prepare a place for you.
> And if I go and prepare a place for you [in my Father's house], I will come again, and receive you to Myself; that where I am, there you may be also.
>
> John 14:2,3

> For the Lord Himself will descend from heaven with a shout. . .and the dead in Christ shall rise first.
> Then we who are alive and remain shall be caught up together with them. . .to meet the Lord in the air. . . .
>
> 1 Thessalonians 4:13-18

Such an event would instantly create a spiritual vacuum that Antichrist could take advantage of.

The coming apostasy (departure from the faith) would then be in full bloom. *The lie* of infinite human potential demonstrated in godlike mind powers will seem to be the wonderful truth giving promise of a New Age. That lie is already at work in the world. According to 2 Thessalonians 2:3, the apostasy *must* occur before the rapture ("our gathering together to Him") can take place or the Antichrist can be revealed. Much evidence indicates that it has already begun.

Among those who call themselves Christians, there have always been many apostates who deny the virgin birth, the divinity and uniqueness of Jesus Christ, the authority of Scripture, the necessity of redemption through the sacrifice of Christ on the cross, and other essentials of the faith. Babylon already exists as apostasy within the church, and it did in Paul's day. Clearly he was not talking about that, however, but about an apostasy that was yet to come, which would be so much worse than anything previously experienced that it would be known as *the apostasy*. It would influence the entire church then upon earth; and it would also be called *the apostasy* because at its heart would be *the lie* that humans can become gods.

Transformation of the Church

Why *must* the apostasy come *first*? Apparently it will be an integral part of the great deception and delusion that will sweep the entire world in preparation for the Antichrist's take-over. Thereafter those who "did not receive the love of the truth so as to be saved" (2 Thessalonians 2:10), will be given a "deluding influence so that they might believe *the lie*." There will be no hope of salvation for them. Therefore, those who will receive Christ during the Great Tribulation and be martyred as a result will not have previously heard and rejected the gospel. This could include many within mainline Protestant denominations and the Catholic and orthodox churches, who think of themselves as Christians but have never heard from their pastor or priest the real message of salvation.

Departure from the Faith or from the Earth?

Paul's prophecy of apostasy seems to fly in the face of the prevailing optimism and predictions of great revival that dominate Christian media. Such pronouncements by many Christian leaders concerning success, prosperity, and Christians taking over the world for Christ, however, are based more upon the popular idea that one must always be positive than upon solid Bible teaching. It is not easy to overcome the temptation to join the excited crowds who eagerly embrace whatever this or that dynamic Christian leader says without checking it carefully against the Bible. Those who accept at face value the many prophecies concerning apostasy, destruction, and judgment are labeled as "negative" or "gloom and doomers."

It is all too common for Christians either to become depressed by those who predict gloom and doom; or to be swept up in the enthusiasm of those who declare that the church is in the midst of a great revival. The Bible seems to indicate that apostasy and revival will go on side by side in the last days. For example, the parable Jesus told of the man who "was giving a big dinner, and he invited many" (Luke 14:16). Those he invited apparently accepted the initial invitation. It was later "at the dinner hour (when) he sent his slave to say to those who *had been bidden*, 'Come, for everything is ready now,' " that they made their pitiful excuses of having "bought a piece of land...five yoke of oxen... married a wife..." and refused to come (Luke 14:18-20).

That was when, in anger, the master sent his slave out to bring in "the poor, the crippled and blind and lame...[from] the highways and hedges, and compel them to come in, that my house may be filled." This could certainly be interpreted to indicate that many who call themselves Christians and are attending church are not really interested in being taken to heaven to participate in "the marriage of the Lamb" (Revelation 19:7). Apparently they are too intent upon making a success out of life here upon earth to take time off for what they consider to be a "pie-in-the-sky" event up in heaven. At the same time, however, multitudes of drug addicts, drop-outs, New Agers, criminals in prisons, and other unlikely candidates are repenting of their sins, receiving Jesus Christ as Savior and Lord, and will be caught up in the rapture.

Regardless of the precise scenario, the Bible makes it very clear that the major sign of the last days prior to Christ's return will be religious deception. That this apostasy must come and that it will mirror within the church the very pattern of delusion that is preparing the secular world for Antichrist not only makes sense but agrees with the weight of Bible prophecy. It also seems to agree with many developments both in the secular world and the church today that we will be dealing with as we proceed.

Antichristianity Posing as Christianity

The Antichrist will be the ultimate fulfillment of Christ's prophecy "Many will come in My name, saying, 'I am the Christ,' and will mislead many" (Matthew 24:5). He will be *the false Christ* for whom the many pretenders to Christhood have prepared the world: Satan's man posing as God's man, the Antichrist posing as the Christ. It would not be surprising, therefore, if the official world religion will be antichristianity posing as the true Christianity. The examples of precisely this are growing in number and strength. Mormonism is one of the boldest and most successful examples; and it has even managed to deceive many Christians, who think the Mormon Church is just another Christian denomination.

Claiming to represent the only true Christianity, The Church of Jesus Christ of Latter-day Saints denies every essential Christian doctrine. [For a full treatment of Mormon beliefs, see Ed Decker and Dave Hunt, *The God Makers* (Harvest House, 1984).] Its leaders declare that Mormonism teaches what "The Mystery Religions, pagan rivals of Christianity [have always] taught...." What is this teaching? "The doctrine that 'men may become Gods.' "[1] There could be no clearer example of antichristianity posing as the true Christianity. Mormonism is literally founded upon the words of Satan to Eve in the Garden of Eden, and top Mormon leaders have frankly admitted this. For example:

> On the afternoon of June 8, 1873, preaching from the pulpit of the Mormon Tabernacle in Salt Lake City, President Brigham Young declared: "The devil told the truth [about godhood].... I do not blame Mother Eve. I would not have had her miss eating the forbidden fruit for anything."[2]

He went on in that sermon to explain that it was through Eve's eating of the forbidden fruit that the pathway to godhood was opened for humanity. Mormonism proudly boasts that obedience to its prophets and precepts and participation in its secret temple rituals is the only way to reach the godhood that Satan promised. The ambition of every active Mormon male is to become a god, manufacture his own world, and through eternal sex with his many goddess wives people that world with another Adam and Eve, have another Lucifer tempt them in their Garden of Eden, another Jesus (Lucifer's brother) redeem them, and on and on forever. Hinduism has 330 million gods, but Mormonism has literally trillions, each of whom was a sinful man living on some other earth, where he was redeemed by the Jesus of that earth, which made it possible for him over eons of time to prove his worthiness through good deeds and occult rituals and finally become a god himself.

Compromise: Seed of Apostasy

If all this sounds bizarre and unbiblical, Christianity seems just as devilish to Mormons. John Taylor, the third Mormon President, said that Christianity was "hatched in hell"[3] and "a perfect pack of nonsense.... The Devil could not invent a better engine to spread his work...."[4] Yet many Mormons seem to be completely sincere in their religion, and their apparent sincerity would indicate that they have been deluded into believing that a lie is the truth. The end-time apostasy will involve an even stronger delusion and will encompass the entire world.

This apostasy will not suddenly spring up in full bloom. It will take time to develop, and the evidence indicates that we are in that development stage right now. Examples are evident throughout the Christian community of acceptance of Mormons as just another denomination. There are Christian television stations and networks where guests are specifically told not to speak negatively of Mormonism, Christian Science, etc. Everything must be "positive."

Another example would be men like Norman Vincent Peale who counts Mormon "prophets" among his best friends. As the keynote speaker at the 85th birthday party of current Mormon President Spencer W. Kimball, Peale praised Kimball as a great man of God and a true prophet of Jesus Christ. One can only wonder what "God" and what "Jesus Christ" Peale had in mind. Brigham Young did not compromise: He plainly declared that the Christian God is "the Mormon's Devil."[5]

Scientology is very similar to Mormonism. Being of more recent origin, however, it incorporates aspects of modern science and psychotherapy into the ancient lie of promised godhood. With a preexistent state that has (like Mormonism) many similarities to Hinduism, Scientology teaches that all humans are uncreated "Gods" called Thetans. After creating the universe, the Thetans incarnated the creatures they had made. As lower forms of life evolved ever higher (evolution is a key doctrine of Hinduism), "we Thetans" reincarnated repeatedly. By the time we had evolved into humans, we had forgotten who we were. Scientology offers a psychotherapeutic process for breaking through the "engrams" picked up from traumas in prior lives, to "realize" once again one's true identity as an "operating Thetan" (God) beyond the limitations of space, time, and matter.

This is *the lie* expressed as a search for the "true Self"—an attempt to "realize" one's inherent godhood or infinite potential. This lie is found in most cults and in much psychotherapy. In the mind science cults (Christian Science, Religious Science, Unity, etc.) *the lie* becomes a Christianized science (psychology) of the mind. Mind science has a much broader appeal than either Mormonism or Scientology. Pretending to be a neutral, scientific, nonreligious methodology for self-improvement, this syncretization of pseudoscience and Eastern religions is gaining increasing credibility in medicine, business, psychology, education, and even Christian thinking. It has the backing of many influential leaders, such as ex-astronaut Edgar Mitchell, who holds a doctor of science degree and was commander of Apollo 14 and the sixth man to walk on the moon.

Mitchell had a mystical experience of "unity consciousness" during his moon mission. This so transformed his life that upon his return to earth he abandoned the outer space program to join the inner space program, the new frontier of modern science.[6] Former astronaut Brian O'Leary, who earned his Ph.D. in astrophysics, had a similar experience that opened him to the belief that "the development and transformation of the human consciousness" would be the next pioneering project of science.[7] In a recent interview, O'Leary said:

> Seven years ago I took a Lifespring training in Philadelphia and it awakened parts of me that I never knew existed. Then I took an Insight training and began studying MSIA (Movement of Spiritual Inner

Awareness) discourses about two years ago, and I've been sailing ever since!...

During a spiritual retreat, I reconnected with a feeling...which I knew had to come from inside myself .... I just *knew* that outer space was a manifestation of inner development....

Outer space for me is a physical metaphor for inner space.... There is so much...we can do to accelerate the new age....

I think that the real quantum leap will be by a spiritually motivated group....[8]

Finding God-in-Us?

This belief in the exploration of "inner space" in order to discover and tap an alleged unlimited human potential is being expressed increasingly by Christian leaders. One of many examples is Rodney R. Romney, senior minister of Seattle's First Baptist Church. Romney has written a book titled *Journey to Inner Space: Finding God-in-Us*.[9] Its message is summarized in bold type on the back cover: "MISSION: To Find God. METHOD: By finding one's self."

Inside the book the message is spelled out: "To understand God is finally to realize one's own godhood";[10] Jesus was not God[11] but "simply a man who knew the laws of God"[12] and who expected His followers to "realize the Christ within their own consciousness."[13] In agreement with Mitchell and O'Leary and the spirit of the New Age movement, Romney states that "along with the inauguration of the Outer Space Age has come the rise of an Inner Space Age, marked by a great meditation movement."[14] Of course the swamis, Yogis, gurus, witchdoctors, and other occultists have been "exploring inner space" for thousands of years before anyone even thought of space travel. Romney knows this, and he recommends such forms of Eastern Mysticism as Zen,[15] Yoga,[16] Sufism,[17] and Transcendental Meditation.[18]

Denying that Christ's death and resurrection provide our only salvation, Romney writes: "He [Jesus] meant to establish a world religion that would embrace every soul and synthesize every creed...."[19] Apparently all religions are equally true; nothing is wrong in any of them. Mother Teresa, who is praised and highly honored by Christian leaders, seems to agree. She is to be commended for her selfless service to the suffering street people of Calcutta; however, she has denied her patients the opportunity to hear the clear gospel. There is something more important than "dying with dignity." She has said:

> Oh, I hope I am converting. I don't mean what you think.... If in coming face to face with God we accept Him in our lives, then we are converting.
>
> We become a better Hindu, a better Muslim, a better Catholic, a better whatever we are....
>
> What approach would I use? For me, naturally, it would be a Catholic one, for you it may be Hindu, for someone else, Buddhist, according to one's conscience.
>
> What God is in your mind you must accept.[20]

A further example of this type of "broad-mindedness" is London's venerable old St. James Anglican Church just off Piccadilly Square, a well-known tourist attraction that calls itself "A Seven Days a Week Church for London and the World" and is a gathering place for New Age activists of all kinds. There one could become involved in regular meetings of the "Sufi Healing Order," or the "Yoga Meditation Class." Special Monday evening lectures have included "Health for the New Age... through meditation, visualization...," "Lifetime Astrology," "New Age Groups, the Collective Unconscious and Networks," and "Personal Religion beyond Dogma: Don't ask a God to bear your cross, but find your God within!" It is shocking and tragic to discover the many other churches that are becoming New Age centers, where the "broad way" which Jesus said "leads to destruction" (Matthew 7:13) is now the message they promote. James Parks Morton, Dean of New York's Episcopal Cathedral of St. John the Divine, stated in a recent interview:

> So at Pentecost we invited the head Rabbi of New York, the Abbot of the Zen Community, Satchidananda—a Hindu Oren Lyons—an American Indian,

the head Immam at the mosque, and we all stood around the altar and prayed for peace in our own languages.

Then we all received communion. Some church people said, "How can you do that? They don't know what they're receiving!"

I say, "Well, I don't really know what I'm receiving either...."

We're increasingly being called to realize that the body of Christ is the earth—the biosphere—the skin that includes all of us.[21]

The Claims of Christ

Not only is such an attempt to deny the obvious differences among religions unscriptural, but it is not even logical. For example, in Buddhism there is no God, and the goal is *nirvana*, which means to be blown out, a return to the void; but in Hinduism there are about 330 million gods, and the goal is "Self-realization," to "realize" that one *is* God. It is therefore irrational to say that even these two teach the same thing, much less that they can be reconciled to Christianity, which is completely different from either of them.

Jesus Christ Himself made definite claims that exclude all other religions. One is free to reject His claims; but one is not entitled to deny the clear meaning of what He said: *"I am the way and the truth and the life; no one comes to the Father but through Me"* (John 14:6). We are not separated from some mythical "higher self" but from the one and only true God, the Creator of all. Nor do we *find* Christ within; we must *invite* Him in. After He died for our sins, rose from the dead, and ascended to heaven, Jesus Christ said:

> Behold, I stand at the door and knock; if anyone hears My voice and opens the door, I will come in to him, and will dine with him, and he with Me (Revelation 3:20).

6

Roots of Seduction

> Beloved...I felt the necessity to write to you appealing that you contend earnestly for the faith which was once for all delivered to the saints.
>
> Jude 3

It requires little insight to realize that in order to establish Antichrist's official world religion in the space age, where science is worshiped, it will be necessary to merge religion with science. Many secular leaders have been predicting this for some time. Catholic priest/paleontologist Teilhard de Chardin and psychologist C. G. Jung both foresaw it. This process is already well-established, not only in the secular world, but also within the church.

One place where science and religion have met is in the growing practice of hypnosis. Though an integral part of occultism for thousands of years, hypnosis has now been accepted as "scientific" and is even being used by hundreds of Christian psychologists. The following statement by two of the leading authorities in the field of hypnosis, William Kroger and William Fezler, should give everyone who uses any form of hypnosis, especially Christians, serious concern:

> The reader should not be confused by the supposed differences between hypnosis, Zen, Yoga and other Eastern healing methodologies.
>
> Although the ritual for each differs, they are fundamentally the same.[1]

More and more Christian psychologists use hypnosis to "regress" clients back into their childhood or even into the womb in order to deal with early traumas. Factual data often come forth, even though the brain of the prenatal, natal, and early postnatal infant is not sufficiently developed to carry memories. The source of these "memories" is therefore suspect at best. This is equally true of the memories often aroused in what Christians call "inner healing" or "healing of the memories," which can be a form of hypnosis and will be dealt with later. However, some of Bernard Diamond's comments about suggestion and memory should be noted now. A professor of law and clinical psychiatry, he is one of the world's leading authorities on hypnosis. Among the questions Dr. Diamond answered in the *California Law Review* were the following:

> Can a hypnotist, through the exercise of skill and attention, avoid implanting suggestions in the mind of the hypnotized subject? No, such suggestions cannot be avoided.
>
> During or after hypnosis, can the hypnotist or the subject himself sort out fact from fantasy in the recall? Again the answer is no. No one, regardless of experience, can verify the accuracy of the hypnotically enhanced memory.[2]

Nevertheless, in the name of science, hypnosis is being called upon increasingly to support psychology's religious beliefs in such things as "infinite potential residing in the subconscious," the conscious direction of humanity's evolution to a so-called "higher" consciousness involving godlike mind powers, and lately even reincarnation. Psychiatrists are now "regressing" patients under hypnosis back through the womb to experience alleged prior lives. Clearly such "memories" do not come from the brain, but from the same seductive source as prenatal "memories." Even factual "memories" of the *future* surface under hypnosis! In one study involving 6000 hypnotically regressed subjects, about 20 percent experienced "earlier existences on other planets."[3]

Evolution plays an extremely important part in the merger of so-called science with religion. Evolution is a theory that did not originate with science, but has been at the heart of the occult for thousands of years. Hinduism with its evil caste system is based upon a cosmic evolution to godhood that works through karma and reincarnation. The growing acceptance of these ideas in Western society is illustrated by the following ad in the Sunday Calendar Section of the *Los Angeles Times*:

SHRI MATAJI NIRMALA DEVI
the most important spiritual figure in
the world today. She will awaken in
you the force that will change your life
and change the world.
This awakening explains and integrates all the
great religions. It grants inner peace, health and joy.
It is the last evolutionary step, promised by
traditions that stretch back to the beginnings
of human spiritual awareness.
FIRST UNITED METHODIST CHURCH
OF HOLLYWOOD

This is Science?

Some psychiatrists are even "regressing" their patients back into earlier forms of life in order to recall the deeper "memories" of their experiences as apes, salamanders, or pollywogs. Jean Houston, who has Ph.D.'s in both religion and psychology, conducts workshops in which she leads participants to awaken these ancient "memories." The following excerpt from a reporter's account of one such session indicates the type of delusion that has become commonplace among educated people who consider themselves too sophisticated to believe in sin, repentance, and forgiveness through the sacrifice of a crucified and resurrected (not reincarnated) Jesus:

"Remember when you were a fish," Houston suggested in Sacramento.
Nearly a thousand people...dropped to the floor and began moving their "fins" as if to propel themselves through water.

"Notice your perceptions as you roll like a fish. How does your world look, feel, sound, smell, taste?"

"Then you came up on land," Houston recalled, taking us through the amphibian stage. . . .

Then Houston suggested, "Allow yourself to fully remember being a reptile. . . . Then some of you flew. Others climbed trees". . . . We became a zoo of sounds and movements made by early mammals, monkeys, and apes.

Houston then called us to remember being "the early human" who loses his/her "protective furry covering" and. . .evolves into the modern human.

The climax of the already intense exercise that had taken us more than an hour followed: "Now I want you to extend yourselves even further—into. . .the next stage of your own evolution." We became a room of leaping, joyous, sometimes alone, often together human beings who eventually joined hands and voices. The impact was electric. . . .

We had become a wriggling sea of bodies—nearly a thousand housewives, therapists, artists, social workers, clergy, educators, health professionals. . . [who] had crawled over and under each other, enjoying ourselves and re-learning what was deep within our memories.[4]

Following encouragement by her close friend Margaret Mead, Jean Houston organized "a symposium for leading U.S. government policymakers entitled 'The Possible Society: An Exploration of Practical Policy Alternatives for the Decade Ahead.' "[5] Houston tells how she guided "about 150 extremely high-ranking government officials for about three days. . .we had these officials on the floor, guiding them into internal journeys, looking for the possible society."[6] With examples such as this multiplying in the name of *science*, the biblical prophecies about deception and delusion just prior to Christ's return are becoming more believable and understandable each day. There is a deep need in the human heart for purpose and meaning. If this is not satisfied in a personal relationship with God through Jesus Christ, the soul will seemingly grasp at any straw, no matter how flimsy or bizarre.

Teilhard de Chardin: Architect of Apostasy

No one person has contributed more to the merger of science and religion than the French priest/paleontologist Teilhard de Chardin. Treated as an apostate by the Vatican, banned from teaching, and forbidden to publish his writings, the controversial Jesuit, (who was known as the father of the New Age) became a hero of sophisticated Protestants and then "returned to the good graces of Rome 26 years after his death" in 1955.[7] Teilhard "was the name most frequently mentioned by 185 leaders in the [New Age] movement when Marilyn Ferguson—preparing her book on the movement, *The Aquarian Conspiracy: Personal and Social Transformation in the 1980s*—asked who was the most influential person in their lives."[8] Teilhard expounded "a new theology in which soul emerged as the driving force of evolution," leading to the "awakening to a [collective] superconsciousness...[and] a new age of the earth."[9] Sociologist/anthropologist H. James Birx explains that Teilhard argued for—

> the coming of a deeply moral super-humanity ennobled by the universal spirit of the cosmic Christ....
>
> Human consciousness, growing ever more complex and interdependent, feeds what Teilhard calls the noosphere, a layer of mind or spirit enveloping the earth.
>
> A future fourth layer, the theosphere, is envisioned by Teilhard as the culmination...when the converging ...human spirits transcend space and matter and mystically join god-omega at the omega point.[10]

Calling himself a Teilhardian, Robert Muller refers to the key turning points in his life during his 36 years at the United Nations as "my Teilhardian enlightenments." He builds his speeches around Teilhard's "philosophy of global evolution, of the noosphere, of metamorphosis, and of the birth of a collective brain to the human species," into which he fits the role of the

U.N.[11] Jean Houston got her start in life as a young girl deeply influenced by long talks with Teilhard in New York City's Central Park.[12] It is understandable that Muller, Houston, and many other New Age leaders were profoundly influenced by Teilhard and became his admirers. It is incomprehensible that this is also true of some people who are looked up to as Christian leaders.

Teilhardianism and Christianity

Perhaps no woman in this century has had a larger influence upon the Christianity of today than prolific best-selling author and teacher Agnes Sanford. Quoted and recommended widely by Christian leaders, Agnes Sanford was largely responsible for bringing visualization and "healing of memories" into the church. We will have a great deal to say about her later, but at this point it should be noted that much of her writing is a clear reflection of Teilhardian philosophy, which she appears to admit. After discussing the healing of the subconscious,[13] she calls God "the very life-force existing in a radiation of an energy...from which all things evolved,"[14] and declares that "God is actually *in* the flowers and all the little chirping, singing things. He made everything out of Himself and somehow He put a part of Himself into everything.[15] Sanford further states:

> If anyone doubts this, considering it an unworthy female conception and too frivolous for serious consideration, let him read *The Phenomenon of Man* and *The Divine Milieu* by that great anthropologist and prehistorian, Pierre Teilhard de Chardin.[16]

Numerous other highly influential Christian authors quote Teilhard favorably without so much as a word of caution, among them Bruce Larson, a well-respected Presbyterian leader and keynote speaker at the recent Presbyterian "Congress on Renewal" convention in Dallas, Texas. Larson is a popular pastor and the author of 15 best-selling books. Oddly enough, he seems to admire Teilhard de Chardin, calling him "a pivotal Christian thinker of our time."[17]

A Smorgasbord of Confusion

In his book *The Whole Christian*, Bruce Larson does make a fairly clear statement that "forgiveness and redemption are possible only through God's love in the death and resurrection of Jesus Christ."[18] Unfortunately, that statement is buried within the context of what he calls "a smorgasbord of answers...all of which are valid."[19] He gives credence to everything from numerous pop psychologies to occultism—all presented as apparently beneficial for Christian living. The book is confusing at best and more likely deadly. Though he presumably is advocating the "wholeness" found only in Christ, Larson presents the transformation of "a middle-aged man" through LSD as one of the "best definitions of wholeness" and an excellent example of "the healthiest kind of conversion...":

> I'm happy and I simply don't think the world is going to hell as so many people seem to. I am once again very aware that there is a supreme power of which all and everything is a part.
>
> Most call this power God. I don't think it makes any difference if I call it love. I only wish that the religious forces could obtain those kinds of results.[20]

Larson lauds a school in Boston for offering, among other subjects, Yoga and belly dancing.[21] He praises Delores Krieger, who teaches nurses "to use their hands like divining rods" in an occult healing ritual, and explains the results in terms of "a force that is called prana" (a Hindu term) that "can be transmitted from one person to another by touch."[22] He quotes favorably numerous questionable sources from Sigmund Freud, C. G. Jung, and Abraham Maslow to Fritz Perls, Tom Harris (*I'm Okay—You're Okay*), and Eric Berne (*Games People Play*) and declares that Carl Jung, an occultist and antichristian, "is one of my heroes."[23] Nevertheless, this book is highly acclaimed by a number of respected Christian leaders.

When will such men realize that their careless recommendations cause many Christians to read books they might otherwise pass by; and to accept false and dangerous ideas such as those we've documented from *The Whole Christian*?

"The Five Year Plan for Evangelism in the Presbyterian Church (U.S.A.)" has the astonishing title *New Age Dawning*.[24] These key words are repeated dozens of times throughout the official booklet presenting this "Plan" to the Presbyterian church. One would like to assume that the slogan *New Age Dawning* was adopted because it seems inspiring. However, it is difficult to understand how the committee responsible could work for two years on this "Plan" without realizing that the words *New Age* already had an accepted meaning that would make their adoption by a Christian denomination confusing at best. The Committee called specific "attention to the Presbyterian Congress on Renewal, January 7-11, 1985 in Dallas, Texas."[25] As keynote speaker at that Congress, Bruce Larson had already gone on record concerning what he means by "new age":

> I had and have now a growing belief that we are in the beginning of an exciting new age...[a] new age which I believe is already imminent...[and will] change life for all people upon this globe...inner space and inter-space will become just as important, if not more important, than outer space....
>
> Mine is not an isolated hope. Carl Jung stated that in Jesus Christ there is made possible a new rung on the ladder of evolution. Pierre Teilhard de Chardin talks about his dreams for the evolution of a new being and a new society.... My dream is that we are on the verge of such a discovery.[26]

The Deification of Man

The "evolution of a new being and a new society" that was Teilhard's and Jung's dream is certainly not what the Bible promises through the resurrection or transformation of our bodies at the return of Jesus Christ for the redeemed. Teilhard dreamed of humanity merging into "God" and each realizing his own godhood at the Omega point. This belief has inspired many of today's New Age leaders. One of the major New Age networking groups is called Planetary Initiative for the World We Choose. It comes out of the United Nations and lists among its founding organizations the Club of Rome and The Association for Humanistic Psychology. David Spangler and Robert Muller are board members. Inspired by Teilhard's beliefs, its logo is the earth with the omega sign around it. Its director, Donald Keys, has written a book intended to be a blueprint for the New Age titled *Earth At Omega*. Like the title, its contents reflect Teilhardian beliefs.

What Teilhard taught, of course, was not unique to him but was a restatement of the ancient lie from Eden. It is therefore not surprising that many people who have never heard of Teilhard have come under the same delusion. What is astonishing, however, is the extent to which this idea of human deification is gaining momentum within the church—and that includes many evangelical groups. Some of the leaders who are now promoting the self-deification idea as true Christianity have been such stalwarts of the faith that one finds it impossible to believe what they are now teaching.

Norman Grubb's ministry for the Lord goes back as far as 1919, when he did pioneer work among unreached tribes in the Congo with the great missionary C. T. Studd, whose daughter he later married. Grubb helped found Worldwide Evangelization Crusade and Inter-Varsity Christian Fellowship, and some of his books are classics, such as *Reese Howells, Intercessor*. The current vehicle for his ministry is an organization called Union Life, which publishes a magazine by the same name. Norman Grubb explains what he now believes, which sounds more like Hinduism than Christianity:

> What we call Union Life has only one foundation... the truth that there is only One Person in the universe, and every thing and every body is a manifestation of Him in one of His millions of manifested forms. That is oneness....
>
> If everything is He in one form or another, negative or positive, then there is nothing in the universe but He.... *Nothing but God exists!* [emphasis in the original].[27]

This is pantheism, and it leads logically step by step into the merger of science and religion. Indeed, science *is* religion if all is God. It also leads to the denial of evil, sickness, and death that one finds in the rosy optimism of the mind-science cults; for even what *seems* evil to us, including Satan, is a form of God. Thus the only problem is our imperfect *perception* of reality. The next step, of course, is to realize the elusive goal of the Yogis: to see ourselves as God in human form. That leads, as *Union Life* editor Bill Volkman has written, to *Living "As Gods" Without Denying Our Humanity*, recognizing that "All humans are incarnations of deity," just as Jesus was.[28] In an interview, Bill Volkman explained what that really means:

> Why do people constantly seek the will of God? Since I have seen this whole thing of union, I have no problem defining the will of man and the sovereignty of God—as far as I'm concerned, they're exactly the same.
> And I no longer seek the will of God, you know, "What does He want me to do?" I say, "What do *I* want to do?"[29]

Exact Duplicates of God?

One cannot possibly investigate what is happening in both the world and the church today without becoming convinced that end-time prophecy is being uniquely fulfilled. The lie that will be believed by everyone when that "deluding influence" sweeps the world during the end times is already becoming the "new truth." Not only is this lie the foundation of the New Age movement, but it is being embraced within the church. One of many examples we could give is a young, dynamic pastor named Casey Treat. His new 3500-capacity auditorium of Christian Faith Center in Seattle, Washington, is already bursting at the seams. One of Casey's favorite verses to preach from is Genesis 1:26, where God said, "Let Us make man in Our image...." Casey's interpretation is startling but clear:

> The Father, the Son and the Holy Ghost had a little conference and they said, "Let us make man an exact

duplicate of us." Oh, I don't know about you, but that does turn my crank!

An exact duplicate of God! Say it out loud, "I'm an exact duplicate of God! [The congregation repeats it a bit tentatively and uncertainly.]

Come on, say it! [He leads them in unison.] "I'm an exact duplicate of God!" Say it again! "I'm an exact duplicate of God!" [The congregation is getting into it, louder and bolder and with more enthusiasm each time they repeat it.]

Say it like you mean it! [He's yelling now.] "I'm an exact duplicate of God!" Yell it out loud! Shout it! [They follow as he leads.] "I'm an exact duplicate of God! I'm an exact duplicate of God!" [Repeatedly]....

When God looks in the mirror, He sees me! When I look in the mirror, I see God! Oh, hallelujah!...

You know, sometimes people say to me, when they're mad and want to put me down..., "You just think you're a little god!" Thank you! Hallelujah! You got that right! "Who d'you think you are, Jesus?" Yep!

Are you listening to me? Are you kids running around here acting like gods? Why not? God told me to!... Since I'm an exact duplicate of God, I'm going to act like God![30]

A Lie Whose Time Has Come

What seems most significant is the fact that only a few years ago Christians would have gotten up and walked out on anyone who tried to suggest to them that they were gods. That no longer seems to be the case. Did anyone notice that Pastor Treat had taken a quantum leap from an "image" to an "exact duplicate"? Clearly this is a lie whose time has come.

Only a very few years ago it was extremely difficult to convince Christians that Mormons hoped to become gods. Anyone who said that was likely to be accused of having it in for Mormons and spreading lies about them. Today many Christians themselves believe not that they are going to *become* gods like the Mormons, but that they *already are gods,* like the Hindus, and just need to "realize" it. And they even support this idea with selected Bible verses.

As Bill Volkman writes:

> It was Jesus Himself who asked the Pharisees this question: "Is it not written in your law that 'I say you are gods'?" (John 10:34, as quoted from Psalm 82:6)....
>
> But why did Jesus say that they were gods? Because all of us are gods! *All humans are incarnations of deity* [emphasis in original].[31]

Norman Grubb, Bill Volkman, and Casey Treat are by no means the only ones who are teaching that we are gods. This belief is foundational to the teachings of the Positive Confession movement. The reason they say we can allegedly "speak the creative word" and "call those things which are not as though they were" just as God does is because we *are* gods.

Yonggi Cho, Charles Capps, and other "faith teachers" repeatedly speak of man as being "in God's class." Popular Los Angeles pastor and TV evangelist/teacher Frederick K. C. Price has written, "I believe that...God made man a god. A god under God."[32] Charles Capps agrees: "...Jesus said 'ye are gods.' In other words, Adam was the god of the earth.... Man was created...to be god over the earth...."[33] Kenneth Copeland has said, "You don't have a God living in you; you *are* one!"[34] Robert Tilton, pastor of Word of Faith World Outreach Center in Dallas, Texas has written:

> You are...a God kind of creature. Originally you were designed to be as a god in this world.
>
> Man was designed or created by God to be the god of this world.... Of course, man forfeited his dominion to Satan who became the god of this world.[35]

"Ye Are Gods"

The Bible never says that God made man a god, or that He promised man that he could become a god. That was Satan's seductive promise to Eve, and it would have been meaningless if Adam and Eve had been created gods. Genesis 3:22,23 says: "Then the Lord God said, 'Behold, the man has become like one of Us, knowing good and evil; and now, lest he stretch out his hand, and take also from the tree of life, and eat, and live forever'—therefore the Lord God sent him out from the garden of Eden." God would not perpetuate man in his fallen state of "godhood."

Disobedience had brought the knowledge of good and evil, and that knowledge (forbidden by God) had destroyed the man and woman whom God had made. They had become as "gods," "knowing good and evil." They were now Satan's followers and children of darkness. Grasping after that knowledge was man's declaration of independence. He wanted to decide on his own what was right or wrong, without having to consult God. Obviously, if everyone comes up with his own standard of good and evil, utter chaos would be the result. The idea that man can know what is right and wrong by consulting himself is a lie that caters to our pride. Man had rejected God as the personal Creator who sets all standards, and in so doing had set himself up as his own god. Moral absolutes were out; doing one's own thing was in.

To prevent complete chaos, God indelibly imprinted moral laws in their conscience. Innocence was gone. The relationship they had known with God of complete trust and perfect love had been shattered. For the first time in their existence, Adam and Eve had the experience of a guilty conscience. That experience haunted them and continues to haunt their descendants. We have all tried to escape, ignore, adjust, or live up to conscience without success. The knowledge of good and evil has been a curse upon the human race, for we "gods" can neither do the good that we should do nor refrain from the evil that we should not do. Paul expressed the tragedy of the bondage to sin that we have all inherited from Adam and Eve:

> For the good that I wish, I do not do; but I practice
> the very evil that I do not wish. . . .
> Wretched man that I am! Who will set me free from
> the body of this death?
> Thanks be to God [for delivering me] through Jesus
> Christ our Lord! (Romans 7:19,24,25).

Genesis 3 teaches the following: 1) Man was not created as a god; 2) he became a "god" through disobedience; 3) whatever that meant, it was something that God didn't want to occur and it was not good; 4) it caused man's expulsion from the Garden, because it apparently destroyed man as God had intended him to be. God would not allow Adam and Eve to eat of the tree of life and thereby perpetuate themselves in their fallen "godlike" condition. In Psalm 82 God's judgment was pronounced against the rulers of Israel because they were acting like gods who were a law unto themselves. In verses 6 and 7 God stated: "I said, 'You are gods. . . . Nevertheless you will die like men.' "

A Terrible Indictment

This Scripture and Jesus' quotation of it has given comfort to cultists and occultists and caused confusion among the unlearned. Mormons, for example, point to it as justification for their goal of godhood and support for their teaching that Satan told the truth when he offered godhood to Eve. Clearly that is a false application, for Psalm 82 does not say, "Ye shall *become* gods," as Mormons hope, but "Ye *are* gods." So whatever is meant by this statement, it refers to something that humans already *are*, not to some new status that we will eventually *attain*.

There is only one true God. All other gods are false and are demonic beings in rebellion against the true God. Through the fall, man had become like one of these false gods. Not only did Jesus say to the religious leaders of His day, "Ye are gods," but He also said, "You are of your father the devil" (John 8:44). It was a terrible indictment.

Satan, who had said, "I will make myself like the Most High" (Isaiah 14:14), seduced Eve into joining his rebellion against the true God. Of course when he promised godhood to Eve, that "father of lies" (John 8:44) had neglected to tell her that she would be a pretender, a grasper after godhood, and a rebel against the true God—and thus subject to His judgment upon all false gods. No wonder the world trembles on the brink of destruction: We now have about 4.6 billion false gods on planet Earth, each trying to rule over his own little empire in a clash of egos that won't quit. The only hope is for these gods to abdicate the thrones of their lives and come under submission to the one true God through Jesus Christ.

It can only be another sign of the growing apostasy that the same verses to which Mormons and other cultists have long pointed to support their self-deification are now being used by many evangelicals as justification for their belief that being gods is something natural, normal, and good for humans. Many of the faith teachers believe that because God gave man *dominion* over the earth, therefore man was created a god by God. They teach that the essence of the fall was the loss of this dominion to Satan, who thereby became the god of this world, and that it is now up to man to take that dominion back from Satan and once again reign as the god over this earth. They attempt to support this from Psalm 82:6.

What Did Jesus Mean?

If man is not intended to be a god, then why did Jesus quote Psalm 82:6 to His accusers? He was doing two things: 1) demonstrating that they didn't understand their own Scriptures, so were in no condition to condemn Him for saying that He was God; and 2) showing them the depths and horror of their rebellion. Jesus was not complimenting the Jews of His day, but reminding them of their rebellion against the true God. Indeed we are gods, just as Jesus said, but it isn't good. Through rebellion man has broken free from God and is now a little god on his own. It is a terrible thing to be called "gods," to be identified with demons who have rebelled against God and are seeking to reign in His place.

The consequences of becoming gods are very clear. Jeremiah reminds Israel that the only true God is the Creator of the universe, and that He has declared that all who aspire to the status of being a god will perish:

> The Lord is the true God; He is the living God and the everlasting King. At His wrath the earth quakes, and the nations cannot endure His indignation.
>
> Thus shall you say to them, "The gods that did not make the heavens and the earth shall perish from the earth and from under the heavens" (Jeremiah 10:10, 11).

The lake of fire, we are told, was prepared not for man but for the Devil and his angels. However, we consign ourselves to the same fate when we not only join Satan's rebellion, as all of us have done, but when we refuse to admit the sin of masquerading as gods. If we are to be saved, then we must make a full confession of the real nature of our sin: that we have tried to play God. Instead of that, a "positive confession" is being preached: "Confess your *healing*, confess your *prosperity*, confess your *dominion* over this earth, confess your *divine right*; *command* God to heal and bless!" Such "confession" is not the repentance that qualifies for the forgiveness which God offers by virtue of the fact that Jesus Christ has paid the full penalty for our rebellion. This "positive confession" is a renewed declaration that we want the same godhood Satan offered to Eve.

This aspiration after godhood is an ambition that has become an apparently incurable (apart from Christ) obsession for the entire human race. It is at the heart of all occultism and shamanism and is the essence of the Human Potential movement and the religion of Antichrist. It is sweeping the world today as part of the delusion that is preparing us for this coming world dictator. And this same delusion has been entering the church as a key element in the growing apostasy.

Self-Deification: Delusion for Today

The noted historian Arnold Toynbee, after studying civilizations across the whole span of history, concluded that self-worship was the paramount religion of mankind, although it appeared in various guises. Man (i.e. self) is the "God" of atheistic humanism. Of course he is not God in the classical biblical sense of the Creator who made everything out of nothing and is separate and distinct from His creation. This true God is denied in the religion of Antichrist, as we have already seen, so that self may be enthroned in His place (2 Thessalonians 2:4). In humanism, as in Mormonism, Unity, Religious Science, Hinduism, and other New Age philosophies, man has become god 1) through an evolutionary process, and 2) by mastering the forces inherent in nature or the cosmos. This was the superman of Nietzsche and Hitler. It is only within the past 25 years, however, that this obsession has become the popular religion of the masses. Historian Herbert Schlossberg has said:

> Exalting mankind to the status of deity therefore dates from the furthest reaches of antiquity, but its development into an ideology embracing the masses is a characteristic trait of modernity.[36]

It should be added that "its development into an ideology embracing the masses" and its spreading in the church would seem to be a clear fulfillment of prophecy and a solemn indication that the second coming of Christ could be very near. For those who reject the Positive Confession point of view, Satan cleverly puts the same lie in a package that will appeal to them: the pseudoscientific language of psychology. The magician's deep silk hat from which Christian intellectuals have been persuaded they can pull forth magic mind powers is called the subconscious. This supposedly holds the key to miraculous healings of body, soul, spirit, mind, and emotions. Satan reinforces his promise of godhood with the lie that we have all we need within us. If we only know how to get in touch with our true self, then we can tap into this power.

The entire smorgasbord of therapies being encouraged by some Christian leaders is being sampled by Christians in one form or another, either out in the secular world or inside the church. Much of this influence has come into the church through Christian psychology and the pseudopsychologies of inner healing and healing of memories. The common denominator is *self*. Not everyone would identify with the desire to become a god, but that is the lie that hooked not only Eve but her descendants. And to whatever extent we seek our own will, seek to use God to bring about our will, pander to our self-centered desires, or in any way are afraid or unwilling to surrender wholly to God's will—to that extent we are exalting ourselves to the position of gods, whether we call it that or not. The teaching is spreading that we don't *ask* God, but *command* Him to give us all that is our *divine right* to possess and enjoy.

Whatever the label on the package, the product inside is the same old satanic ploy: "The answer is within ourselves." We can "do it" if we only learn the "laws" and "principles" that apply and put them into operation by "faith." The goal is always to reward *self* in some way. Though called by many names, it is still the lie that the Bible prophesies will become the new "truth" upon which Antichrist's kingdom will be built and which will eventually prove to be a foundation of sand. From this root of delusion the entire tree of sorcery has sprung forth and blossomed, and is now bearing the evil fruit that is so greedily being devoured by this generation.

7

Sorcery, Scientism, and Christianity

> Just as Jannes and Jambres opposed Moses, so these men also oppose the truth.
>
> 2 Timothy 3:8

> There was a certain man named Simon...practicing magic [sorcery] in the city, and astonishing the people ...[who were] saying, "This man is what is called the Great Power of God."
>
> Acts 8:9,10

It should be profoundly disturbing to Christians that growing numbers of pastors and Christian leaders are teaching that humans are destined to be gods. The fact that this belief is spreading within the church at the same time that it is being embraced by increasing millions in virtually every area of secular society as part of the growing New Age movement can hardly be coincidence. Meanwhile, there are those in science who have added their prestigious endorsement to the pursuit of godhood. The related beliefs in evolution and infinite human potential lead logically to the twin conclusions that God as Creator of all does not exist, and that man can eventually become a god himself.

Eastern mysticism provides the psychospiritual technologies for apparently *experiencing* oneself as God through so-called higher states of consciousness. Having had this experience through drugs and various forms of Yoga, millions of people are now convinced. And now that science has given its endorsement to the exploration of inner space, the seduction has moved into high gear.

An Arrogant Scientism

As one of the world's leading astrophysicists, Robert Jastrow has expressed the popular theory that evolution could have been in process on some planets out there for 10 billion years longer than on earth. Therefore beings could exist who are as far above humans as we are beyond worms. Jastrow suggests that if and when we meet them, they would seem like gods to us, with powers of omnipotence and omniscience.[1] It is to such beings—or to ourselves—that we are to look for salvation, not to the God of the Bible.

This is not *science* but what historian Herbert Schlossberg calls "an arrogant *scientism* that went far beyond the evidence at its disposal."[2] The religion of scientism requires a leap of faith unsupported by evidence. It has been popularized by persons such as Carl Sagan, who has unlimited faith in the Cosmos to produce ever higher forms of life. The Bible condemns this religion and describes its followers as "fools...[who] exchanged the truth of God for the lie, and worshiped and served the creature [creation] rather than the Creator" (Romans 1:22,25).

The popular image of scientists as cool intellects free of personal bias who base everything strictly upon solid facts is unfortunately false. Noting that there can be "no simple appeal to the 'facts,' for factuality cannot be considered apart from a philosophy by which the facts are interpreted,"[3] Schlossberg documents that eventually "the scientific scabbards fall away to reveal ideological swords."[4] Even Aldous Huxley admitted that science is "that wonderfully convenient personification of the opinions, at a given date, of Professors X, Y, and Z."[5] Referring to the reluctantly admitted prejudice of scientists, C. S. Lewis implied that—

> ...the whole vast structure of modern naturalism [seems to] depend not on positive evidence but simply on an *a priori* metaphysical prejudice...[and is] devised not to get in facts but to keep out God.[6]

Scientism, Evolution, and Reincarnation

While professing atheism, scientific materialists could be considered polytheists. Their gods are spawned by alleged evolutionary processes and natural forces, with whom they hope (or fear) to make contact someday through the space program, and even aspire to become like them. What the occultist has traditionally hoped to accomplish through mystical practices the scientific materialist has dreamed of doing through technology: to conquer the atom and space, to discover the secret of life, to eradicate all disease, and eventually to reign supreme over all the forces of nature as captain of his own fate and master of the universe.

The Human Potential movement offers a growing number of techniques for allegedly taking charge of one's own evolution—to advance the species not *physically* but *metaphysically* through releasing the powers that allegedly lie hidden in other states of consciousness that sorcerers have always known of but modern man is only now beginning to explore seriously. This humanistic religion that substitutes a "higher self" for God and requires blind faith in impersonal and unexplained forces that have guided evolution in the past but which we can now take charge of is being passed off as science. The Institute For Conscious Evolution, for example, offers "evolutionary counseling services" at its San Francisco Counseling Center and provides courses in Conscious Evolution toward M.A. or Ph.D. degrees, in spite of the fact that no one can explain or demonstrate what "conscious evolution" really is. The Institute publishes a quarterly called *GAIA* as well as the widely distributed New Age resource magazine *Common Ground*. It also sponsors seminars, workshops, and special projects such as its recent 125,000-dollar grant to study cultural transformation as part of its Earth Community Network Project—all in the name of science.[7] Jean Houston's blend of Darwin and Freud into a bizarre therapy that seeks to create inspiration for the future of the race by "remembering" when we lived as reptiles, amphibians, and apes is just one more example of directions in which this "science" is heading.

Realizing, as British Museum of Natural History senior

paleontologist Colin Patterson has begun to admit, that "statements about ancestry [of species] are not applicable in the fossil record...[but] are made up stories...not part of science,"[8] many scientists are increasingly being drawn to evolution's mystical roots. Far from being scientific, evolution has been an integral part of occultism/mysticism for thousands of years, where it has always been understood to be the mechanism behind reincarnation. That concept, largely confined to the East until recently, is gradually replacing the once-dominant belief in resurrection in the West.

As we have already noted, this has largely come about through "proof" for reincarnation being established under hypnotic regression to alleged prior lives by growing numbers of psychiatrists. One wonders how Christian psychologists and assorted practitioners within the church of "healing of the memories" can justify their promotion of regression into infancy and the womb, when the same method can be extended to produce just as vivid and factual "memories" of alleged prior lives. At least as important, if not more so, is the question why it should be necessary to develop and pursue techniques for making Christianity "work" that were unknown to earlier generations of victorious Christians and are not found in the Bible. It is obvious that there would be no takers for these methods unless multitudes of Christians were failing to find the joy and fulfillment they seek. This can only mean that Christianity is deficient and needs outside help, or else that biblical Christianity is not being taught and lived in many of our churches.

As part of the exploding self-improvement movement, self-hypnosis tapes by the thousands are now available for reprogramming the subconscious, experiencing psychic power, and reaching a better reincarnation. Though they would avoid those involving reincarnation and obvious occultism, Christians are using similar self-improvement tapes recommended on the job, unaware of the subtle satanic influence they may exert. The following statement by Dick Sutphen, one of the largest distributors of self-help, Human Potential tapes, is typical of a growing delusion that is nevertheless still considered by many people to be scientific:

...let's go back to the beginning...there existed in the non-physical realms a great energy gestalt. We'll call the gestalt God, but any name would do as well....

So, as an expansion of the energy gestalt called God, the cells within the great body of God divide and subdivide always creating new energy...for human beings are in reality structures of energy.

Let's call the new God cells "oversouls".... As man evolved from ape to human he developed to the point he could support intelligence...thus providing oversouls with another channel to expand their energy...all who would follow in their lineage would retain a deep subconscious memory of other star systems....

Your oversoul was from a direct lineage of cells or souls that lead directly back to the energy gestalt we called God. Thus, you are part of God...YOU ARE GOD. Every living and discarnate individual is God. Together we are an energy gestalt called God....

If you are hypnotically regressed to your most recent past life, you are experiencing the life of your oversoul [emphasis in the original].[9]

"Religion In Science"

The obvious similarity between Sutphen's occult explanation for human consciousness and famed psychologist Carl Jung's "collective unconscious" (which many Christian leaders and practitioners of inner healing have accepted) ought to be a warning that something is wrong. It is astonishing how easily those Christians who have rejected evolution can be persuaded to accept a blend of Darwin and Freud or Jung as an "additive" to make up for what biblical Christianity seems to lack. Though supported by most scientists today, the incredible theory of ever-higher cosmic evolution resulting from natural forces inherent in the universe is not the product of scientific investigation but a restatement of the Serpent's seductive offer of godhood in modern, scientific terms. Those who accept and promote this theory do so on the basis of a *religious faith* that has nevertheless gained acceptance as the latest science, medicine, psychology, sociology, and education. In such forms Christians encounter and absorb Satan's lie without even knowing it.

"Evolutionists—like the creationists they periodically do battle with—are nothing more than believers themselves," according to paleontologist Colin Patterson, who recently came to this unsettling conclusion: "I had been working on this stuff [evolution] for more than twenty years, and there was not one thing I knew [that was true] about it. It's quite a shock to learn that one can be so misled for so long."[10] Since then he has been cautiously reminding his fellow paleontologists that "statements about ancestry and descent are not applicable in the fossil record,"[11] which is not what his colleagues want to hear. Growing numbers of scientists doubt evolution, but their rejection of God leaves them no alternative. Is it their unwillingness to accept moral responsibility to their Creator that causes many scientists to cling to evolution in face of the abundant evidence to the contrary? In an unusually candid confession for a public speech, D.M.S. Watson, popularizer of evolution on British television (as Carl Sagan has been on American TV), reminded his fellow biologists of the common *religious faith* they all shared:

> Evolution itself is accepted by zoologists not because it has been observed to occur or . . . can be proved by logically coherent evidence to be true, but because the only alternative, special creation, is clearly incredible.[12]

Those who worship at the altars of scientism were shocked and offended by Robert Jastrow's speech at the 144th national conference of the Association for the Advancement of Science. Director of NASA's Goddard Institute for Space Studies, Jastrow reminded some 800 of his fellow scientists that the evidence is overwhelming that the universe had a beginning that seems to demand a Creator exactly as the Bible states.[13] Though a professed agnostic, Jastrow has written:

> Astronomers are curiously upset by . . . proof that the universe had a beginning. Their reactions provide an interesting demonstration of the response of the scientific mind—supposedly a very objective mind—

when evidence uncovered by science itself leads to a conflict with the articles of faith in their profession. . . .

There is a kind of religion in science; a faith that. . . every event can be explained as the product of some previous event. . . . This conviction is violated by the discovery that the world had a beginning under conditions in which the known laws of physics are not valid. . .the scientist has lost control.

If he really examined the implications, he would be traumatized. As usual, when the mind is faced with trauma, it reacts by ignoring the implications. . . .[14]

Religious Science and Laws

So at the heart of science is what Jastrow admits is "religion." This blind and unsupported faith that "every event can be explained. . .[by] some previous event" has had serious and far-reaching consequences for humanity. This is the classic argument of atheism: No "God" exists (certainly no "God" is needed) if everything can be explained by natural processes governed by scientifically explicable laws. Yet many Christians make God Himself subject to law without realizing that they have destroyed Him in the process; for who needs God if everything happens according to laws that even God must obey? This eliminates true miracles (what *seems* to be a miracle is the result of some "higher law") and turns prayer into a technique for releasing divine power by following certain principles, rather than submitting to God's will and trusting His wisdom, grace, and love.

This belief that all is governed by higher law thus eliminates God completely for the atheist, turns Him into an impersonal Force for the occultist, and relegates Him to a secondary position for those who are into Positive Confession.

This is not only the faith of scientism but is also the foundation of all occultism, the Mind-Science cults, Positive and Possibility Thinking, and the growing Positive Confession movements within the church. Although Kenneth Hagin and Kenneth Copeland are unquestionably the leaders of the Positive Confession movement, Charles Capps is the popular teacher who lays out the basics of this theology in its clearest terms. Capps presents what appears to be an evangelical version of Christian Science founder Mary Baker Eddy's teachings: that Jesus was a *scientist* who simply applied the *laws* inherent in the universe, and that we can "demonstrate the same truth" in our own lives by a scientific application of the spiritual laws. Capps has written:

> God's Word is *spiritual law*. It functions just as surely as any natural law.... Words governed by spiritual law become *spiritual forces* working for you....
>
> *Man was created in God's class*...a spirit being very capable of operating on the same level of faith as God.... *God released His faith in words.... To imitate God, you must talk like Him and act like Him....*
>
> THE NATURAL WORLD IS TO BE CONTROLLED BY MAN SPEAKING GOD'S WORDS.... There was creative power that flowed out of the mouth of God and you...have the same ability dwelling or residing on the inside of you....
>
> This is not theory. It is fact. *It is spiritual law*. It works every time it is applied correctly...concerning confessing the Word of God aloud [so] you can hear yourself saying it...[God] said, "It is a scientific application of the wisdom of God to the psychological makeup of man [emphasis in the original].[15]

Activating Spiritual Power That Works For Anyone

The belief in laws that control spiritual forces, which in turn control the physical world through the power inherent in spoken words, is the essence of sorcery. Occultists promote exactly the same concepts as Positive Confession leaders. Charles Capps declares that "words are the most powerful thing in the universe." From a statement such as this are we to conclude that words are even more powerful than God? God Himself activates the incredible power inherent in words by speaking them, and so can you because you are "in God's class." Thus you "get what you say," whether positive or negative, because "words are containers," having in and of themselves a spiritual power that is released no matter who speaks them.[16] True faith grows out of a relationship with God that turns us into channels of His love, grace, and will; it has nothing to do with releasing "power" through speaking certain words. What His words mean to me, whether of comfort or correction, and how I speak them to others, depends upon that personal relationship with *Him*—not upon some power inherent within *words*.

Occultists repeat a *mantra* (a special word with spiritual power) and practice *decreeing*, which is the repetition of "positive confessions" to create what is being spoken. The Soka Gakkai (more commonly known outside Japan as Nichiren Shoshu) chant the mantra "Nam-myoho-renge-kyo" to "fuse the ultimate eternity of the life within with the essence of the eternal Law without."[17] Those in the I AM groups, such as Elizabeth Claire Prophet's Church Universal and Triumphant, get together not to pray but to "decree" because they believe in "the science of the spoken word, the creative power of the spoken word."[18]

In the mind-science cults one doesn't pray but makes "positive affirmations," which is what the Positive Confession movement also teaches. It used to be that "confession" meant repentance of and turning from sin. However, some would consider that a "negative confession," which is the worst thing one could do. One idea prevalent in Christian practice today calls this "praying the problem,"[19] whereas it says that we should only pray the solution: "Make a positive affirmation." Since power is inherent in the words themselves, a "negative" confession is just as powerful as a "positive" one. The relationship between "positive thinking" or "possibility thinking" and Christian Science ought to be clear. In contradiction to the facts presented in Scripture ("my soul is exceeding troubled unto death...let this cup pass from me...nevertheless, not my will but Thine be done"), Capps says of Jesus:

> He spent much time in prayer, but He never prayed
> the problem, He prayed the answer....
> He always spoke the end results, *not the problem*.

Never—did He confess *present* circumstances. He spoke the *desired results*.[20]

Sorcery, Ritual, and the Church

In contrast to the biblical doctrine of grace, this insistence that God Himself must work even His own miracles within a framework of laws that enables us to tap into and dispense spiritual power by what we think, speak, or do is the basis for all ritualism and occultism. When the witch doctor slits the rooster's throat, sprinkles the blood in a certain pattern, and chants a formula, the gods *must* come through because they are bound by "spiritual laws" to do so. The same delusion underlies all religious ritual, even though done in the name of Christ. Leading occult authority Manly P. Hall explains:

> Ceremonial magic is the ancient art of invoking and controlling spirits by a scientific application of certain formulae. A magician, enveloped in sanctified vestments and carrying a wand inscribed with hieroglyphic figures, could by the power vested in certain words and symbols control the invisible inhabitants of the elements and of the astral world. . . .
> By means of the secret processes of ceremonial magic it is possible to contact these invisible creatures and gain their help in some human undertaking.[21]

In sorcery everything works by established esoteric formulas. By his knowledge of the spiritual laws, the priest (whether wizard, medicine man, witch doctor, etc.) has become the special intermediary between the people and the gods. The arrangement between the priest and the spirit world is called the "magician's bargain." What seems to the awestruck people to be a "miracle" is actually the result of this "inside deal," which is believed to be produced by the spiritual laws that govern not only the occultist but the spirits as well (who sell power for human souls).

The Bible forbids humans to attempt any contact or bargaining with the spirit world (Deuteronomy 18:9-14). It can only lead to disaster, even though at first there may seem to be genuine healings and feelings of love and peace. There is no cause-and-effect relationship between man and spirits, whether angels or demons, any more than between man and God; evil spirits encourage this idea in order to deceive and enslave. We must never forget that our *only* approach to God is as unworthy sinners relying upon His grace and love. Whatever is governed by *law* cannot be grace. This idea of spiritual "law" to which even God is subject is the basis of all ritual and occultism. Although they may not intend it, the Positive Confession teachers often present in a biblical framework basic occult theory and methodologies that lead to delusion. The biblical teaching of *supplication* has been replaced by the idea that we can get God to do whatever we want to by following the rules of the game. In reference to a house she wanted to buy, Gloria Copeland relates:

> I began to see that I already had authority over that house and authority over the money I needed to purchase it. I said, "In the Name of Jesus, I take authority over the money I need. (I called out the specific amount.) I command you to come to me...in Jesus' Name. Ministering spirits, you go and cause it to come."
> (Speaking of angels...when you become the voice of God in the earth by putting His Words in your mouth, you put your angels to work! They are highly trained and capable helpers; they know how to get the job done.)[22]

We do not believe the leaders of the Positive Confession movement are deliberately involved in sorcery. However, the terminology, while sounding biblical, promotes concepts that cannot be found in the Bible, but are found in occult literature and practice. Moreover, some of the Positive Confession leaders not only admit but teach that the methods, laws, and principles they use are also used successfully by occultists. Nowhere in the Bible does it indicate or even imply that the people of God are to use the same methods or power as the pagans. Yonggi Cho, however, not only says that miracles must all conform to his "Law of the Fourth Dimension,"[23] but that *anyone*, including occultists, can "apply the law of the fourth dimension and...perform miracles."[24]

It sounds like the "dark and light sides of the Force." Nevertheless, pastor Cho assures us that he learned this from "the Holy Spirit" when he asked in prayer why occultists could do miracles just like Christians.[25] Cho commends the Japanese Buddhist occultists, the Soka Gakkai, for performing "miracles" through visualizing "a picture of prosperity, repeating phrases over and over [and]...develop[ing] the human spiritual fourth dimension."[26] And he scolds Christians for not doing likewise.[27] *Prophecy & Economics Newsletter* publisher Frank Goines states that anyone, Christian or not, can—

> totally control his own flow of God's riches [because there] is a law of Prosperity...[that] can be used by *anyone*.
>
> ...Prayer is a scientific application following an exact law [emphasis in the original].[28]

The New Testament warns that sorcery will be revived in the last days prior to the second coming of Jesus Christ and that the world will refuse to repent of it (Revelation 9:21; 18:23; 21:8; 22:15). Two Greek words are used, both translated "sorcery" in the King James Version: *mageia* (from which we get our word "magic") and *pharmakeia* (from which we get "pharmacy" or "drugs"). A sorcerer takes drugs or practices forms of Yoga in order to reach an altered state of consciousness and to thereby contact "spirits" from whom he can gain "magical" knowledge and power. This revival of psychic power produces the counterfeit "great signs and wonders so as to mislead, if possible, even the elect" (Matthew 24:24) that Jesus warned would be performed by false prophets immediately prior to His return. Paul provided further insight by indicating that in the last days modern "miracle-workers" would oppose the truth with occult powers like those of Pharaoh's court magicians (sorcerers) Jannes and Jambres, who were able up to a point to duplicate the miracles that God did through Moses (2 Timothy 3:8).

In the physical realm, God sends rain "upon the just and the unjust." But in the spiritual realm, God's blessing and power are by grace, not law, and are reserved for His own who walk by faith and in obedience to His will. Anything of a spiritual nature that can seemingly be performed by non-Christians is a deception from Satan and has nothing to do with any legitimate power given to man by God.

The Real Issue

Robert Jastrow called the belief that every event is the result of previous events (all governed by scientifically explicable laws) the "religion in science." It is clear that out of a naive deference to science and a penchant for success, many leaders within the church are seduced into attempting to make Christianity scientific. If *everything* is part of a cause-and-effect process governed by physical or spiritual laws, then it follows that: 1) anyone or anything, including God or gods, must be part of this process and bound by these laws; 2) there is no act of creation out of nothing and thus no Creator separate and distinct from His creation; 3) there can be no supernatural, for *everything* (including the actions of the gods) would be governed by *natural* laws; and 4) godlike powers are available to anyone.

On the other hand, if creation was not the result of a *natural* process governed by *natural* laws, then it must have been a *supernatural* event requiring a Creator. This fact forces us to the following conclusions: 1) since the very origin of the universe is a miracle, it is clear that miracles can repeatedly occur; 2) if miracles are to occur, they can only result from the *independent action of the Creator*; and 3) since miracles by very definition are not governed by laws of any kind, there is no ritual, formula, prayer, or demand that anyone can use to bring about a miracle; it must be by grace alone. We can rely upon God's *promises* because of His integrity and love—not because He is bound by "scientific law."

The Creator God of the Bible is not subject to such laws, nor is He in a cause-and-effect relationship with His creation, or else He would be part of a problem to which there would be no real solution. Because He is outside of nature, God is not affected by the disease, decay, and death that now exist and are bringing inevitable destruction upon the entire universe. Indeed, the cosmos has the stamp of death upon it because it is separated from its Creator by the rebellion of Satan and of man and is therefore under God's judgment: "The wages of sin is death."

But the transcendent God of the Bible can reach in from outside, effecting His miracles. These include the whole range of triumph over natural law; but the most important miracles are forgiveness of sin, redemption, resurrection, and the creation of new creatures for a new universe that He will someday bring into existence for the redeemed to inhabit. Having given us the power of choice so that we could freely choose to respond to His love, He will not violate our wills. And unlike the bargaining and appeasing involved with pagan gods, our approach to the God of the Bible must be as unworthy sinners relying upon His grace and mercy, recognizing that there are no formulas that we can think or speak that will require Him to respond to us in a certain way.

We must come to God on His terms, believing that through the virgin birth He became a man to die for our sins, and that having paid the penalty we could never pay, He rose from the dead and is now alive, seeking an entrance into the hearts of all who will receive Him as Savior and Lord. To admit that the true God is not bound by laws opens the door to miracles and closes the door on occultism and ritual magic, which are man's attempt to play God. In doing this man no longer has *control* of himself or the universe. That is the issue.

8

The Temptation to Power

The Spirit explicitly says that in later times some will fall away from the faith, paying attention to deceitful spirits and doctrines of demons.

1 Timothy 4:1

Even Satan disguises himself as an angel of light.

2 Corinthians 11:14

Unfortunately, Christians who have tasted genuine miracles often succumb to the temptation to be able to control the occurrence and increase of God's power through methods, principles, and laws. Perhaps many are not aware that they have thereby denied the true miraculous and have locked God in a box where He *must* respond in a predetermined manner to their positive or possibility thinking, positive confession, visualizations, and affirmations. The fact that they may have stepped over the line into the occult without realizing it doesn't help either them or their followers to escape the consequences.

Using God for Our Ends

The sorcerer masks his rebellion by postulating in place of the personal God of the Bible, who holds us morally accountable and whose will we must obey, an impersonal metaphysical "Force" that can be manipulated as "scientifically" as tapping into the energy of the atom. Often without realizing it, sincere Christians accept the same basic idea presented in psychological and pseudochristian terminology. Like positive confession, positive and possibility thinking are further examples. In his most famous best-seller, *The Power of Positive Thinking*, of which more than 3 million copies have been sold, Norman Vincent Peale reveals the fact that his entire system is based upon this same foundation. For example, he declares:

> Prayer power is a manifestation of energy. Just as there exist scientific techniques for the release of atomic energy, so are there scientific procedures for the release of spiritual energy through the mechanism of prayer. Exciting demonstrations of this energizing force are evident....
>
> It is important to realize that you are dealing with the most tremendous power in the world when you pray.... New and fresh spiritual techniques are being constantly discovered...experiment with prayer power....[1]

Many who claim they want to know God very often do not want to know the true God, but a god whose power they can use to their own ends. The very title of such popular booklets as *God's Creative Power Will Work for You*, by Charles Capps, and *How To Write Your Own Ticket With God*, by Kenneth Hagin, would seem to set a tone that panders to man's basic weakness, no matter how much good they may otherwise contain. Our selfish ambition blinds us to the fact that God is not a "genie in the bottle" who exists to do our bidding whenever we summon him, but is the Creator of all, who calls us to turn from our folly to submit to His will.

With some of those who speak a great deal about submitting to God's will, much of the language they use and the basic premise behind it denies this submission. A prophet of God can speak with authority, but only as God's servant performing His will, and not as a magician who has mastered cosmic forces by his knowledge of the laws that govern them. The basis of answered prayer is not a "positive confession," but what John explains:

> And this is the confidence that we have before Him, that if we ask anything according to His will, He hears

us. And if we know that He hears us in whatever we ask, we know that we have the requests which we have asked from Him....

And whatever we ask we receive from Him, because we keep His commandments and do the things that are pleasing in His sight. And this is His commandment, that we believe in the name of His Son Jesus Christ, and love one another, just as He commanded us (I John 5:14; 3:22,23).

The Bible contains many promises of God's blessing to His own. Whether to Israel or Christians, however, and whether for healing or prosperity, these promises are always conditioned upon God's wisdom and will in the particular situation and upon the obedience of His people. It is our natural inclination to make the only condition our ability to "believe" that God will give us what we want. Those who try to develop a "faith" that always gets one's interpretation of a "promise" to work out may in fact not have the genuine faith to trust God's love and the true wisdom to let Him work all according to His will and not ours. His answering "exceeding abundantly above all that we ask or think" (Ephesians 3:20 KJV) may therefore not be what we "confessed" but something that would be even better for us in the end, though our limited view may not see it that way at the time.

Death of Materialism: Birth of Scientific Mysticism

Sorcery and materialistic science have the same goal, and differ only in the means of attaining it. Intending to be no less "scientific" than a physicist or chemist, the occultist deals with *spiritual* laws and metaphysical forces (which he believes govern the physical elements) while the materialistic scientist has generally confined himself to dealing with *physical* laws, because he denies that anything nonphysical exists. That attitude is changing, however. Mortimer J. Adler, guiding genius behind *The Encyclopaedia Britannica* and *Great Books of the Western World,* has predicted that a belief in a nonphysical reality will soon be considered orthodox science.[2] As a result, science and sorcery will become much more difficult to distinguish from each other. In our opinion, the confusion between science, scientism, and sorcery will be an important factor in the growing seduction.

The major premise behind occult methodologies, that mind creates reality, is now considered by a number of top scientists to be implied by quantum mechanics. Such theories are even affecting the arts. "Commenting on the religious mysticism so evident in his paintings, Salvador Dali told an interviewer that he was influenced by the spirituality of the new physics [quantum mechanics]. 'I realized that science is moving toward a spiritual state,' said Dali."[3] After interviews with leading scientists in Europe and America, philosopher John Gliedman reported that "several leading theorists have arrived at the same startling conclusion: their work suggests a hidden spiritual world."[4] The indirect effect upon the church of this swing by science to mysticism promises to be staggering. Dr. Gliedman explains the view of certain scientists:

> Some [scientists] agreed with the distinguished physicist, Fritz London, that [John] von Neumann's rigorous formulation of quantum mechanics showed that physical reality was a figment of the human imagination and that the only true reality was thought....
>
> "It could be," London and a collaborator wrote...
> "that the scientific community is a kind of *spirit society* that devotes itself to studying imaginary phenomena, and that the objects of physics are ghosts produced by the observer himself."[5]

Not long ago such ideas were confined to a relatively few esotericists and considered madness by the vast majority. Today, however, although no more logical or factual, this basic occult belief that mind creates its own reality (and the practices it leads to) are the essence of the *new* physics and the *new* (transpersonal) psychology. These ideas are expressed in popular form in the New Age movement, known also as the Holistic, Human Potential, or Consciousness Movements. No longer seen as a machine, the universe is now viewed, as Eddington said, "more like a thought." In his excellent work, *Idols For*

Destruction, historian Herbert Schlossberg explains what has happened:

> Many physicists have become. . .idealists who believe that *mind* is the ultimate reality with *matter* the epiphenomenon. . . .
> Sir James Jeans said that things seem objective due to their "subsisting in the mind of some eternal spirit."[6]

Christians often quote such statements from leading scientists as support for the biblical belief in spiritual reality, as though this proves that humans have infinite, untapped potential in the form of astonishing "mind-powers." However, instead of finding comfort in statements by scientists inferring "spiritual" power, Christians need to recognize the dangers. For example, Nobel Laureate Max Planck's remark, "I regard consciousness as fundamental and matter as derivative from consciousness," is far from Christian. It elevates the human mind to godhood, endowed with the capacity to create its own reality through manipulation of consciousness. The new science has jumped out of the frying pan of materialism into the fire of mysticism/occultism, which is beginning to have devastating consequences for both secular society and the church.

The New Religious Science

There is increasing acceptance among scientists of what William Tiller, Stanford University Professor of Materials Science, describes as "new energies, which we have never dealt with before in physics."[7] Whatever these "new energies" are, there is a growing consensus that they are not "physical" in the materialistic sense, but are somehow connected to human consciousness. Science has stumbled into the realm of "spirit," where its instruments and methodologies are hopelessly irrelevant, making it the inevitable victim of its own misconceptions.

Many scientists are concluding, as Tiller himself believes, that "at some level of the universe, we are all connected. . .time, space and matter are all mutable."[8] Hinduism has been saying this for thousands of years. If actually true, then each of us is not just potentially but in fact God, and "Self-realization" (i.e. "God-realization") may well be attainable, as the Yogis have so long insisted, simply by looking within to discover who we really are. Although a turn to mysticism may actually involve only a minority of scientists, they are the most vocal and represent the popular view of science held by the general public. Because it is worshiped like a sacred cow by almost everyone, including many Christians, science is influencing the church in its slide toward sorcery.

By calling itself *science,* Yoga (which is the very heart of Hinduism) has within the last 20 years become an integral part of Western society, where it is taught in nearly every YMCA or YWCA, in clubs, in public schools, in industry, and in many churches. Dressed in Western clothes, Yoga has gained acceptance in medicine, psychology, education, and religion under such euphemisms as "centering," "relaxation therapy," "self-hypnosis," and "creative visualization." Yoga is designed to lead to the "realization" of one's true "godhood" through an inward meditative journey that finally locates the ultimate source of everything within the human psyche. Once ridiculed as pure nonsense by educated Westerners, this belief is being taken seriously by millions in the West, including increasing numbers of top scientists. For example, Cambridge University's Brian Josephson, recipient of the 1973 Nobel Prize in Physics, "has staked his enormous scientific reputation on the possibility that he can gain insights into objective reality by practicing traditional Eastern meditational techniques."[9]

Holograms and Godhood

Far from being as absurd as it seems at first, this idea appears to have an intriguing scientific basis. We may soon be seeing holograms in theaters: three-dimensional images spreading the action from the big screen out into the auditorium among the spectators. The amazing thing about a hologram is that no matter how many or how small the pieces it is cut into, although the resolution becomes distorted, each one retains the entire image of the whole. The same is true of single cells in the body: Each one has the entire DNA formula for replicating the whole, which is why it is theoretically possible to clone an entire human being from a single cell.

The next logical step is to suggest that each of us is a little holographic image of the entire universe—a "God" that contains within itself everything that is. Christians will need to get back to the Word of God and know what they believe and why they believe it in order to deal with such ideas in the days ahead. Unfortunately, much popular teaching in the church today, instead of refuting Eastern mysticism, seems to support it. One example is Yonggi Cho's teaching about his "fourth dimension." Stating that a line is one-dimensional, a plane is two-dimensional (the two include the one), and a cube is three-dimensional (the three include the two), he then declares:

> Then God spoke to my heart, "Son...the spirit is the fourth dimension. ... [as] the third dimension includes and controls the second dimension, so the fourth dimension includes and controls the third dimension, producing a creation of order and beauty."[10]
>
> There are three spiritual forces in the earth. The Spirit of God, the spirit of man, and the spirit of Satan.... All three spirits are in the realm of the fourth dimension, so naturally spirits can hover over the material third dimension and exercise creative powers....
>
> The Holy Spirit said, "My son, man still does not realize the spiritual power that I have given to him."
>
> Yes, I said, realizing what God was referring to.... False prophets had power in the realm of the spirit because they had come to realize their potential.[11]

The "Fourth Dimension"

It contradicts logic and science as well as the Bible to say that spirit is a fourth dimension that "includes and controls" the three-dimensional universe. This not only denies God's transcendence by placing Him in a dimensional/cause-and-effect relationship with the physical universe, but it also presents the Hindu concept of God, who is the All and made everything out of Himself. The most disturbing part about Yonggi Cho's "fourth dimension" is his claim that the Holy Spirit revealed this to him. He even gives us his conversation with God on the subject. Coming up with a mistaken idea on one's own can be dismissed as poor logic, but to have a voice (audible or inaudible) that one believes comes from God present false information is far more serious. Not only must we reject this "revelation," but it should be a reminder to "prove all things; hold fast to that which is good."

Out of this error comes another equally serious one: the claim that the Spirit of God, angels, demons, and man's spirit all inhabit the same dimension. Again the transcendence of God is denied. This, in fact, is the basis for Satan's claim, "I will make myself like the Most High" (Isaiah 14:14), which in turn became the basis for his promise to Eve that she could be like the gods also. On the contrary, the Bible presents God as totally in a class and realm by Himself: ". . . who alone possesses immortality and dwells in unapproachable light; whom no man has seen or can see" (1 Timothy 6:16).

Man's spirit is intended by God to function within his body, which operates in the physical space/time/matter universe and is subject to the laws that determine order in that realm. We are forbidden to attempt to make contact with disembodied spirits, whether angels, demons, or spirits of the dead. They live in another dimension that is bound by its own laws, which we can neither measure with our scientific instruments nor understand on the basis of our material experience nor manipulate by formulas or rituals. When these entities intrude into the physical world in forms of psychic phenomena, the things they do seem like supernatural miracles to us, but are as natural to that spiritual dimension of nature they inhabit as everyday events in the physical world are to us.

God does not inhabit, nor is He part of, the spirit world any more than the physical world. He is in a realm of pure existence totally other than anything else: The Creator and His creation, whether physical or spiritual, are separate and distinct from each other. The true supernatural comes from Him alone; psychic phenomena originate with Satan and his minions and are intended to deceive humans into thinking that they have made contact with the genuine supernatural power of God. It is essential that we know the difference.

Visualization: "Like a Hen Sitting on Her Eggs"

Although he probably does not realize it, pastor Cho has laid out basic occult theory, an apologetic for nature religion, or witchcraft. He states that because God "includes" the entire physical universe, He can therefore create matter out of Himself. How does He do it? By "incubating," which is Cho's term for visualizing: "In Genesis the Spirit of the Lord was incubating . . . like a hen sitting on her eggs. . . ."[12] The Bible never suggests, much less teaches, that God creates through any technique, visualizing or other. To suggest *how* God creates is to confine His power to a particular methodology, which is clearly inappropriate, since God cannot be limited in any way.

This sets us up for the delusion that if we can somehow use the same technique, we can do what God does. Thus the next error in Cho's reasoning process is, if possible, even worse than its predecessor: that because man is also a "fourth-dimension" spirit being, we too can visualize, incubate, and create reality just as God does. In his sequel to *The Fourth Dimension,* pastor Cho writes:

> We've got to learn how. . .to visualize and dream the answer as being completed as we go to the Lord in prayer. We should always try to visualize the end result as we pray.
>
> In that way, with the power of the Holy Spirit, we can incubate that which we want God to do for us. . . .
>
> God used this process of visualizing the situation to help Abraham. . . . By that visualization through the associated thought Abraham. . .could incubate his [future] children and dispel the doubts from his heart. . . . The main thing is that we should know the importance of visualization.[13]

If visualization is so all-important, one would expect that the Bible would have a great deal to say about it. But in fact the word does not occur even once in the entire Bible, and the concept is never so much as mentioned, much less explained or taught. We will have more to say about this later. However, at this point it should be clearly understood that the whole idea of visualizing a vivid image in the mind in order to produce an effect in the physical world is not just missing from the Bible but is present in all occultic literature as far back as we can go (and is in fact one of the most basic shamanistic devices). Yet it is being taught not only in the way Cho uses it but also by Christian psychologists in therapy and by success/motivation teachers, and is the major technique used for inner healing or healing of the memories and even for healing at a distance.

Mind Magic: Latent Power of the Soul?

Throughout its history, humanity has been obsessed with the pursuit of power—from the despots (who have perpetually sought to wield power over others) to the alchemists and modern scientists (who have sought the source of power in physical substances) and the mystics (who have been convinced that the greatest power lies within). It is this latter myth of infinite power within and the search for self-fulfillment that is in vogue today. After extensive investigation of psychology, journalist Martin L. Gross declared: "One of the most powerful religious ideas of the second half of the twentieth century is the Great Unconscious.... In this religion of the Unconscious, our conscious mind is a second-class being...a mere puppet of the unknown true self...."[14]

Today's most attractive myth, unproven but sold to the masses as scientific fact by thousands of psychologists and psychiatrists, is the theory that somewhere hidden at the deepest depths of the psyche lies an untapped and unlimited power potential. This is the basic idea behind the Human Potential movement, and hundreds of methodologies are being foisted upon a gullible and needy public, each touted as the fastest, surest, and most effective technique for releasing this fabled power of the mind. Christians have also begun to believe this theory, which is being perpetuated by popular leaders in the church who ought to know better. Pastor/author C. S. Lovett has written:

> Would it shock you to learn that God's healing power is available through your own mind and you can trigger it—by faith!...
>
> If you had DIRECT ACCESS to your unconscious mind, you could command ANY DISEASE to be healed in a flash. That's how much power is at hand. Jesus obviously had access to it, for He produced COMMAND healings.
>
> But God has purposely placed this power beyond our awareness. That way fallen man can't tamper with it. However there is a way to get to it—indirectly—BY FAITH....
>
> SOUNDS LIKE MIND SCIENCE? I admit that. It's true that the cults have discovered certain of God's healing laws and use them to lure people into their webs.... But let me ask, should born-again believers be denied healing simply because certain cults exploit these laws...?
>
> That's like throwing the baby out with the bathwater. It's ridiculous to say, "I can't use these laws because the Science of Mind people use them" [emphasis in the original].[15]

There are obvious fallacies in the above, which by now should be recognized as common errors taught widely in the church that are in fact ancient sorcery dressed up in Christian terminology. Similar to the teaching which advocates having "faith in your faith," Lovett urges us to have faith in our subconscious. Moreover, he suggests that it was not through the power of God but through tapping into the power of the human unconscious that Jesus healed. However, Jesus said, "Have faith *in God*."

Made in the "Image of God"

The first thing we are told about man in the Bible is that he was created "in the image of God" (Genesis 1:26,27). An image is reflected in a mirror. Being like a mirror of God's glory, man was intended to reflect a reality *other than his own*. It is just as absurd for a man as it would be for a mirror to try to develop a "good self-image"! If the image is distorted, the proper solution is for the mirror to get back into a right relationship with the one whose image it was designed to reflect, and not to pursue self-improvement, self-confidence, etc. These ideas of modern psychology turn us to ourselves rather than to God, where the only true solution lies. Man is totally dependent upon God, having been created to reflect the character of God and not some goodness or power of his own.

Satan's promise to Eve that she could "be like God" would have had no meaning to her if she already had godlike powers within herself. Furthermore, we know that this promise was a lie, which would argue against the possibility of such powers being acquired then or now. Psychic powers do not represent something inherent within man, but an intrusion from the demonic realm. Satan wants man to imagine that this power comes from his own psyche, mind, or subconscious—some source within himself—in order to hide the fact that he is thereby making man a slave by the temptation to power. This popular idea has caught on even among Christians, for whom ESP (extrasensory perception) is often confused with the gifts of the Spirit which Ralph Wilkerson has described as "HSP" (Holy Spirit Perception). In his book *ESP or HSP?—Exploring Your Latent Seventh Sense*, Wilkerson, who pastors Melodyland Christian Center in Southern California, writes:

> Why are some more gifted with HSP—hearing the voice of God, discerning demons, speaking words of wisdom and knowledge—and others less so, only manifesting it occasionally? Certain people appear to be more naturally sensitive than others to the seventh sense.
>
> Those with American Indian ancestry, such as Oral Roberts, often exhibit a special openness to both the sixth [ESP] and seventh [HSP] sense. I believe this can be traced to the keenly developed perception necessary for primitive Indian's survival....

> Women are apparently more aware of hidden realms beyond.... Perhaps this explains why so many psychics are female.[16]

If Adam, the first man, had psychic powers before he sinned, then surely Jesus, the Second Man, who was without sin, would have displayed these same powers. He always said that He Himself was not doing the works, but His Father was doing them through Him. In John 1:47-51, when Jesus told Nathanael that He had seen him "under the fig tree" when this had been physically impossible, Nathanael acknowledged this as evidence that Jesus was the Son of God. Christ accepted that recognition. He didn't assure Nathanael that this was a display of "clairvoyance" made possible by the psychic powers that He possessed as the last Adam, the perfect man. Much less did he encourage Nathanael or anyone else to develop psychic powers, as some church leaders are now recommending.

Psychic Powers Versus Miracles

The only supernatural powers that Christians are to exhibit are called "gifts of the Spirit." It is evident that they do not result from some latent power within man that has been awakened, but that man has once again become, through the Holy Spirit, a channel of God's life and image. Scripture would indicate that no such latent power resides within man; the source of both psychic phenomena and true miracles lies outside of man, who is like a channel of power. This analogy fits 1 Corinthians 12:7, which calls the display of the miraculous gifts a "manifestation of the Spirit."

The display of supernatural powers by psychics and other shamans are not gifts of the Holy Spirit coming to them on the conditions of repentance, redemption, faith, and obedience set forth in the Bible. These are manifestations of evil spirits, of demons or Satan himself. Samson manifested supernatural power that was clearly not his own, feats of strength that cannot be explained except as the supernatural power of God working through him. Likewise, the demoniac in Mark 5:2-13 who could not be bound, but who broke iron chains like thread, was not displaying any power that has its source within human beings; he was displaying demonic power.

It is clear that humans do not have supernatural powers of their own. When such are displayed through a human, they are manifestations either of the Holy Spirit or of demons, and they relate to the spiritual battle between God and Satan for human souls. There is no neutral ground that man can claim as his own. The explanation of psychic power is not some universal, impersonal Force with a dark and a light side. There are two spiritual beings—the almighty God and Satan—in conflict with each other, and man is the prize in this battle. God has all power, but He will not violate the free will He has given man: We must choose whom we will serve. Satan's weapon to get man to opt for his side is the lie that apart from God we can awaken an infinite potential that lies within each of us.

A Serious Confusion of Terms

Even hard-core secular humanists are now speaking of "spiritual" powers as more than a metaphor. Whatever the atheistic meaning of "spiritual," it is metaphysical and certainly not biblical. For example, in a recent *Newsletter* of the Association for Humanistic Psychology, AHP Executive Director Francis U. Macy reported that recent "AHP conferences included sessions on such topics as psychological and spiritual responses to planetary peril...."[17] Leaving open the question of Humanistic Psychology's definition of "spiritual," the newsletter went on to declare:

> AHP has always held spiritual concerns close to its heart.... We have been open to spiritual practices both east and west. We have championed the return of spirit to therapy.
>
> We who appreciate (and participate) in the mystical quest can be of great service.[18]

This is atheistic mysticism, a religion that denies it is a religion, claims to be scientific, and is adamantly opposed to biblical Christianity. Nevertheless, the church has so wholeheartedly embraced psychology that few Christians seem to question what atheistic humanists mean by "spiritual concerns" held close to the "heart." This is religious language. Psychiatrist Thomas Szasz declares: "...modern psychotherapy...is not merely a religion that pretends to be a science, it is actually a fake religion that seeks to destroy true religion."[19] In keeping with the trend in science itself, the pseudoscience of psychology has also turned to mysticism. In *From Shaman to Psychotherapist*, Walter Bromberg writes:

> Whereas in previous generations "altered consciousness" was considered a mark of bohemian depravity if sought voluntarily or one of madness if involuntary, nowadays a "high" is the essence of psychologic sophistication.[20]

Modern medicine has taken the same blind leap of faith into mysticism. With its deceptive and seductive claim that it involves the treatment of "mind, body, and spirit," Holistic medicine is growing in popularity and acceptability. In fact the new concern for "spirit" in health and education has come about as part of the astonishing transformation of Western society through its acceptance of Eastern mysticism.

Many Christians are usually only too eager to assume that anyone using such words as "God," "Christ," or "spirit" agrees with their own understanding of these terms, especially if such an assumption would appear to put "science" on their side. Obviously, however, "spirit" is not a scientific or medical term, but a religious one. Yet how many Christians ask their doctor or psychologist what religion involving "spirit" he is passing off on his patients in the name of the latest medical science? Psychologist Jack Gibb has put it plainly:

> The absolute assumption that a lot of us are making in the Holistic Health Movement is that all of the things necessary to create my life are in me....
>
> I believe that I am God, and I believe that you are....[21]

Although some Christian doctors, like non-Christians, may use the term "Holistic" simply because everyone else is, without understanding it, the vast majority of those involved in the Holistic (or Wholistic) movement are practicing some form of sorcery. One of the leading authorities in his field, anthropologist Michael Harner of New York's Academy of Science, explains that the religion behind Holistic medicine is in fact ancient shamanism revived. Says Harner, "The burgeoning field of holistic medicine shows a tremendous amount of experimentation [with]...techniques long practiced in shamanism.... In a sense, shamanism is being reinvented in the West...."[22] Harner makes this statement not as a critic but as a believer. Like Mircea Eliade, who thoroughly documents in his classic work *Shamanism* that witchcraft's basic premises and practices are identical *everywhere* and always have been, Harner declares:

> Shaman (pronounced SHAH-maan) is a word from the language of the Tungus people of Siberia and has been adopted widely by anthropologists to refer to persons in a great variety of non-western cultures who were previously known by such terms as "witch," "witchdoctor," "medicine man," "sorcerer," "wizard," "magician"....
>
> Shamanism represents the most widespread and ancient methodological system of mind-body healing known to humanity.... These shamanic methods are strikingly similar the world over even for peoples whose cultures are quite different in other respects and who have been separated by oceans and continents for... thousands of years....[23]

It is not surprising, therefore, that shamanism is taking exactly the same form in its current revival in the modern and sophisticated Western world of today. What is most alarming is the staggering extent to which basic shamanistic practices are being accepted in the church under psychological labels. Obviously there has always been and still is a common source of inspiration behind shamanism no matter where it was or is practiced. The

Bible leaves no doubt that the one masterminding this worldwide seduction of the human race to accept false religion is none other than "the god of this world," Satan himself, aided by his followers, both human and demonic.

9

Shamanism Revived

> I solemnly charge you in the presence of God and of Christ Jesus...preach the word...reprove, rebuke, exhort, with great patience and instruction.
>
> For the time will come when they will not endure sound doctrine; but wanting to have their ears tickled, they will accumulate for themselves teachers in accordance to their own desires, and will turn away their ears from the truth, and will turn aside to myths.
>
> 2 Timothy 4:1-4

"Visualization" and "guided imagery" have long been recognized by sorcerers of all kinds as the most powerful and effective methodology for contacting the spirit world in order to acquire supernatural power, knowledge, and healing. Such methods are neither taught nor practiced in the Bible as helps to faith or prayer. Those who attempt to do so are not following the leading of the Holy Spirit or the Word of God, but are practicing an ancient occultic technique. Legitimate uses of the imagination would involve such things as seeing mental images of something being described in a book; designing, planning, or rehearsing something in our minds; or remembering a place or event. Such mental processes are normal aids to everyday activities and do not involve an attempt to create or control reality through mind-powers. When dealing with visualization in the following pages, we do not mean any of the many nonoccultic uses of the imagination.

The visualization we are concerned with is an ancient witch-craft technique that has been at the heart of shamanism for thousands of years, yet is gaining increasing acceptance in today's secular society and now more and more within the church. It attempts to use vivid images held in the mind as a means of healing diseases, creating wealth, and otherwise manipulating reality. Strangely enough, a number of Christian leaders teach and practice these same techniques in the name of Christ, without recognizing them for what they are.

Agnes Sanford's "Metaphysical Method"

Much of the credit for bringing these occult methodologies into Christianity must go to Agnes Sanford, who has probably influenced the church, and particularly charismatics, as much as any woman of this century. John and Paula Sandford, who are among today's leading "inner healing" teachers, have said of Agnes Sanford that she was "for all of us the forerunner in the field of inner healing by prayer, [and] she was also our own first mentor in the Lord, our friend and advisor.... A sound church woman, she...founded the School of Pastoral Care...[where] many pastors, doctors, nurses and others came and learned; among them were Francis MacNutt, Barbara Shlemon, Tommy Tyson, Herman Riffel, Paula and myself, and others who have since written or become noted concerning the healing of the inner man."[1] This "sound church woman" who "founded the School of Pastoral Care" explained her doctrinal view of sin and redemption in the following metaphysical/Jungian terms, with which any mind-science cultist would agree:

> God's love was blacked out from man by the negative thought-vibration of this sinful and suffering world.... So our Lord in the Garden of Gethsemane undertook the great work we call the Atonement—the at-one-moment which reunited man with God.
> He literally lowered His thought-vibrations to the thought-vibrations of humanity and received into Himself man's thoughts of sin and sickness,

pain and death.... So He cleansed the thought-vibrations that surround this globe....

Therefore since He became a very part of the collective unconscious of the race, when He died upon the cross a part of humanity died with him...[and] a certain emanation or an invisible and personalized energy of our spirits has already ascended with Him into the heavens....

His blood, that mysterious life-essence...remains upon this earth, in plasma form, blown by the winds of heaven to every land beneath the sun, exploding in a chain reaction of spiritual power....

But how can we direct this great flow of life into a closed mind?... By doing penance for the sins of the world, or for the sins of that particular world leader for whom we pray. And by taking that one to the cross of Christ and there receiving for him forgiveness, healing and life....

I have learned to combine the sacramental with the metaphysical approach...[but] not everyone has the open mind and the visioning faculty necessary if one is to use the metaphysical methods.[2]

In her books, which are so blatantly pagan as to be astonishing, Agnes Sanford makes no distinction between truth and error; anything that seems to tap into what she calls "this flow of energy,"[3] this "high voltage of God's creativity,"[4] is acceptable. Saying that "we are part of God...He's in nature and He is nature,"[5] and calling Him that "primal Energy"[6] and Jesus "that most profound of psychiatrists,"[7] Sanford taught that we can literally create virtues in other people by the power of our minds,[8] heal people at a distance,[9] and even forgive their sins[10] through visualization. Sanford gives her approval both to "the savage dancing in the jungle...primitive people who create an atmosphere of faith by war paint and feathers" and to the mind-science cultists "who already have a way of faith wrought by the denial of all that is not good."[11] Though she finds no fault with paganism or Christian Science, which others are perfectly free to follow as far as she is concerned, Mrs. Sanford explains that personal preference has led her to adopt a different technique, which she introduced into the church as the key element in what became known as inner healing or healing of the memories:

> How, then, shall I create in myself the atmosphere of faith: the feeling that God is answering my prayer? The method that I use is the training of the creative imagination....
>
> In the healing of the memories one must firmly hold in the imagination the picture...of this person... [regardless of] perversions...[as] a saint of God, and turn in the imagination the dark and awful shadows of his nature into shining virtues and sources of power.
>
> Indeed, they can be thus turned. This is redemption![12]

This is an ancient witchcraft or shamanistic method of healing that had already been "Christianized" by pseudochristian mind-science cults such as Religious Science and Unity. In fact it was probably from a woman Unity minister that Agnes Sanford learned this technique. In her first book, *The Healing Light,* she commends "Unity and other modern schools of prayer" for their metaphysical methods by which they were able mentally "to project the power of God into the being of man." Then she tells how she inquired of an open-minded "lady minister" why she couldn't project healing power through prayer over a distance. She was given this advice:

> "Oh my dear, you're seeing them sick," cried the beautiful old minister. "...if your subconscious mind does not really believe he's going to be well...you only fasten the illness on him. When you pray for someone, dearie, you must learn to *see* him *well.*"[13]

The Influence of Sanford

Richard Foster, who is one of Agnes Sanford's many admirers and was heavily influenced by her, states: "I have been greatly helped in my understanding of the value of the imagination in praying for others by Agnes Sanford and my dear friend, Pastor Bill Vaswig.'' Foster says that he took "the idea for some of the...visualizations" he presents from Vaswig's book;[14] and Vaswig got them from Sanford.[15] The arousal of the power of the imagination through fantasy and visualization is one of the major themes of Foster's best-selling book *Celebration of Discipline,*[16] which, nevertheless, is to be commended for encouraging devotion to the Lord and greater discipline in the Christian life. Later Foster says again: "This advice...[of] prayer through the imagination...picture the healing...and much more, was given to me by Agnes Sanford. I have discovered her to be an extremely wise and skillful counselor.... Her book *The Healing Gifts of the Spirit* is an excellent resource."[17] Whatever Sanford said as a "skillful counselor" concerning her favorite topic, "prayer through the imagination," was rooted in her basically pagan beliefs onto which she merely superimposed Christian and psychological terminology, especially Jungian. This ought to be clear to anyone reading her writings. For example:

> Wise men of India for many centuries have trod the lofty peaks of meditation developing their psycho-spiritual powers and giving birth to their oversouls.
>
> Spirits of those [dead] for whom we have prayed on earth are working through us....
>
> One conveys that healing force to the inner being [of the sick] through the law of suggestion....
>
> He [the person doing the healing] has made a thought-track between his spirit, subconscious mind and body; and the body, the subconscious mind and the spirit of the patient....[18]

Though so highly recommended by numerous Christian leaders, the message of Sanford's books is consistent with the basic teachings of occultism. This is clear not only from the books themselves, but from such endorsements as the following from the major champion of Hindu/Buddhist occultism, *The American Theosophist:* "...an inspiring handbook for developing one's own capabilities for richer living and giving."[19] Yet the writings of Agnes Sanford continue among the most consistent sellers in

Christian bookstores everywhere. Christian magazines periodically reprint excerpts from her books. *Charisma* recently featured an entire chapter. It is of great concern that Christian leaders such as Richard Foster, who is a Christian university and seminary lecturer, could embrace what Agnes Sanford has written without rejecting her blatant occultism, and instead of warning others of her dangerous teachings, recommend her books highly!

Pantheism, Jungianism, and Inner Healing

We have already pointed out that Agnes Sanford was a pantheist. This shamanistic philosophy colors all of her basic ideas and teaching, such as her statement that "every cell in the body has a rudimentary mind and will hear your words,"[20] and her apparent belief in an eternal preexistence for humans before we came to earth trailing "a cloud of glory" with an "unconscious memory of that land from whence we came."[21] This form of pantheism is also reflected in her Universalist belief that "the entire race must rise to a higher awareness of God before all things that are possible with God become actual,"[22] as well as her Jungian/ occult teaching that Jesus Christ "became forever a part of the mass mind of the race...a part of His consciousness is forever bound up with the deep mind of man."[23] The fact that Jungian occultism became the basic framework for the shamanistic system of inner healing that she picked up from the metaphysics of the mind-science cults and passed on to the evangelical church is very clear:

> There is a mysterious connection between the unconscious being of one person and the deep mind of another. Moreover, this connection can reach back through time and forward....
>
> Now in the speaking with tongues, this power latent in the unconscious mind of all people is...quickened, so that the unconscious may make rapport with the unconscious mind of someone else living anywhere upon this earth or of someone who has lived before or of someone who will live in the future or even of someone from heaven; some great...messenger of light

that He [God] may lift us out of darkness into the light
of immortality.[24]

Her naive trust in psychotherapy and Jungian philosophy led
Sanford to believe that through His incarnation Christ entered
"into the collective unconscious of the race, into the deep mind
of every person, there being available for healing and for help."[25]
This in turn led to her development of "inner healing" and
"healing of the memories,"[26] which now heavily influences
Christianity. Any apparent recognition of her occultic practices
and false beliefs, or even any cautionary warning about her
syncretistic teachings, is conspicuous by its absence from the
writings and talks of Christian leaders who recommend her,
usually in glowing terms. With such ideas spreading everywhere,
the individual Christian who fails to take responsibility for
checking everything out in prayerful study of the Word of God
will be easily led astray by sincere but misguided shepherds who
themselves failed to test what Agnes Sanford (and others like her)
taught. Concerning inner healing, pastor/author Robert Wise
writes:

> The name and the idea began with the ministry of
> Agnes Sanford...one of those rare, highly gifted
> people of the Spirit, Agnes was able to coin phrases
> and find metaphors that helped bring insight into how
> God's healing power works. Her inspired reasoning led
> her into this realm of prayer therapy.[27]

Consistent with her shamanistic beliefs, Mrs. Sanford tells of
her "baptism of the Holy Ghost" that came "through the sun
and the waters in the lake and the wind in the pine trees,"[28] and
explains that this is possible because even "a rock emanates an
invisible energy...the light of the Creator,"[29] which she also
describes as the "life-force...from which all things evolved."[30]
In one of her most astonishing statements, Agnes Sanford wrote:

> It is no longer possible for me to do this work [of
> prayer] individually, person to person, for the field has
> grown too wide. The Lord has therefore guided me to
> a broader and more subtle way of prayer.

It baffles me in a way, because I cannot tell what my spirit does and whither it goes. But that it does travel and that God does work through my spiritual body even when my mind is quite unaware of it, becomes more and more apparent.

Therefore, simply call in your mind to me, or to someone else as a human channel for the love of Christ.[31]

Morton Kelsey's Benign Witchcraft

Among the many Christian leaders who promote the same seductive philosophy as Agnes Sanford, one of the most influential is Episcopalian priest and Jungian psychologist Morton Kelsey, who was also a friend of Sanford. Agnes was a simple woman whose homespun accounts of remarkable experiences drew her many admirers (and through them a large segment of the church) into shamanistic practices. Kelsey, however, is a sophisticated thinker and a prolific and persuasive writer. His basic Jungian belief (usually disguised by orthodox-sounding language) that good, evil, Satan, angels, and demons are archetypal constructs of the human psyche[32] gives Kelsey's arguments a confusing but at the same time peculiarly irresistible flavor. What Sanford taught by experience, Kelsey persuades the church to believe by seductive reasoning: that witchcraft, sorcery, and other forms of shamanism are not evil in themselves, but are legitimate so long as we use them lovingly and for good.[33] He writes:

There is nothing intrinsically evil about...psi [psychic power] or its use.... Psi experiences themselves are not something from beyond. They are simply natural experiences of the human psyche, which mankind shares with other living things and which can sometimes be developed....

When people have deep and abiding experiences of God, ESP experiences often occur. Clairvoyance, telepathy, precognition, psychokinesis, and healing have been observed in and around the lives of many religious leaders and nearly all Christian saints. . . .

This is the same kind of psi power Jesus himself had.[34]

Kelsey and "Christian" Shamanism

As one would expect, the many Christian leaders within the inner-healing movement who recommend Sanford also generally quote and admire Kelsey, even though he believes in and practices alleged communication with and guidance from the dead,[35] equates the Holy Spirit with "the self,"[36] and equates shamanistic psychic powers with the gifts of the Holy Spirit,[37] which *"simply occur* where there is vital Christianity."[38] Kelsey, who believes that his mother died for him "as did our Lord,"[39] declares that the shamanistic "view of evil. . . was a part of the total point of view of Jesus of Nazareth."[40] Moreover, a shaman (witch doctor, etc.) is not evil, but "one in whom the power of God is concentrated and can thus flow out to others."[41] Based upon this belief, Kelsey states:

> Jesus was a man of power. He was greater than all shamans.
>
> My students begin to see the role Jesus was fulfilling when they read Mircea Eliade's *Shamanism* and Carlos Castaneda's *Journey to Ixtlan*. . . .
>
> This is the same kind of psi power Jesus himself had.[42]

As we have already noted, "shaman" is a word that anthropologists now use for those who were formerly called witch doctors, medicine men, wizards, and sorcerers. The apostle Paul wrote, "The things which the Gentiles sacrifice [to idols], they sacrifice to demons and not to God" (1 Corinthians 10:20). Like Agnes Sanford, however, Kelsey doesn't seem to think of shamans or idol worshipers as involved in anything that is *inherently* evil. According to Kelsey, clairvoyance, telepathy, out-of-body experiences, psychokinesis, and any other forms of what he calls ESP are manifestations of the power of God. Thus involvement in the psychic realm by whatever means could lead to evil only if one's motives are wrong. Moreover, the use of drugs, crystal balls, tarot cards, astrology, I Ching, hypnosis, mediumistic trances, Yoga, or other methods of Eastern meditation are all neutral and legitimate methods for getting in touch with God's power.[43] In a similar vein Robert Schuller writes:

> A variety of approaches to meditation...is employed by many different religions as well as by various non-religious mind-control systems. In all forms...TM, Zen Buddhism, or Yoga or...meditation...of Judaeo-Christian tradition...the meditator endeavors to overcome the distractions of the conscious mind....
>
> It is important to remember that meditation in any form is the harnessing, by human means, of God's divine laws.... We are endowed with a great many powers and forces that we do not yet fully understand.
>
> The most effective mantras employ the "M" sound. You can get the feel of it by repeating the words, "I am, I am," many times over.... Transcendental Meditation or TM...is not a religion nor is it necessarily anti-Christian.[44] [TM is in fact pure Hinduism, and will lead to eternal separation from Christ. See *The Cult Explosion* for details.]

Jesus, Shamanism, the Unconscious, and "Spiritual Reality"

To Kelsey, the important thing is that most major religions believe in spiritual reality and that people can personally experience God, never mind what they call Him or it.[45] He commends "Hinduism, the disciples of Zarathustra...Chinese folk religions" for this common faith,[46] believes that the occult Oracle of Delphi was a legitimate way of getting in touch with God,[47] and compliments the ancient Greeks and Romans because they "were as sure of their gods as we are of electrical power today."[48] He says, "The old shamans, the medicine men, were confronted with an unheard-of power [of God] that nearly overpowered them. These men and women were amazing healers

who mediated these strange unknown powers to other people."[49]
According to Kelsey, this shamanistic tradition was carried on
by Jesus:

> Christianity maintains that the only safe way to
> pierce the unconscious, or enter spiritual reality, is with
> a leader—Jesus. Shamanism shows us that even before
> Jesus, though, God worked among people.[50]

The impression one gets is that this "power" that seemingly
permeates the universe and can be tapped into for good or evil
has its roots in Jung's collective unconscious; it is considered by
Kelsey to be analogous to the Christian concept of God. To
Kelsey, who has arrived at his understanding of Christianity
through insights received from Jung's "depth psychology,"
"spiritual reality" is merely a construct of the human "unconscious," and this "power" behind psychic phenomena is the
ultimate integrative archetype. Those who are looked to as the
mediators of this psychic power for the good of others are called
shamans. After a lengthy and favorable discussion of shamanism,
Kelsey lets us know once again that Christianity is just another
form of this ancient and universally practiced witchcraft, which
he recommends:

> When we look at the ministry of Jesus, we shall
> see...that his life and acts, his teaching and practice,
> are rather akin to shamanism based on an intimate
> relationship with a loving father god. In fact, an
> important study might be made comparing the ministry
> of Jesus with that of shamanism....
>
> Those who are taken aback by his healing min-
> istry...are ignorant of the experiences of healing
> universally known...in most forms of shaman-
> ism.
>
> The shaman is the mediator between the individual
> and spiritual reality, both good and evil, and because
> of this the healer of diseases of mind and body. In
> stepping into his healing role Jesus picks up the
> prophetic and shamanistic strand of the Old Testament
> tradition already mentioned.[51]

Shamanism and Visualization

New York Academy of Science anthropologist Michael Harner places visualization at the head of the list of now-popular psychospiritual technologies that he says represent a revival of shamanism,[52] which he defines as sorcery or witchcraft.[53] Harner says this not as a critic but as one who has, like so many other "transpersonal" anthropologists and psychologists, become a convinced believer in shamanism. The use of visualization, which is by far the most effective and powerful form of shamanism, is literally exploding throughout the secular world, and, since its introduction by Agnes Sanford, is gaining increasing acceptance and use in the church. Explaining the central role that visualization plays in shamanism, Harner states:

> A shaman is a man or woman who enters an altered state of consciousness—at will—to contact and utilize an ordinarily hidden reality in order to acquire knowledge, power and to help other persons....
>
> It is in the SSC (Shamanic State of Consciousness) that one "sees" shamanically. This may be called "visualizing," "imaging," or as expressed by Australian aborigines, using "the strong eye."...
>
> As the distinguished Australian anthropologist A. P. Elkins observes, the vision of an aborigine shaman "is no mere hallucination. It is a mental formation visualized and externalized, which may even exist for a time independent of its creator...."[54]

Psychologists argue that our minds can't tell the difference between the "real" world (depending upon what that means) and something vividly imagined. In a recent book, psychologist William Fezler goes one step further to say that there *is* no real difference.[55] In his latest book, Carl Rogers argues for a reality that is purely subjective and created by each individual. He suggests that "there are as many realities as there are persons," and urges us to prepare ourselves for a world without "solid basis, a world of process and change...in which the [individual] mind...creates the new reality."[56]

Such theories espoused by highly honored psychologists such as Rogers are nothing more than ancient shamanism restated in academically respectable language. Scores of pop psychologies and self-help cults represent the working out in modern society of the old occultism made acceptable by psychology. Psychiatrist C. G. Jung, whom Morton T. Kelsey raised to the level of a Christian leader and saint,[57] believed that images originating within the mind were as real as those coming from external objects. Heavily involved in the occult, including seances for communicating with the dead, Jung explained the "ghosts" he saw on more than one occasion as "exteriorizations" of archetypal images within his mind originating in the deep psyche of the human race. Refusing to believe in a real spirit world of demons or angels, psychologists play mind-games with visual images that Christians then pick up as "scientific," unaware that they are opening themselves to demonic spirits. According to Barbara Hannah, a Jungian analyst and teacher at the C. G. Jung Institute, imagery or visualization is—

> ...considered the most powerful tool in Jungian psychology for achieving direct contact with the unconscious and attaining greater inner knowledge.[58]

Witchcraft under "scientific" labels has now become an integral part of modern society. There is a conscious effort to merge science with shamanism. Under the heading, "Scientists, shamans to convene, explore common ground," Marilyn Ferguson's *Brain/Mind Bulletin* announced one of a growing number of gatherings for this purpose. Held at Ojai, California, April 29—June 3, 1984, and organized by anthropologist and New Age leader Joan Halifax, this unusual "residential program tracing the pattern connecting scientific and sacred traditions" was supported by such luminaries as psychologist R. D. Laing and plant physiologist Rupert Sheldrake. It brought together "biologists, physicists, psychiatrists, and neuroscientists with American Indian and African healers, Tibetan lamas, Sufi mystics, Zen teachers and martial arts specialists."[59]

Almost no one connects it with its pagan roots when it comes clothed in psychological terminology as a "personal development'' course, a self-hypnosis tape, or a PMA (Positive Mental Attitude) or success/motivation seminar for business executives. Shamanism is even less likely to be recognized for what it really is when it is naively presented by Christian leaders with apparent biblical backing. Today its swelling ranks of committed believers include growing numbers of medical doctors, psychologists, university and seminary professors, sociologists, theologians, Christian leaders, and other well-educated and sophisticated persons of wide influence.

10

Mental Alchemy

In spite of your many sorceries, in spite of the great power of your spells evil will come on you which you will not know how to charm away.
Isaiah 47:9,11

It is now recognized by most researchers who have studied the exploding revival of mysticism that the Western world has its own witch doctors. They wear business suits, clerical collars, or white smocks, and many of them have M.D., D.D., or Ph.D. degrees. Nearly all claim that what they believe and practice is truly scientific; and many deny the existence of God, Satan, angels, or demons as independent entities. As a result, they attribute the source of the psychic powers to the unlimited human potential that allegedly lies within the unconscious of each of us. Their "mind magic" is *powerful* and it *works*. In his introduction to William Fezler's book *Just Imagine: A Guide to Materialization Using Imagery*, Beverly Hills psychiatrist William S. Kroger says:

As modern day fields of psychology and medicine grow we become more and more amazed at just how much power the mind really does exert.... Nowhere in man's writings has it been explained *how* to imagine something strongly enough to produce a concrete result in reality.

Just Imagine fills this gap. It describes definite ways to structure a new and better reality. The method involves using images...that can be developed and

137

embellished in a progression till they influence reality to such an extent that they become reality!

Over the past ten years I have worked with and watched Dr. Fezler teach patients how to produce images strong enough to materialize.... [1]

Creative Visualization

Shamanistic visualization is an attempt to create or manipulate the physical world by the practice of "mental alchemy." It is based upon the ancient sorcerer's belief that the entire universe is an illusion (called *maya* in Hinduism) created by the mind. Adelaide Bry, one of the leading proponents of shamanistic visualization, describes it as "the deliberate use of the power of your mind to create your own reality. You can use visualization to have whatever you want.... [2] This is the stuff of ancient ritual magic that voodoo priests and witch doctors still use, both for curses and cures, but it is now looked upon as a neutral mind-power included in the alleged unlimited human potential we all possess if we only know how to make it work. New Age activist Laurie Warner explains that this belief runs "through all the literature of the New Age." She explains further:

> All the methods of the New Age...meditation, yoga, aerobics, ionics, crystallography, nutrition, trans-actional analysis and many other systems all...can be seen as tools for amplifying and transmuting energies ...[and] release[ing] our innate spiritual potentials.
>
> We are learning that "energy follows thought" and that through inner work of symbolic alchemy and mental programming we can move through altered states of consciousness and experience new interactions with our realities. [3]

After labeling such beliefs primitive superstition for years, modern man is at last discovering that there is incredible power in "creative visualization" and is applying it in a variety of ways. Popular and powerful occult methodologies such as Silva Mind Control, est (Erhard Seminars Training), and Mind Dynamics, for example, all rely heavily upon visualization. A special report by the Psychosynthesis Institute states that "the use of the imagination is one of the most rapidly spreading new trends in psychology and education...."[4] In the opening paragraphs of his book, psychologist William Fezler presents the seductively appealing possibility of mental alchemy in a persuasive manner:

> All scientists agree that matter can be converted to energy. Surely the reverse is possible. Energy must be capable of converting to matter. Mind is energy. Thought is energy.
>
> We eat an apple and it becomes energy, it becomes mind. Why is it so difficult for some to grasp that the thought is capable of becoming apple again? Not an imagined apple, but a real one.... materialization is possible.[5]

To use imagery effectively in healing the sick, says Agnes Sanford, "mental training" is required to develop "the creative faculty, that part of the creative imagination that is most like God."[6] This is the teaching of Christian Science and other mind-science cults. Unfortunately, it is also what Yonggi Cho teaches in *The Fourth Dimension*:

> God spoke to my heart, "Son...the fourth dimension includes and controls the third dimension, producing a creation of order and beauty. The spirit is the fourth dimension.
>
> "Every human being is a spiritual being.... They have the fourth dimension as well as the third dimension in their hearts."
>
> In Genesis the Spirit of the Lord was incubating, brooding over the water; He was like a hen sitting on her eggs, incubating them and hatching chickens. In much the same manner the Holy Spirit incubates the third dimension, so does the evil spirit incubate....
>
> You may wonder how we can incubate our subconsious...the only way for us to incubate is through our imaginations.... Through visualizing and dreaming you can incubate your future and hatch the results....

So men [Christians or occultists], by exploring their spiritual sphere of the fourth dimension through the development of concentrated visions and dreams in their imagination, can brood over and incubate the third dimension, influencing and changing it.

This is what the Holy Spirit taught me.[7]

Visualization: The Ancient Tradition

According to Hermetic tradition, the Egyptian god Thoth, known to the Greeks as Hermes Trismegistus (The Thrice-Powerful), was the originator of alchemy. He taught that the physical world could be transformed through mental imagery. Equally as ancient, the use of visualization in Yoga to create reality with the mind and achieve union with The All (Brahman) dates back thousands of years. In a recent interview reported in *The Journal of Transpersonal Psychology*, the Dalai Lama declared that "the use of the imagination to generate or visualize an image in the mind's eye" is an integral part of tantric Yoga; and he explained how this ancient practice is related to similar techniques recently adopted in modern psychotherapy.[8]

Christian leaders who promote and defend visualization seem unwilling to admit that it lies at the heart of religious beliefs that are demonically inspired and unalterably hostile to Christianity. They suggest instead that shamanistic visualization is a counterfeit of God's truth that they teach. However, there is no true visualization taught or practiced in the Bible for Satan to counterfeit; visualization is as absent from Scripture as it has always been present in the occult. Neither Isaiah, Jeremiah, nor any other biblical prophet created his visions through visualization, but received them by *inspiration* from God. Jesus didn't teach that His disciples could get Him to appear at will by visualizing Him, or that we should visualize what we are praying for. Yet this is being taught by Christian leaders today who without intending to lead anyone into occultism are, nevertheless, pointing them in that direction by some of the methodologies they promote.

Just as in the church today, throughout history shamanistic visualization has been associated with healing, both physical and spiritual. Common threads of belief and practice can be traced from ancient times down to the present. There is no more obvious link between paganism/occultism and modern psychological/religious practices than visualization. Biblical Christianity alone stands outside of and in opposition to these pagan traditions. Medical doctor Mike Samuels and his wife, Nancy, who are practicing occultists and experts in this area, point out in their definitive study of visualization:

> For the Egyptian followers of Hermes, who believed that everything is mind, disease was thought to be cured by visualizing perfect health.
>
> Among the Navaho Indians elaborate, concrete visualizations, in which a number of people participate, are used for healing a sick person. The rite helps the patient visualize himself as healthy....
>
> Paracelsus, a Swiss alchemist and physician of the sixteenth century, believed that "The power of the imagination is a great factor in medicine. It may produce diseases in man and it may cure them."
>
> In the late 1800's Mary Baker Eddy discovered Christian Science...based on the concept [that]... disease is essentially a product of the human mind... "the origin of all disease is mental...all disease is cured by divine Mind."[9]

Shamanistic Visualization in Modern Western Society

Psychic healers Bill Henkin and Amy Wallace stress that "visualization is one of the most potent and widely used techniques in [psychic] healing."[10] Steller declares that the exercise of "visual imagination is a regular part of the training for psychics and healers in...Spiritist churches."[11] Shakti Gawain says, "Creative visualization is the technique of using your imagination to create what you want...a state of consciousness in which you know that you are the constant creator of your life."[12] In her acknowledgments, Gawain gives special thanks to her "inner guide who keeps showing me the way...and who actually is responsible for writing this book."[13] In his *Magic: An Occult Primer*, leading occultist David Conway explains the absolute necessity of visualization for performing ritual magic:

> ...the technique of visualization is something you will gradually master, and indeed must master if you are to make any progress at all in magic...it is our only means of affecting the etheric atmosphere.
>
> It enables us to build our own thought forms, contact those already in existence and channel the elemental energy we need down onto the physical plane.[14]

Bry says that visualization is "being used by a growing variety of people: physicians, psychotherapists, athletes, teachers, dieters, artists, business people and lovers to name just a few."[15] A recent handout to engineers and executives taking a self-improvement course at Hughes Aircraft in Southern California announced that projecting a "mental picture...upon the 'screen of the mind' " to effect personal transformation is the "wonderful 'secret'... known and practiced by all the great teachers of the truth."[16] In June 1984, the Rockwell California Chapters of the National Management Association sponsored a "New Age Thinking" program titled "Visualization Training to Expand Life's Potential" that was taught by psychotherapist Rita Uniman, who directs the Institute of Holistic Psychology. The course was billed as a combination of Eastern religion, Western psychology, Holistic health, and human potential training.[17] Such courses are legion throughout the business world. Their true religious nature is betrayed in this statement from the Psychosynthesis Institute that through imagery and visualization—

> ...we are capable of transcending the worldly order, of participating in eternal life and in the energy of the super-celestial. It is through this principle, therefore, that we will be liberated from the bonds of fate itself.[18]

In spite of the apparent initial benefits, Satan eventually gets his pound of flesh from anyone who plays his mind-games. This is not only true in the case of individual horror stories that could be told. The evidence is overwhelming that there is a much larger purpose behind the drug/occult revival, of which shamanic visualization is an integral part. In his book *Occult Preparations for a New Age,* Theosophist Dane Rudhyar lays out some of the strategy and hopes of those promoting such techniques:

> The spreading use of L.S.D. and other psychedelic drugs...[had] a powerful cathartic effect, breaking open doors of the mind and the usual ego-defenses built by our traditional culture....
>
> The field of action of the present aspect of counter-culture is increasingly defined by "psychic" research of all kinds, and by the modernizing of old yoga techniques and spiritual-mental disciplines....
>
> The number of persons using or claiming clairvoyance and contacts with inner guides, spacepeople, or discarnate healers is steadily increasing...these manifestations...challenge the validity of our Euro-American cultural main stream....
>
> ...we are living in a period of transition between the old Western civilization...and a new type of culture presumably of a global nature.[19]

Fantasy Versus Exegesis

Whether practiced by Christians or non-Christians, visualization is purely an occult technique offering a substitute source of power, knowledge, and healing, which, if it could be realized, would make man a god in his own right, independent of his Creator.

Yonggi Cho tries to manufacture examples from the Bible, but they are built from unwarranted assumptions. Because God had Abraham look up at the night sky and told him that his seed would be innumerable as the stars in the heavens, Cho imagines that Abraham began to visualize countless descendants and that this fantasy is what brought about the birth of Isaac! On such speculations Cho has built his entire visualization teaching. He writes:

> I imagine that Abraham...when he looked up at the stars, all he could see were the faces of his children,

> and suddenly he felt that he was hearing them call to
> him, "Father Abraham!"
>
> . . . He could not sleep when he closed his eyes, for
> he saw all the stars changing into the faces of his
> descendants. . . . Those pictures came to his mind again
> and again. . . [and] became part of his fourth dimen-
> sion. . . .
>
> These visions and dreams carried dominion over his
> one-hundred-year-old body, and it was transformed as
> if it were like a young body.[20]

This is not biblical exegesis but pure fantasy. We are not questioning Cho's motives, but we must question his methods and
teaching. Unfortunately, Cho's conclusions are in perfect agreement with occult tradition. Yet they are accepted by multitudes
of Christians. Uncritical acceptance of whatever Christian leaders
teach, instead of checking it carefully against the Word of God
(as did the Bereans with Paul's preaching), is one of the seeds
of apostasy. This is how visualization and other forms of sorcery
are entering the church.

Some Christian writers quote the Scripture "Where there is
no vision the people perish" to support their use of visualization.
But God is clearly referring to the visions He gives by His own
initiative to His chosen prophets in His own time and way for
His own purpose, and not to someone initiating his own "vision"
by fantasizing a vivid image in his imagination. Yet this verse
is used to support the false teaching that anyone can conjure up
his or her own visualized "vision" and that God must honor it.
In Jeremiah 23:16 God warns against this very perversion:

> Do not listen to the words of the prophets who are
> prophesying to you. They are leading you into futility.
>
> They speak a vision of their own imagination, not
> from the mouth of the Lord.

"What You See is What You'll Be"

We will have more to say in the next chapter concerning the
growing trend of conjuring up in the imagination a fantasy

"Jesus" or "God," who then literally comes alive in the mind. Any shaman would acknowledge that visualizing someone or something in the mind is the fastest way to make contact with spirit entities. Shamanism in the form of visualization is being introduced into the church today by numerous Christian leaders who are not recognizing it for what it is.

Foster's *Celebration of Discipline* has been a favorite among many conservative evangelicals. Yet *Celebration* teaches that visualization can be used to transcend time and space and ascend into the very presence of God: "In your imagination allow your spiritual body, shining with light, to rise out of your physical body. . . up through the clouds and into the stratosphere. . . deeper and deeper into outer space until there is nothing except the warm presence of the eternal Creator."[21] Foster assures us that this is not mere fantasy or imagination, but *reality* created with the mind.[22] Christians are unwittingly falling into an old occult practice attempting to create reality and even manipulate God through forming vivid mental images. Yonggi Cho writes:

> We should always try to visualize the end result as we pray. . . . If you have not visualized clearly in your heart exactly what you hope for, it cannot become a reality to you. . . .
>
> We have taught our people how to. . .visualize success. . . . Through visualizing and dreaming, you can incubate your future and hatch the results.[23]

That unbiblical use of the imagination would give humans godlike powers can be seen in the following portrayal by William Fezler:

> In Galilee a man called Christ imagines a few fish and loaves of bread are many and feeds a multitude. His faith, his belief, becomes reality. The thought is father to the deed. The image always precedes the manifestation.
>
> At a hospital in Los Angeles a young woman with cancer imagines her white blood cells are knights in shining armor vanquishing cancer cells which

she pictures as rotten hamburger. Much to the staff's amazement the cancer disappears....

First mind, then matter. Matter is the materialization of mind. And the two are inseparable. Mind and body, energy and matter, are one.[24]

Norman Vincent Peale calls visualization "positive thinking carried one step further."[25] This is quite an endorsement from the man who has spent his life promoting Positive Thinking! Amway Crown Direct Distributor Bunny Marks, explains the power of visualization in a motivational tape titled "What You See Is What You'll Be":

So the first thing we must do if we wish to achieve and live the life of success, the life of plenty and happiness, is first of all to visualize it.

We actually create reality by what we visualize.

...The picture you hold in your mind will develop the same way a film develops.... If you start visualizing what you desire, you shall have it! You can have anything you desire if you want it badly enough and begin to visualize it....

So the picture's the secret, that is the key; for *the picture you hold is the picture you'll be!*[26]

Some Serious Problems

It is astonishing that those who promote visualization never seem to deal with the obvious problems it creates. Aside from the fact that it is one of the fastest ways into occultism, there are ethical considerations that are ignored. What right does anyone have to shuffle God's universe about with the power of his mind? And what about controlling the actions of other persons by imposing one's will upon them? Apparently oblivious to the serious implications, Agnes Sanford declared:

After a few months of practice, I found that I could influence my children by "remote control"...in less than a minute, the child would change and the thing that I had seen in my mind would be brought forth.

It was like writing and staging a play, and seeing the picture that one had created in mind come to pass on the stage.

We are indeed made in His image...He is first of all a Creator—and so are we.[27]

Like so many Christian leaders today, Agnes Sanford believed that "there is a power and it does work" for anyone, Christian or not, because God works "through the application of laws and of powers that He has created...."[28] This is contradicted by both the Bible and logic. The classical argument of the atheist is, "You just think that's a miracle because you don't yet understand the law of nature that governs in that situation." Everyone instinctively knows that anything governed by scientifically explicable laws is a *natural* process, whereas miracles are *supernatural* acts of God entirely outside the influence of the laws of cause-and-effect. Redemption, resurrection, forgiveness of sins, and instantaneous healing of organic illness are miracles beyond the limitations of physical laws and are thus acts of God's sovereign grace.

Agnes Sanford told of a young mother to whom she tried to teach visualization "in the name of Jesus Christ." The woman protested that she wasn't a Christian, to which Sanford replied that it didn't matter, since this power works for *anyone*: "Make the picture [in your mind] of the child as you want her to be...."[29] From the stories Mrs. Sanford told, it appears that if we would all begin to visualize a world of harmony and love, planet Earth would be transformed into a paradise. She taught that "by sending forth the forgiving love of Christ," we could "bring out the natural goodness in those we meet."[30] According to some of the experiences she related, Agnes was even able, through visualization, to zap an unsuspecting person with powerful thoughts and change him on the spot, even forgiving his sins and setting him free without speaking a word.[31]

Gods Indeed?

If, by applying certain principles or laws, we can change

God's universe and remold those living in it to conform to our desires, then we are gods indeed. Norman Vincent Peale tells how visualization compelled members of his congregation to fill the church on a stormy Sunday night[32] and even to give him large sums of money. To illustrate this power further he writes:

> Brother Andrews said: "There's a doctor downtown ...we're going to pray that he will give you...five thousand dollars. We'll not only pray, we'll visualize him doing it."
>
> [Norman Vincent Peale returned triumphantly with the five thousand dollars to tell his waiting friend that after refusing him at first, the doctor suddenly changed his mind and gave him the money.]
>
> Brother Andrews explained: "I just sent a thought hovering over you all the way down there that he *would* do it, and my thought hit him right between the eyes."
>
> [Dr. Peale] exclaimed, "You know, I saw it hit him!"
>
> He said, "It penetrated his brain and it changed his thinking. But this should change your thinking, too. Just remember, when you want to achieve something, hold in your mind the picture of yourself achieving it. Paint in all the details. Make it as real as you possibly can."[33]

Dr. Peale has been involved in visualization ever since, apparently without realizing that he is using a shamanistic technique in attempting to impose his will upon God and other people. Peale writes, "Imaging has been...implicit in all the speaking and writing I have done...only recently has it begun to...be recognized by scientists and medical authorities...."[34] If reality can actually be created or manipulated by visualization, this would allow everyone to play God with the universe. What would happen when competing realities were being visualized by different persons? If visualization taps into some power inherent within the universe and available to anyone, it would be the ultimate weapon to hand over to human egos; and the result would not be paradise, but hell on earth.

11

Christianized Idolatry?

> To obey [God] is better than sacrifice.... Rebellion is as the sin of divination [witchcraft], and insubordination is as iniquity and idolatry.
>
> 1 Samuel 15:22,23

> Therefore, my beloved, flee from idolatry.... The things which the Gentiles sacrifice, they sacrifice to demons, and not to God.
>
> 1 Corinthians 10:14,20

Shamanism promises power to heal and transform through contact with a parallel universe of the spirit, from which this mysterious energy is allegedly drawn. That contact is said to be made in our minds: The thoughts we think and the words we speak become the vehicles of spiritual power. Those who accept this concept become victims of the great delusion that displaces God with self. In seeking power for self, they have become susceptible to the power of Satan. Nevertheless, even as the irrefutable evidence mounts documenting its destructive and evil power, shamanism's popularity and general acceptance is exploding in the secular world, and in "Christianized" forms is gaining increasing acceptance within the church. This is due to ignorance of biblical warnings against occultism and a willingness to accept psychological theories and success formulas. Failing to recognize that shamanistic visualization is neither scientific nor biblical, many Christian leaders surprisingly promote it as both. *The Wall Street Journal* recently commented:

Another trait of Korean Christianity that disturbs some is the tendency, encouraged by prelates like Mr. Cho, to see Christianity as a path to material prosperity. That tendency, critics say, is a residue of shamanism, the native folk religion in Korea and other northeast Asian countries for centuries. In Shamanism, you ask the shaman, a sort of medicine man or woman, to...intercede with the spirits to ensure your health or business success.

There is in Korean shamanism a great spirit, above the other spirits, who couldn't be contacted by the shamans. That helped Christianity get off the ground, says David Susan, a Lutheran missionary, because "when the early Christian missionaries came and said, 'There's an almighty God who judges you at your death,' Koreans said, 'Ah, yes, we've heard of that God before.' " But in a sense it made Christianity too easy for Koreans to accept.... Many Korean Christians still consider the gods of shamanism and the God of Christianity kindred spirits.[1]

This affinity for shamanism is not unique to Koreans, but is the same everywhere in the world, as Michael Harner documents.[2] Even among evangelicals, we are seeing an astonishing acceptance of heresies that are reminiscent of the radical teaching of the Transcendentalists (Ralph Waldo Emerson, Henry Thoreau, William Channing, Bronson Alcott, et al), who introduced an intellectualized form of shamanism into America in the early 19th century. The Transcendentalists sparked a successful revolt against then-dominant New England Fundamentalism. Similar teaching is being revived today, but this time Fundamentalism itself is being revolutionized from the inside.

New Thought: The New Revival

Transcendentalism helped spawn what became known as New Thought, which emphasized that *thought* controls everything. The power of *thinking*, whether negative or positive, was believed to be sufficient even to create physical reality or to destroy it.

God was not personal, but a great Mind which was activated by our thoughts and would actualize them into concrete form. The corollary to this axiom is obvious: Man is divine. Forced out of the church at that time as heresy, New Thought became the basis for such mind-science cults as Christian Science, Religious Science, and Unity. Today's church is being swept by a revival of New Thought, now called Positive Thinking, Possibility Thinking, Positive Confession, Positive Mental Attitude, and Inner Healing. We are very concerned that this time New Thought, which represents inside the church what New Age is in the secular world, will not be forced out, but will remain within the evangelical church to contribute to the growing confusion and seduction. One of the most basic New Thought techniques is visualization, which is now firmly entrenched within the church.

Even after it was forced out of mainstream Christianity early in this century, New Thought survived on the fringes of the church in extreme Pentecostalism and in organizations such as Camps Farthest Out (CFO). Through CFO founder Glenn Clark, a surprising amount of basic mind-science has come into the evangelical church. Clark taught that evil was to be overcome by dismissing it from one's mind completely.[3] Out of this belief Clark developed a shamanic approach to prayer.

New Thought historian Charles Braden writes:

> Hundreds of prayer groups all over America, largely the result of attendance of Clark's Camps Farthest Out, employ many of the techniques which New Thought employs, and the interest in healing which they carry into the churches, healing not only of souls but also of bodies of men, is quite in the pattern of New Thought...
>
> The importance of these camps...[is] that through them...New Thought teaching and practice...has been accommodated to the vocabulary of the orthodox Christian faith, and so made an effective part in the ongoing life of the church without most persons ever being aware that it is so.[4]

Speakers popular in CFO in the 1970s included Ruth Carter Stapleton, Rodney Romney, Agnes Sanford, Tommy Tyson, Francis MacNutt, Norman Grubb, and John Sandford. Their influence within the church continues to be strong, though CFO itself has waned in popularity.

CFO was the early staging area for what is known today throughout the church as Inner Healing or Healing of Memories, of which we will have more to say later. Even more influential in keeping New Thought alive within the church have been Robert Schuller and Norman Vincent Peale. As we have noted, Peale credits Religious Science founder Ernest Holmes with making a positive thinker out of him. "Positive Thinking" is a phrase that Peale borrowed from Charles Fillmore, the cofounder of Unity School of Christianity.[5] Dr. Peale has written, "The world you live in is mental and not physical," and, "Change your thought and you change everything."[6] According to Charles Braden, Peale's father once told his son:

> You have evolved a new Christian emphasis out of a composite of Science of Mind, metaphysics, Christian Science, medical and psychological practice, Baptist Evangelism, Methodist witnessing and solid Dutch Reformed Calvinism.[7]

In an April 1984 newspaper interview, Norman Vincent Peale called the virgin birth "some theological idea" of no importance to salvation.[8] On the Phil Donahue TV show in October 1984, he denied the necessity of being born again. "I have my own personal relationship with God, you've got yours," he told a questioner. "I know a Shinto temple in Japan where I found eternal peace one day in my soul."[9] The connection between Positive and Possibility thinking and Mind-science cults such as Unity School of Christianity is clear.

At Unity headquarters near Kansas City, Missouri, Dr. Robert Schuller addressed a large audience of Unity ministers and ministers-in-training, sharing with them how his ministry had grown and showing them how they could apply the same principles to improve the growth of Unity. In response to questions, Schuller gave some very revealing answers. Asked what was the "one single thing that has most contributed to the success of [his] ministry," he replied, ". . .it's our positive approach."[10] What he meant by that became clear from his response to another question.

"Dr. Schuller," he was asked, "we hear a lot of talk these days about the New Age, the Age of Aquarius, the type of New Age thinking that we are involved in with Holistic healing and various other things that are part of what is called the New Age. Will you describe the role of what you might consider the New Age minister in the '80s and beyond?" Schuller made no protest that he knew nothing of the New Age or that he wasn't a "New Age minister." Without hesitating, he replied:

> Well, I think it depends upon where you're working. I believe that the responsibility in this Age is to "positivize" religion. Now this probably doesn't have much bearing to you people, being Unity people, you're positive. But I talk a great deal to groups that are not positive. . .even to what we would call Fundamentalists who deal constantly with words like sin, salvation, repentance, guilt, that sort of thing.
>
> So when I'm dealing with these people. . .what we have to do is positivize the words that have classically only had a negative interpretation.[11]

Today New Thought is being revived once again in the church; but this time its basic techniques of "thinking, speaking, and visualizing" come clothed in language that Christian psychology has conditioned us to accept. Kenneth Hagin, Jr. writes:

> Somebody will argue, "You're talking about positive thinking!"
>
> That's right! I am acquainted with the greatest Positive Thinker who ever was: God! The Bible says that He called those things that be not as though they were. . . .
>
> The two most prominent teachers of positive thinking are ministers.[12]

While it is true that our thoughts influence us in many ways, it is not true that "thinking," "speaking," and "visualizing" contain the virtually unlimited power attributed to them; nor are they biblical methods for "releasing God's power." Mind-manipulating techniques for solving human problems and creating health and wealth have always been part of the occult.

The Power of "Self-Talk"

One method advocated for reinforcing positive affirmations is called "self-talk." This idea was pioneered by Emile Coue in the early 1900s. His magic phrase "Every day and in every way I am becoming better and better" swept Europe and America, healed organic diseases, and transformed lives before falling into disrepute.[13] Under different labels this idea is being revived again on the Positive Mental Attitude, and success/motivation circuits, and Christian psychology has brought it into the church. Although he tries to differentiate his brand of "self-talk" from Positive Confession, pastor and clinical psychologist David Stoop states:

> The power released by our Self-Talk is incredible. Not only do our thoughts and words create our emotions, they have the power to make us well or sick, and to determine our future.
>
> This renewed emphasis on the power of the mind reflects a swing back to ancient ideas concerning the interrelationship of the body and the mind....
>
> These principles are universal.... Think you're getting a cold? Watch out, you've got it!... Think your kids are going to act up at Grandma's house? Never fails.[14]

Here not only psychosomatic symptoms are alleged to be produced by what one thinks, but even the behavior of the "kids at Grandma's"! Such ideas used to be termed superstition, but are now deemed scientific because they have become incorporated within psychology's conflicting mind/spirit theories and therapies. Agnes Sanford writes: "...a vibration of very, very high intensity and an extremely fine wave-length, with tremendous healing power, caused by spiritual forces operating through the mind of man, is the next thing science expects to discover."[15] Such ideas, once the dream of the ancient alchemists, are today the Holy Grail of psychology. Although they are no nearer to finding it and no more scientific than their predecessors, many Christian psychologists hold out this "carrot on the stick" to anguished souls seeking a peace and joy that earlier Christians found in the crucified and risen Christ alone. Denis Waitley counsels:

> Perhaps the most important key to the permanent enhancement of self-esteem is the practice of positive self-talk. Every waking moment we must feed our self-images positive thoughts about ourselves and our performances, so relentlessly and vividly that our self-images are in time molded and modified to conform to new, higher standards.[16]

The New "Science of the Mind"

Biblical truth is no longer the solution, but flattery and fantasies of the mind. What used to be called pride is now called "positive self-talk," and is as diligently cultivated today as it was formerly struggled against. The almost canonical authority given to psychology within the church makes what would otherwise be obviously erroneous seem sensible to Christians and even scientific. In another of his books hailed by top Christian leaders, Waitley suggests that "positive self-talk" be recorded and listened to repeatedly to improve "health, self-esteem, and creative growth."[17] The seductive manner in which shamanism is deliberately masqueraded as "science" in order to give it wide acceptance can be understood from the following statement in *New Thought* magazine:

> Something wonderful has been happening behind the scenes in both science and non-denominational worship...researchers are able to show that we ARE spiritual beings, creatures of light and cosmic substance, and that our lives are the product of our thinking apparatus and how we use that computer-like device to create holograms of our "reality"....

The growing demand for self-help products indicates that the time has come for this information to be a basic topic from kindergarten upward. But, unless we name it something else—like "bioenergetic physics"—it's going to remain a religious idea and subsequently stay out of our schools....

This should not be blacked out of our schools. This is not religion. This is a science. In the final analysis, perhaps it is the only science there is.[18]

This same guise of calling basic sorcery "science" has brought shamanism into public schools. Lutheran pastor Bill Vaswig declares: "Agnes Sanford has believed in God's 'light' in terms of real energy for many years. In many ways her belief has been sustained by modern physics and psychology."[19] As an example of how this works, Vaswig writes: "We visualized the light and energy of God entering the woman's body and healing her completely. We held her up in our imaginations...[and] thanked God that it was so."[20]

In the world of success/motivation seminars, imagination is considered to be the key that unlocks infinite human potential—and this is passed off as the latest scientific discovery coming out of the new physics. Waitley suggests that "positive self-talk" should not be listened to consciously, but that the "right-brain" should be allowed to "record" it in the unconscious as "images and feelings about yourself...." He adds emphatically: *"Who you see in your imagination will always rule your world."*[21] This is no suggestion that we focus our attention upon our Lord. Instead of "being transformed into Christ's image" through meditating upon His glory by faith (2 Corinthians 3:18), we are being taught to visualize ourselves as we want to be in order to transform ourselves into the likeness of this fantasy image. Waitley declares: "As you see yourself in the heart of your thought, in your mind's eye, so you do become."[22] Pastor/author C. S. Lovett states:

Imagination is the key to creation. Everything God is doing he first sees in His mind. And so it is with men made in His image....

> While our faith allows us to accept what we can't
> see...imagination takes us a step beyond, allowing us
> to PICTURE what we cannot see. Isn't that remark-
> able! [emphasis in the original.][23]

From Words to Images

The mental images that one is able to *picture* or visualize are
no longer looked upon as mere figments of the mind, but as reality
created by the mind that can even impact the physical world. The
intimate relationship between *thinking*, *speaking*, and *seeing* (and
the power thereby produced) has formed the basis of occult theory
for thousands of years. The metaphysical philosophy underlying
Positive Thinking and Possibility Thinking as well as major
aspects of the Positive Confession movement is founded upon
the alleged power inherent within thoughts and words. Charles
Capps says, *"Words are the most powerful thing in the universe."*[24] God presumably used this power residing within words
to create the universe, and that same power is allegedly available
to us as creatures *"in God's class very capable of operating in
the same kind of faith."*[25] How does this work? Explains Capps:

> *Words are containers. They carry faith, or fear, and
> they produce after their kind.... God is a faith God.
> God released His faith in Words* [emphasis in orig-
> inal].[26]

In shamanism, thoughts, words, and mental images have the
same power as idols and are closely linked. New Thought brought
this basic shamanism into Christianity, which is where Agnes
Sanford picked it up, and this is the source of the prayer techniques that she taught to so many who are now leaders in the
church. Hindu occultism is the most ancient and universal form
of shamanism. In his definitive work, *Hindu Polytheism,* Alain
Danielou explains: "To the original or true language belong the
sacred utterances used in worship and called *mantras.* The word
mantra means 'thought-form.' "[27] The Hindu scriptures declare:
"...they go to Hell who think that the image is merely a stone
and that the Mantra is merely a letter of the alphabet. All letters

[words] are forms of Shakti [force] as sound-powers."[28] There are numerous cults in America today that represent attempts to syncretize Hindu mantra power with New Thought and pseudo-Christianity. The Church Universal and Triumphant headed by Elizabeth Clare Prophet (Guru Ma) is one of the best known. Prophet declares:

> With the science of the spoken Word...incisive invocations in the form of decrees to the ascended Masters help in solving specific problems....
> Since the essence of prana does extend and permeate all of Matter...by the spoken Word we can also send it out into a world in need of healing. So sound is the great command.[29]

The Bible does not teach such methods. Their danger lies in the fact that these shamanistic mind techniques produce mental states that become a substitute for the real solution, which the Christian is to find through his relationship with Christ in the walk of faith.

Visualizing the Deities

The most powerful way that occultists use thoughts is to visualize some particular "thought-form" in the mind. This shamanistic methodology has been adopted by Humanistic and Transpersonal psychologies; and under the umbrella of Christian psychology has come into the church. Dardik and Waitley state: "Visualization works because the mind reacts automatically to the information we feed it in the form of words, pictures and emotions.... The act of vividly imagining a scene in your mind makes it a real experience."[30] Originator of Silva Mind Control Jose Silva agrees: "If you operate according to some very simple laws, the imaginary event will become real.... The better you learn to visualize, the more powerful will be your experience with Mind Control."[31]

Occultists have long held that through visualization, thoughts can thereby be materialized into existence on the physical plane. In their book *Thought-Forms*, Annie Besant, successor to

Theosophical Society founder H. P. Blavatsky, and her close adviser C. W. Leadbeater, declare that "the creation of an object is the passing out of an image from the mind and its subsequent materialization. . . [which] becomes for the time a kind of living creature. . . [called] 'an elemental.' "[32]

Visualization brings surprisingly easy contact with what witch doctors and other shamans have always called "spirits." Harner explains that "the shaman has at least one, and usually more, 'spirits' in his personal service. Without a guardian spirit it is virtually impossible to be a shaman. . . . "[33] Modern man follows the same shamanistic procedures and contacts the same "spirits" but calls them "inner guides" or "imaginary guides." This ancient method has produced remarkable results for Dr. O. Carl Simonton and his wife, Stephanie. The Simontons have become famous for their success with terminal cancer patients, some of whom have apparently been healed through the power of "inner guides" which the Simontons have taught them to visualize. It used to be axiomatic that scientists considered *why* something happened to be extremely important. Harner expresses the modern attitude when he argues that to use—

> techniques long practiced in shamanism. . . such as visualization. . . we do not need to understand in scientific terms why it works, just as we do not need to know why acupuncture works in order to benefit from it.[34]

In his popular *The Well Body Book*, Mike Samuels, M.D., tells how to get in touch with one's own inner "imaginary doctor" through visualization. However, his identification of this mysterious and apparently all-knowing and all-powerful entity is contradictory and hardly satisfying. On the one hand, Dr. Samuels parrots the psychological explanation so popular today in suggesting that this apparently infallible "doctor" that speaks with its own, independent "inner voice" is simply one of many forms which the Infinite Wisdom allegedly residing in each of us takes in order to communicate with us. Yet in *Spirit Guides: Access to Inner Worlds*, Samuels seriously declares that his "imaginary doctor" is actually his personal "spirit guide," whom he contacted through instructions from "Rolling Thunder," a native American Indian shaman (medicine man).[35]

In visualizing "God" or "Jesus" or the thing being prayed for, the average Christian is not aware that he is following the same procedure that shamans insist opens a "magic doorway" in the mind that leads to the sorcerer's world. This simple but powerful technique (long used by shamans for entering the spirit realm in order to contact and bargain with spirit entities) has gained acceptance in today's medicine, psychology, success/motivation, and education. It is also being promoted and taught by an alarming and increasing number of Christian leaders, who urge us to visualize our concept of "Jesus" and promise that the image we create in our minds will become the *real* Jesus, who will then make genuine contact with us. C. S. Lovett writes:

> Around 300 years ago there was a French monk by the name of Brother Lawrence, who...developed the art of VISUALIZING the Lord Jesus, and it revolutionized his life....
>
> THE MOST NOBLE AND GLORIOUS PURPOSE OF THE IMAGINATION IS GIVING REALITY TO THE UNSEEN LORD!...
>
> As you know, many tend to be superstitious about picturing the Lord.... But you see, the Lord doesn't care ONE BIT how we visualize Him.... Picture Him any way you wish, but love Him...I know from experience your enjoyment of Him is going to be greatly enhanced by giving Him arms with which to hold you [emphasis in original].[36]

How to Meet Your Own Jesus?

Those pursuing healing and success often fall prey to the temptation to accept whatever seems to work, and to adjust their interpretation of the Bible accordingly. Christians are being taught to "visualize" themselves on a beautiful, sandy beach or a peaceful, grassy knoll, and to "see" Jesus approaching them. All over America, specialists in healing of the memories are leading entire congregations to visualize Jesus as present at some traumatic childhood or even prenatal event, which He sanctifies, forgives, or changes—and in the process delivers them from their past. Others who are not necessarily advocating the same type of inner healing, also promote a similar visualization of Jesus.

Calvin Miller, who is one of today's most honored Christian writers, promotes the dangerous idea that we can visualize into existence with the power of our imagination even God and Christ. In a book that also presents much beneficial teaching, Miller writes:

> One door opens to the world of the spirit: imagination. . . . To follow Christ, we must create in our minds God's unseen world, or never confront it at all. Thus we create in our minds the Christ. . . .
>
> We cannot commune with a Savior whose form and shape elude us. Whenever I speak long distance to my son or daughter, I use their voices to hang a thousand images of who they are.
>
> Likewise, in my conversation with Christ, I see him white robed, yet at ease in my own time. I drink the glory of his hazel eyes, thrill to the golden sunlight dancing on his auburn hair. I see his calloused hands reaching out for me and for all the world he loves.
>
> What? Do you disagree? His hair is black? Eyes brown? Then have it your way. His lordship is your treasure as it is mine. His image must be real to you as to me, even if our images differ. The key to vitality, however, is the image. . . .
>
> Bit by bit, block by imaginary block, we define him and we adore him. The Bible writers did the same.[37]

Is this visualized "Jesus" merely an aid to faith, like an icon in a Greek Orthodox church? If so, are mental images of deity allowed while those made out of wood or stone are forbidden? Or is this actually Jesus Himself coming to us whenever we image Him in our minds, as some are teaching? If that is the case, would it not seem that we have Jesus on a string and can make Him appear at will? The Bible teaches that Christ has come to live within those who have opened their hearts to Him, receiving Him as Savior and Lord. Jesus has promised never to leave or forsake the individual Christian, and has promised His presence in a special way wherever two or three are gathered together in His name. For Him actually to *appear* to His own, however, is something altogether different, and has only happened on rare occasions. When Jesus suddenly appeared to the ten disciples who were hiding behind locked doors after His resurrection, it was a miraculous event initiated by Him for His own purposes. Doubting Thomas, who was not present on that occasion, had to wait a week before the risen Lord appeared again and allowed him to put his fingers in the nailprints and his hand in the spear wound in His side. We are being taught today, however, that Thomas need not have waited five minutes. He could have had the *real* Jesus appear to him by simply visualizing Him; and we can do the same any time we wish.

Jesus carefully told His disciples that He was going away, and that He would send the Holy Spirit to be with them. The Comforter has come, and we know His presence in our lives by faith in His promise and by the experience of the fruit of the Spirit. *Visualization* of God or Jesus plays no part in this, is not necessary, and in fact is an attempt to make Him *appear* rather than to know His abiding presence. Our Lord certainly gave no instruction nor even hinted that anyone should *visualize* Him and that He would then appear.

The New Testament records a number of appearances of Jesus to His disciples during the 40 days after His resurrection and prior to His ascension, and even afterward to Paul on the Damascus road. Never is there a hint that any of these appearances were initiated by anyone except the Lord Himself, much less that they were brought about by visualization. Indeed, had they been caused by visualization, Paul's argument in 1 Corinthians 15 that these appearances proved the resurrection would have lost most of its power. Anyone who fantasizes contact with other humans, rather than making genuine contact with them, would be considered at the least eccentric. If he insisted that he was thereby making *real* contact with friends and family, he would surely be considered insane.

There is a genuine contact with Christ through faith, a communion in the heart that He gives to His own. He may even appear as He wills for some specific purpose. But to create a fantasy Jesus in our minds and insist that this is the *real* Jesus and that talking with this figment of our imagination is the way to genuine spiritual experience is to be deluded indeed. It is only marginally different, but still a delusion, to attempt to create an atmosphere of high suggestibility that will enable us to "feel" His presence or somehow encourage Him to appear. In any such techniques, the definite possibility exists of opening the door to demonic contact or even of acquiring a "spirit guide" that we think is the real Jesus.

"But It Works!"

C. S. Lovett reminds us that "no one on earth knows, of course, what Jesus really looked like in human form."[38] Therefore each person involved in this visualization process has fantasized his own individual "Jesus," with whom he now carries on a relationship in his imagination. Yet it seems to *work*. Rita Bennett led her husband Dennis, an Episcopal priest, through a healing-of-the-memories session in which he visualized Jesus with him in the past. "Dennis testifies, 'In the one simple piece of visualization, Jesus was able to change my whole basic feeling...about my childhood [and] about life in general.' "[39] Like Lovett, Calvin Miller says that it doesn't matter what the Jesus one visualizes looks like; yet he says, "The key to vitality, however, is the image [visualized]."[40]

One can only wonder why the "image" is so important if it need bear no relationship to the actual appearance of the One it represents. It sounds like Christianized idolatry. Hindus would argue, for example, that the thousands of varying images depicting their concept of deity are equally valid, for it isn't the form of the image but its utility in reminding the worshiper of the higher reality it supposedly represents. For charismatic Catholic priests Dennis and Matthew Linn and Sheila Fabricant the visualized image brings actual contact with Jesus Himself. They declare: "Although she was using her imagination, it was not just her imagination but really Jesus touching her...."[41] Richard Foster promises that through visualization we encounter the real Jesus Christ:

> ...you can actually encounter the living Christ in the event. It can be more than an exercise of the imagination, it can be a genuine confrontation.
> Jesus Christ will actually come to you.[42]

In spite of the fact that it is obviously not biblical, the visualization of Jesus is an increasingly popular tool for Christian psychologists and inner healers. Ruth Carter Stapleton writes: "But as the guided meditation continued, Betty suddenly saw in her imagination Jesus standing before her. His arms went around her and he was saying he loved her. Such a mystical moment is not open to critical analysis. These spiritual dimensions lie far above the rational faculties."[43] Some Christians even have very real experiences through visualizing themselves in God's presence, in spite of the fact that the Bible declares that He "dwells in unapproachable light; whom no man has seen or can see" (1 Timothy 6:16). Richard Foster writes:

> In your imagination allow your spiritual body, shining with light, to rise out of your physical body. Look back so that you can see yourself...and reassure your body that you will return momentarily....
> Go deeper and deeper into outer space until there is nothing except the warm presence of the eternal Creator. Rest in his presence.
> Listen quietly...[to] any instruction given.[44]

The Danger of the Mental Picture

Rita Bennett argues that if it is wrong to visualize Jesus simply because we don't know what he looks like, then it must also be wrong to paint pictures of Jesus.[45] Of course, few Christians claim to receive guidance and healing from pictures of Jesus. Moreover, if all we have is a "picture" we have painted with the imagination in our minds, then it is just as foolish to commune with it as with a picture on the wall. It was for this reason that A. W. Tozer insisted that "we must distinguish believing from visualizing. The two are not the same. One is moral and the other mental."[46] Humans vary in their ability to visualize; some cannot do it at all. If depth of spiritual experience or reality depended upon visualizing a vivid image of Jesus, many would be at a disadvantage. Moreover, the real disadvantage would be to those who visualize, for they have been led to trust in their own imagination rather than in God. Tozer went on to explain:

> Unwillingness to believe proves that men love darkness rather than light, while inability to visualize indicates no more than lack of imagination, something that will not be held against us at the judgment seat of Christ....
>
> The ability to visualize is found among vigorous-minded persons, whatever their moral or spiritual condition may be.... The wise Christian will not let his assurance depend upon his powers of imagination.[47]

The danger of the mental picture is that it *seems* to be real, and therein lies its greater potential for seduction. For Brother Lawrence and Frank Laubach, the experience validates itself and this mystical "meeting God soul to soul and face to face" transcends any objective evaluation, even the Bible. Laubach declares that, dangerous though it may be, he is "going to take the risks...to achieve God-consciousness...[for that] is what made Christ, Christ."[48] We do well to heed the words of John Calvin:

> ...when miserable men do seek after God...they do not conceive of him in the character in which he is manifested, but imagine him to be whatever their own rashness has devised....
>
> With such an idea of God, nothing which they may attempt to offer in the way of worship or obedience can have any value in his sight, because it is not him they worship, but, instead of him, the dream and figment of their own heart.[49]

There is an additional and more obvious (yet seemingly overlooked) problem. Since no painting of Jesus can claim to be accurate, it is clear that many—and perhaps all—such pictures could be misleading Christians by influencing the way they think of Him. Referring to a favorite picture of Jesus painted by his daughter Linda, C. S. Lovett admits, "Yes, it influences my concept of Jesus. I just love it."[50] Yet not only Lovett but other advocates of visualizing Jesus and God seem unconcerned that, like paintings, visualized mental images of Jesus are also misleading—and the more seriously so, because they are mistaken for the *real* Jesus. Is the church being seduced by a new "Christianized" idolatry that is being taught and popularized today? J. I. Packer makes the following interesting observation:

> ...we take the second commandment—as in fact it has always been taken—as pointing us to the principle that (to quote Charles Hodge) "idolatry consists not only in the worship of false gods, but also in the worship of the true God by images."
>
> In its Christian application, this means that we are not to make use of visual or pictorial representations of the Triune God, or of any person of the Trinity, for the purposes of Christian worship.
>
> What harm is there, we ask, in the worshiper surrounding himself with statues and pictures, if they help him to lift his heart to God?... If people really do find them helpful, what more is there to be said?...
>
> ...it is certain that if you habitually focus your thoughts on an image or picture of the One to whom you are going to pray, you will come to think of Him, and pray to Him, as the image represents Him. Thus you will in this sense "bow down" and "worship" your image; and to the extent to which the image fails to tell the truth about God, to that extent you will fail to worship God in truth. That is why God forbids you and me to make use of images and pictures in our worship....
>
> To follow the imagination of one's heart in the realm of theology is the way to remain ignorant of God, and

to become an idol-worshiper—the idol in this case being a false mental image of God, "made unto thee" by speculation and imagination.[51]

Idolatry and Demons

Paul gives a powerful reason against idolatry when he explains that in worshiping idols the Gentiles are really worshiping devils: "No; but I say that the things which the Gentiles sacrifice, they sacrifice to demons, and not to God; and I do not want you to become sharers in demons" (1 Corinthians 10:20). Scripture makes it clear that we must know the true God for who He really is, and that we must come to Him on His terms. Satan or demons, however, will hide behind any mask and answer to any image or name. They are very broad-minded in their various ruses to get humans under their power. Paul seems to be saying that not just *some* idols but *all* idols are fronts for demons. This is what makes visualization of Jesus or God not just a minor error but extremely dangerous. That visualization is ideally suited for contact with demons can be demonstrated in the fact that it has been used for that very purpose for thousands of years in various forms of shamanism. And the shaman will always tell you that it doesn't matter what image you conjure up, but conjure up an image you must.

Few idol-worshipers of any kind would say that they intend to worship devils. Most would protest that they look upon the idol as a symbol of the true God. Yet they get involved with devils because they are using a methodology that God has forbidden. Would "sincerity" in visualizing "Jesus" or "God" be any better an excuse? Demons would certainly not mind being mistaken for Jesus; that would serve their purpose extremely well. C. S. Lewis sums it up in his allegory *The Screwtape Letters*. Screwtape is a senior devil advising his nephew Wormwood how better to seduce Christians. On this subject Screwtape says:

> Whenever they are attending to the Enemy Himself we are defeated, but there are ways of preventing them from doing this. The simplest is to turn their gaze away

from Him toward themselves. Keep them watching their own minds and trying to produce *feelings* there by the action of their own wills....

The humans do not start from that direct perception of Him which we, unhappily, cannot avoid. They have never known that ghastly luminosity, that stabbing and searing glare which is the source of permanent pain in our lives. If you look into your patient's mind when he is praying, you will not find *that* image.

If you examine the picture on which he is concentrating, you will find that it is a composite of many quite ridiculous ingredients. There will be images derived from pictures of the Enemy as He appeared during the discreditable episode known as the Incarnation. In addition, there will be more vague, and perhaps quite barbaric, images associated with the other two Persons of the Trinity. There will even be some of his own reverence (and of bodily sensations accompanying it) attributed to the beloved image.

I have known cases where what the patient called his "God" was actually *located* up and to the left at the corner of the bedroom ceiling or inside his own head or in a crucifix on the wall. But whatever the nature of the composite object, you must keep him praying to *it*—to the thing that he has made, not to the Person who has made him. You may even encourage him to attach great importance to the correction and improvement of his composite object. Suggest that he keep it steadily before his imagination during the whole prayer.

He must never come to make the distinction between the object and the Person. If he ever consciously directs his prayers, "Not to what I think Thou art but to what thou knowest Thyself to be," our situation is, for the moment, desperate. If this ever happens, he may cast aside all his thoughts and images. Or, he may retain them with a full recognition of their merely subjective nature. Then the man will trust himself to the completely real, external, invisible Presence, who is with him in the room. This is the worst thing that could happen.[52]

12

Psychological Salvation

> See to it that no one takes you captive through philosophy and empty deception, according to the tradition of men, according to the elementary principles of the world, rather than according to Christ.... These are matters which have, to be sure, the appearance of wisdom in self-made religion...but are of no value against fleshly indulgence.
>
> Colossians 2:8,23

The very power of the experiences that can be initiated through visualization seems to "prove" that they are genuine not only to non-Christians but even to Christian leaders as well. Writing in *Christian Life* magazine, Robert L. Wise, a well-known pastor and leader in the Presbyterian Renewal movement, explained a "new method of prayer therapy," which he said was "pioneered in the mid-1960s by the doyenne of Episcopal renewal theology, Agnes Sanford."[1] Wise told what happened when he first visualized "Jesus" during a "Healing of the Memories" session under the direction of a Christian leader who had learned the technique from Sanford:

> I began to visualize myself as a boy of eight. I was startled to see...myself carrying a large bundle on my back, [which] apparently...symbolized my past needs and worries.
> "Now see if you can imagine Jesus appearing," she instructed. "Let him walk toward you."

Much to my amazement, I—an ordained Reformed clergyman with a doctorate in psychology—found this happening to me. An image of Jesus moved slowly toward me out of that dark playground. He began to extend His hands toward me in a loving, accepting manner....

I no longer was creating the scene. The figure of Christ reached over and lifted the bundle from my back. And he did so with such forcefulness that I literally sprang from the pew.[2]

A Spirit Guide Called "Jesus"?

Is this the real Jesus? Rita Bennett says, "When we pray and encourage a person to visualize Jesus, the accuracy of the picture isn't important.[3] See Him as your favorite artist pictures Him if you like."[4] Nevertheless, Mrs. Bennett seems to be convinced that more than the imagination is involved in such experiences. Referring to this fantasized Jesus that is initially created in the imagination, but who thereafter comes alive like a motion picture on a screen in the mind, she says, "It's necessary to follow His guidance."[5] If this is indeed the real Jesus, then she is giving sound advice. However, there is neither example nor teaching in the Bible to indicate that Jesus ever appeared or ever will appear to anyone because he or she visualized Him. He is not a magic genie to be conjured up through the power of our minds.

Then who or what is this figure that becomes so real? What is going on in the visualizer's mind? In some inner-healing experiences, such as Robert Wise describes, it would appear that contact has been established with some spirit being. Moreover, what this "Jesus" says or does, as this fantasy motion picture being played on an imaginary mental screen begins to roll on its own, seems to give valid answers to questions and solve perplexing problems. Is it possible that the same demonic beings who pose as "spirit guides" for occultists could appear to Christians as "Jesus"? Would demons be above using such a tactic?

It should be clear that 1) this procedure is not biblical; 2) it has been used for thousands of years in numerous forms of sorcery; 3) something more than imagination is taking place; and 4) those who practice it run the real risk of opening themselves to demonic influence.

"Spirit guides," which have been an integral part of occultism for thousands of years, are contacted through the very same visualization techniques and are equally as real as the Christian's visualized "Jesus." Nor is their guidance any less accurate or compelling. Although God is merciful, Christians who persist in techniques designed to make Jesus appear are on dangerous ground. Pastor/author C. S. Lovett writes:

> Turn on your imagination screen.... We're going to do an EXERCISE that can help you visualize the Lord. I want to make sure you have a clear mental picture of Him....
>
> But you see, the Lord doesn't care ONE BIT how we visualize Him.... Anyone willing to humble Himself on a cross for us isn't going to fuss over the way we picture Him in our minds....
>
> Thank you for alerting me to this glorious use of my imagination...my visualization of You is going to get clearer and clearer as we spend more time together [emphasis in the original].[6]

Psychospirituality on the Move

Lovett thus agrees with Calvin Miller that everyone is free to visualize Jesus in whatever mental image he finds most appealing. Richard Foster says, "We simply must become convinced of the importance of thinking and experiencing in images."[7] Remember, we are not addressing the many valid uses of the imagination, such as visual images used by artists, architects, or ordinary persons in "seeing" what is being described, remembering or rehearsing in their minds. It is only those techniques specifically designed to manipulate reality or evoke the appearance and help of Deity that we must avoid. Within this inner world created by the mind, the same fantasy visions that have deluded occultists and mystics for thousands of years are encountered by modern man through adopting the same occult techniques. Morton Kelsey reminds us of Jung's description of what he called "entering into the unconscious":

> An incessant stream of fantasies had been released, and I did my best not to lose my head but to find some way to understand these strange things.[8]
>
> [Kelsey then adds his own comment]:
>
> Mystics of all religions have engaged in the same journey and have described the same kind of encounters. The shamans of many primitive religions are led through dismemberment and death toward renewal. They understood "these strange things."[9]

So in the name of the latest psychology we are being led back into primitive paganism/shamanism, which then enters the church because psychology is embraced as scientific and neutral. Tragically, this is often done by sincere Christian leaders who imagine that they are bringing revival to the church. Unaware that they are actually adopting psychologized shamanism in their concern to restore God's power in the experience of physical and emotional healings, these men are creating a powerful New Age "paradigm shift" that is changing the way thousands of pastors and future pastors view Christianity and the Bible. In his latest *Signs and Wonders Lecture Notes*, John Wimber writes:

> At the time of the preparation of this manual, Dr. C. Peter Wagner and I have been teaching MC510 for three years. It has been one of the most invigorating and exciting adventures of our lives.
>
> At this date, January 1985, we have had in excess of 700 students take the course at Fuller Seminary School of World Missions. The results have been astounding. Better than 90 percent of the students have indicated a paradigm shift in which they are now ministering in an altered worldview.[10]

Wimber's seminars are being attended by thousands of pastors and Christian leaders. John Wimber is very sincere in his desire to bring biblical teaching. It is the extra-biblical sources he and others draw upon and recommend that creates the major problem. Under the influence of writers such as Sanford, Kelsey, et al more and more Christian leaders interpret Scripture through a grid of mysticism blended with Jungian psychology.

Just Imagine!

There is a definite "paradigm shift" taking place in the thinking of a very wide spectrum of church leaders. Catholic priests Dennis and Matthew Linn state, "Whatever I vividly relive in my imagination affects me as if I really experienced it."[11] Lutheran pastor William Vaswig writes:

> Perhaps the most important thing Agnes Sanford taught me about prayer is that it has to do with the imagination.... I always thought of imagination in somewhat negative terms. I often heard imagination disparaged: "Oh, don't let your imagination run away with you...." Genesis 6:5 says that the imagination of man was exceedingly corrupt....
>
> I believe imagination is one of the most important keys to effective praying.... God touches me through my imagination.... Imagination is one of the keys to the relationship of prayer with God.[12]

Since *imagination* is the key, then the exact *image* one visualizes is not important. Such an idea can hardly be reconciled with *inspiration* from God; yet there is a growing trend among Christian writers to equate the two. Napoleon Hill, as we have already noted, visualized great figures out of history such as Darwin and Voltaire, who put him in touch with an infinite source of wisdom, yet he insisted that it was all just *imagination*. Medical doctor O. Carl Simonton encourages cancer victims to visualize "inner guides," and some patients experience apparently miraculous cures on that basis. Consulted by other physicians, who refer their impossible cases to him, Dr. Irving Oyle teaches patients to visualize "power animals," such as the coyote so popular with American Indian shamans—and incredible results are achieved.

In view of the above and further examples that could be given, today's popular practice of visualizing "Jesus" is undeniably similar to occult practices.

This is not to deny that God in His mercy may protect Christians from occult involvement who have out of ignorance used shamanic techniques. One would hardly expect, however, that God would honor occult methodologies by manifesting Himself to those using them. It is one thing for the Lord to protect Christians who innocently play with a Ouija board, but it is something else entirely to suppose that God would speak to them through this or any other divination device even once, much less on a habitual basis. Many Christians have tried to use a Ouija board, and without knowing the power behind it were disappointed that it didn't work for them. Later they were glad that it hadn't worked, and thanked the Lord for protecting them. The same thing has been true of Christians who have tried to visualize Jesus and nothing happened. For those who make contact with "Jesus" in this manner, we can only warn that there is no biblical support for the idea that the *real* Jesus would appear to them on that basis. In fact it is all to the contrary. Numerous places in the Bible, such as Deuteronomy 18, make it clear that all occult practices are absolutely forbidden to the people of God.

This is not to say that everyone who gets involved in occult practices immediately comes under the power of Satan. Some may have a cathartic and very emotional psychological experience that convinces them that everything is genuine and of God. While this is not *directly* demonic, it definitely draws them in that direction. Some inner-healing practitioners attempt to explain even apparently real appearances of "Jesus " in psychological terms, attributing everything to the power of the imagination. This conveniently removes any fear of contact with demons or seduction by Satan, and of course, is not biblical. If an *imagined* experience has the same effect upon us as an actual experience (as we are repeatedly told by Christian leaders who are promoting within the church basic PMA and success/motivation theories and practices), then one need not even be concerned whether it is the real Jesus or not, since an imaginary one will do just as well. We are back to Hinduism and Christian Science (which teaches that *everything* is an illusion created by our minds), and the door is wide open for every kind of deception.

Jesus, Mary, and Other "Inner Guides"

Miraculous cures, ecstatic experiences of universal love and personal transformation have been effected not only through visualizing "Jesus," but also by visualizing spirits of the dead, the great saints, ascended masters, and religious leaders from the past such as assorted ancient Hindu gurus or Buddha. What is the difference? Jung would say there is none; and this seems to be the teaching not only of Kelsey but of a number of other Christian leaders.

Morton T. Kelsey writes: "Thanks to Jung's advocacy of the active imagination, plus his understanding of the deceased as living on in reality, I was able to have this kind of meeting with my [dead] mother...it seemed real to me."[13]

If it doesn't matter whether we visualize Jesus or Buddha, then it must not matter whether we *believe* in Jesus or Buddha; it is all a mind trip; imagination is as real as actual experience. Although it may be denied by some who practice it, that is the only premise upon which inner healing can be said to rest. *Imagination* is the Creator of a whole new past, present, and future; and is somehow confused with *revelation* from God.

Some of the Vineyard Christian Fellowships, headed by John Wimber, are heavily involved in the use of imagination, visualization, and inner healing. Christian Research Institute has written that spiritual experiences are frequently viewed as "self-authenticating" in Vineyard Fellowships; and there seems to be an assumption "that whatever transpires in their midst is from God."

John Wimber's recommendation of authors such as Kelsey, Sanford, MacNutt, the Sandfords, and the Linns is consistent with the growing reliance upon psychospiritual pseudoChristian techniques as necessary implementations to biblical Christianity in order to experience full deliverance and victory. Francis MacNutt says, "If the person missed out on a mother's love in any way I ask Jesus (if the person is a Catholic) to send His mother Mary...to do all those...things that mothers do to give their children love and security."[14] The Jesuit Linn brothers are among the most prominent leaders in the inner healing movement. Referring to a specific example, the Linns and Sheila Fabricant have written:

> Judy joined Mary at the foot of the cross, watching [in her imagination] as Jesus died. . . she began to feel how Mary felt. . . . Judy let Mary cry against her. . . .
>
> So Dennis [Linn] encouraged Judy [in her fantasized vision] to tell Mary all the things about her [own] mother's death that were hard for her. Judy remembered how frightened she felt in her mother's hospital room. But now as Judy saw that same hospital room, Mary was there holding her. . . .
>
> After remaining in that room and filling herself with Mary's love, Judy asked Mary to be with her at the moment when her mother died. Judy saw Mary bring Jesus into the room also.
>
> [Referring to another case, Linda, who hated her sexual identity, and earlier under "Guided Journaling" visualized a "Jesus who had encouraged her, 'Go ahead and cuss me out.' "]
>
> Thus each week we asked Jesus to take her home to be loved by His parents, Mary and Joseph. . . . In our prayer, we asked that Mary and Joseph become Linda's adoptive parents. We asked also that their wholesome love for each other. . . enfold Linda as it did Jesus, penetrating her subconscious mind and memory from the moment of conception, and reforming her sexual identity in light rather than the darkness in which she had been raised.[15]

One can only wonder how evangelicals, who would reject the idea of Mary and Joseph being involved in healing anyone today, reconcile this practice by inner healers whom they recommend. Since visualizing Mary seems to be just as effective as visualizing Jesus, how do evangelical inner healers differentiate between the two? How do they explain the apparently miraculous healing power of a visualized Mary? It seems that there has been considerable adjustment made to what used to be viewed as Biblical standards in order to embrace the inner healing movement. In recommending them, Wimber writes:

> Fathers Dennis and Matthew Linn...are Jesuit priests who have written four books which deal with physical, psychological and spiritual wholeness.
> They are highly trained in psychology and combine the best insights in this field with theological understanding, shared by Charismatic experience.[16]

It is absolutely necessary to allow the Bible to judge every experience. If there is not clear teaching in the Bible to support a practice, it should not be adopted by the church today, *regardless of how beautiful and seemingly miraculous the experiences are that it produces.* Unfortunately, to an alarming degree, the Scriptures are no longer looked upon as the full and sufficient guide given by the Holy Spirit for doctrine, for reproof, for correction, for instruction in righteousness, that the man of God may be complete, thoroughly equipped for every good work (2 Timothy 3:16,17).

Two major attitudes have opened the door to error in the church: 1) Experience is taken as self-authenticating, so that the need for biblical authentication is considered to be marginal at best; and/or 2) psychological theories are accepted that provide the authentication of experiences and practices which cannot be justified from the Bible. Both of these attitudes are becoming widespread in the church.

Primal Delusion

According to the Ojai Foundation, a Southern California organization that promotes Eastern mysticism, shamanism involves visualized "journeys" into the past accompanied by a "spirit guide" through "archetypal exercises and rituals" to "awaken dormant human capabilities and forgotten connections ...including the extraction of spiritual pain and illness."[17] Substitute "Jesus" for "spirit guide" and inner healing with "archetypal exercises and rituals," and shamanism's connection with Christian inner-healing techniques and psychology's "secular form of salvation" is undeniable. Both secular and Christian therapies share the common delusion that salvation or healing comes through uprooting memories of "hurts" from early childhood and even the womb that are supposedly deeply buried in the subconscious from where they dictate our present behavior without our knowing it. Thus the blame is too often placed in the past and upon others rather than ourselves.

There may indeed be something in the past that must be dealt with, which is causing bitterness against those who may have wronged us and we have never forgiven, or guilt for things we have done to others and never apologized for or made right. No Christian should continue for one more moment with anything like that on his conscience, and need not. All that we need for dealing with such problems is found in the fact that Christ died for our sins and has risen from the dead to live His life in us. No one who has truly received God's love and forgiveness as a sinful rebel can possibly withhold that same love and forgiveness from those who have wronged him. We love and forgive others because of God's love and forgiveness to us. It is that simple. This is the "fruit of the Spirit" that results from Christ living in us. If we are willing to face this truth, then He will give us the strength to carry it out. Inner healing is based upon a denial that this is all we need; "something more" must be involved, and that "something" is borrowed from a variety of psychotherapies, most of which are related to shamanism.

Many of these therapies involve fantasy reenactments of past traumas induced by methods that range from breathing techniques and guided imagery to psychodrama. The available brands cover everything from Primal Scream (developed by Arthur Janov) and its "Christian" equivalent, Primal Integration Therapy, (systematized by Cecil Osborne), to the varying substitutes practiced in the church by traveling specialists in healing of the memories or inner healing. Primal Scream is so outrageous that most inner healers would denounce it. Nevertheless it is true to the basic deterministic theories that underlie psychotherapies and most forms of healing of the memories, secular or Christian. Moreover, some Christian psychologists use Primal Scream. The description given by Martin and Deidre Bobgan in *The Psychological Way/ The Spiritual Way,* shows how Primal Scream fits into the general framework of deterministic psychology and also how it relates to its "Christian" counterparts:

> The sacred words of Primal Therapy are *Primal Pain*...[which] the child accumulates...from unmet needs, such as not being fed when hungry, not being changed when wet...the conflicts between self-need and parental expectation...result in what Janov calls the "Primal Pool of Pain."
>
> When the Pool gets deep enough, just one more incident supposedly pushes the child into neurosis. This single significant incident is labeled the "major Primal Scene,"...[which] occurs between the ages of five and seven and is buried in the unconscious....
>
> Janov theorizes that to be cured, the neurotic must return to his major Primal Scene...experience the emotions, the events, and...accompanying Pain in order to be cured....
>
> In group sessions there is...utter chaos and outright bedlam...some adults sucking baby bottles, others cuddling stuffed toys, still others in adult-sized cribs.... Then there is the birth simulator for those who want to experience the Primals that go all the way back to the womb and the birth process...others on the floor, gagging, thrashing, writhing, gurgling, choking and wailing..."Daddy, be nice!" "Mommy, help!" "I hate you! I hate you...."
>
> This sick, sick psychotherapy is only one of a host of similar therapies that are attracting a large number of adults seeking to find solace for the troubled soul.[18]

Another pioneer in a similar form of fantasized regression closely related to Christian inner healing is Stanislav Grof, who "started out as a strict Freudian, but moved into the Jungian and transpersonal modes to justify his findings...."[19] Through "research in Czechoslovakia during the 60s" using "psycholytic (LSD-based) therapy," Grof discovered that schizophrenics "spontaneously acted out powerful rebirth fantasies under the influence of hallucinogenic drugs."[20] Thus Grof verified with LSD the theories that Freud and Jung discovered through the equally shamanic practice of hypnosis. Such theories form the "scientific" basis for psychotherapy and Christian inner healing.

Deifying the Birthing Process

LSD-induced fantasies have become the foundation of a new secular therapy called "rebirthing." It has become one of the fastest-growing pop psychologies, with everyone from individual practitioners to Unity and Religious Science ministers performing the ritual for "healing of the memories." Often the rebirthing takes place in water, and seems to be the mind-science cults' answer to Christian baptism.

Rebirthing is a Westernized version of ancient mythology that is closely related to the fertility cults: It attributes mystical significance and godlike powers to the birth process. Although Grof and other psychologists, in justifying their secular salvation, suggest that "rebirth imagery [is] the core of mystical experience,"[21] they insist that inducing and interpreting it is *science*. Moreover, they persist in this in spite of the scientific evidence, to which we have already referred, that the pre-natal, natal, and early post-natal brain is not sufficiently developed to carry memories. And now similar ideas have entered the church. Rita Bennett calls her particular brand of healing of the memories "Reliving the Scene With Jesus." Her method purports to relive the past through visualizing Jesus present within the womb, at birth, or during early childhood traumas. Her list of "matters to pray about [for healing] during the important first two years of the person's life" include: "If he was unduly left hungry or wet, or in pain, needing to be burped. . . ."[22]

The increasingly popular Christianized rebirthing rituals seem to produce basically the same "memories" as Stanislaf Grof has aroused through LSD or consciousness-altering breathing. As part of the ritual for healing such questionable "memories," Rita Bennett offers detailed "meditations": "Dear Lord, please wash away any false guilt of feeling responsible for his mother's birth pains. . . visualize your parents and thank them for their part in bringing you into existence, visualize Jesus in the scene," etc.[23] Is this effective? As evidence of that, Mrs. Bennett quotes testimonials, such as the following from a "prayer counselor at the Cathedral of Saint Philip, Atlanta":

> I want to tell you that *nothing* has helped our inner healing counseling as much as learning to pray from the moment of conception, thru the fetal period and birth process.
> We are grateful for these insights.... What a blessing to just be a *part* of this ministry! [emphasis in original].[24]

Many of the leaders in the inner healing movement teach and nearly all seem to imply that the past is actually being *recreated* through visualizing Jesus moving back through the "memories" and changing history. MacNutt explains that "Jesus, as Lord of time, is able to do what we cannot...[we] ask Jesus to walk back with us into the past...it is the inner child of the past who is being healed...."[25] Ruth Carter Stapleton, who, like most of the other leaders in the movement, learned her inner healing from Agnes Sanford, tells of a young woman who became involved in drugs and crime because of the "self-loathing" she felt at being "an illegitimate child." Ruth's solution was to take the young woman back in "a guided meditation" in which Christ was visualized as "present" during the act of fornication that caused her conception and making it "holy and pure, an act of God...ordained by her heavenly Father."[26] The knowledge that one was conceived illegitimately may be very painful, but what really matters is one's present relationship to God through the Lord Jesus Christ. Nevertheless, instead of leading the young woman to the resurrected and risen Christ as Savior and Lord, Stapleton led her to fantasize an imaginary Jesus, who journeyed into the past to turn fornication into a holy and pure act of God! Francis MacNutt writes:

> The idea behind inner healing is simply that we can ask Jesus Christ to walk back to the time we were hurt and to free us from the effects of that wound in the present....[27]

It should be clear by now that what is being taught is a Christianized form of the mental alchemy that lies at the heart of shamanism. This is basic sorcery, the attempt to manipulate reality, whether past, present, or future. At the very least this unscriptural practice denies God's omnipotence by implying that He needs our "creative visualization" to apply effectively His forgiveness and healing; and at worst, it sets us up as gods who can, through prescribed rituals, use Him and His power as our tools. Addressing the congregation at Christ Universal Temple in Chicago, a large Unity church, Mrs. Stapleton presented the underlying basis for her inner healing methodology that explains why we can remake the past:

> God is wholeness; and *you are God*. In you He lives and moves and has His being.[28]

Freud's Myth of Psychic Determinism

The primary foundation for inner healing is a misinformed acceptance of Freud's discredited theory of "psychic determinism." Psychology textbooks describe this as the belief that "human behavior. . . [occurs] in accordance with intrapsychic causes"[29] and is actually "controlled by impulses, many of which are buried in the unconscious, below the level of awareness."[30] These two Freudian/Jungian ideas, *psychic determinism* and the *unconscious*, form the foundation of inner healing, both in the secular world and in the church. It is obvious, however, that if Freud's theory about the past determining the present and future is true, then man does not have a free will, but is ruled by unconscious forces. It would follow that he cannot be held personally accountable for his actions. Inner-healing methodologies sometimes provide a means for putting the blame on others (parents, friends, and even God) and then forgiving them, using Freud's theory of the unconscious as a rationale. Psychologist and author Martin Bobgan has said:

> Among the greatest criticisms of Freudian psychology today—and there are more criticisms today than there ever have been—have been criticisms

aimed at the whole idea of the unconscious.

So from a Biblical basis and from a scientific basis there really is no support for the use of the unconscious as used in Freudian psychology and as borrowed by the inner healers.[31]

To support his theories, Freud contended "that the unconscious is *the* major motivating force behind all human behavior."[32] Accepted as scientific, this Freudian concept has played a large part in turning the West to an Eastern world view centered in selfism. Morton T. Kelsey writes: "One can hardly overemphasize the importance of this theory for all later thinking about the nature of personality...."[33] Typical of secular college textbooks is the following:

Whether one agrees with Freud's theory or not, it is clear that Freudian concepts have completely revised the way we look at human nature. In fact, it is probably accurate to say that no single individual has so revolutionalized the way we view ourselves as Freud did.[34]

Another invention of Freud's that has deeply influenced society and is now seducing Christianity was the idea that "for all practical purposes the adult personality is formed by the end of the fifth year of life"[35] through "certain psychosexual stages of development" that "determine what kind of personality he or she will possess as an adult."[36] It is important to know that it was through "memories" of past experiences aroused in their patients under the influence of the ancient shamanic practice of hypnosis, which we have already noted are at best unreliable and most likely demonic, that both Freud and Jung developed their primary theories. (For a full discussion of hypnosis, see Martin and Deidre Bobgan, *Hypnosis and the Christian* (Bethany, 1984) and pp. 111-28 of *Peace, Prosperity, and the Coming Holocaust,* by Dave Hunt.) Kelsey confirms that through hypnotic regression Freud "discovered" that his patients "were driven by ideas, feelings, and emotions that had been repressed and buried since childhood...."[37] In the same seminar address quoted above, Martin Bobgan reminded his audience:

> The use of the past—this is another insidious psych-
> ological concept, which is amalgamated with Christian
> doctrines in order to be used on unwitting Christians.
> I don't find any Biblical basis for it.[38]

Even Christians have accepted this theory, in spite of the fact that the Bible teaches that present moral choices rather than past traumas determine our current condition and actions. Nor does the Bible offer any example of prophet, priest, or apostle dealing with anything even vaguely related to buried or repressed emotions or memories. If this were the great truth that inner-healing practitioners insist it is, then surely the Bible would have both teaching and example to offer. On the contrary, Paul, whose legalistic upbringing and crimes against the church prior to conversion would seem to make him a primary candidate for healing of the memories, was not only free from any bad effects but declared, "Forgetting what lies behind and reaching forward to what lies ahead, I press on toward the goal for the prize of the upward call of God in Christ Jesus" (Philippians 3:13,14). Nevertheless, John and Paula Sandford, authors of "the most comprehensive book on inner healing today,"[39] declare:

> We need to remember carefully to search out the
> whole history of the person.... We are not ministering
> merely to the grown person, but to the child yet living
> in the heart....
> Frequently, resentments lie totally beneath both the
> heart and mind, having originated either in the spirit
> in the womb or at birth.[40]

While we would not deny that a past event may have some influence upon present attitudes, it is neither biblical nor reasonable to assume that "the whole history" must be searched out, including "resentments" that "lie totally beneath both the heart and mind." It is not so much the event but *how one reacts to it* that is of primary importance in a person's life. One's reaction is not set in concrete to remain forever what it was initially, but is modified as one grows in the Lord. Thus to attempt a reenactment of a past trauma as though it remains as a self-contained unit somewhere in the unconscious, complete with the initial reaction to it, could do more harm than good. It would be an endless chore to dig up every past experience. We are not chained to the past until therapy in some form sets us free. We are free in Christ. He is our life. That life does not need "inner healing" or any other unbiblical therapy. We become born again the day He comes into our hearts.

Since that day the Holy Spirit works in the life of every child of God, transforming his heart and mind. What counts is our love for Him, our simple faith in His Word, and our obedience to the leading of His Spirit in the present. The secret to joy and fruitfulness as a Christian is our dynamic relationship to Christ living in our hearts *right now*. Yet the Sandfords teach that sins we have committed, including resentments we have held, *as spirits within the womb* must be "remembered" and repented of in order to give us the blessings of the cross:

> By now the reader must understand that in our spirits we know and comprehend whatever is happening around us in the womb. . . . In her spirit [referring to a particular case history] in the womb she had judged her father and her mother for fornication, her father for drinking and adultery and for rejecting her mother and her.
>
> That doomed her to: a) reject someone (her husband) as she was rejected; b) drink; c) commit adultery. . . .
>
> As she had hated being in that womb of shame during the nine months and had hated becoming a person, so her girl child forming within her triggered into her hatred of herself, and she subconsciously projected her self-hatred onto her baby.[41]

It cannot be denied that many Christians are suffering in varying degrees from one or more of the following: frustration, worry, habits, regrets, guilt, resentment, jealousy, insecurity, fear, lust, etc. One of the greatest needs in the church is for those who have the compassion, time, and training to help such sufferers. An excellent book on this subject is *How To Counsel From Scripture* by Martin and Deidre Bobgan. We must have counseling for one another. But it must be based upon the Bible and not upon questionable psychological theories. Unfortunately in the area of psychology we have adopted beliefs and practices that have neither a scientific nor biblical basis. As psychologist Carol Tavris has said:

> Now the irony is that many people who are not fooled by astrology for one minute subject themselves to therapy for years, where the same errors of logic and interpretation often occur.[42]

"Solving" the Problems It Creates

Inner healing is simply a Christianized psychoanalysis that uses the power of suggestion to "solve problems" which it has oftentimes actually created. The same can be said for other forms of psychotherapy. Like thousands of others, Dr. Carney Landis, of the Psychiatric Institute of Columbia University, found himself much worse after psychoanalysis. His analyst frankly admitted to him that "the analytic procedure would create a neurosis" in any "really normal person." Landis eventually concluded:

> I believe that . . . the childhood fantasies, memories, the feelings of unreality, the love transference—are actually *produced by analysis rather than revealed by it*.[43]

Such has been the case with many sincere Christians who have become the victims of inner healing. The glowing testimonies hide this very real problem. In churches where inner healing has begun to be practiced, members who seemed quite normal and happy in their Christian life have become depressed after accepting the destructive idea that they were in fact driven by deeply buried hurts and resentments of which they were not even aware. The healing-of-memories process that was intended to deliver them has in fact created pseudomemories that have confused them. No longer can they rely in simple faith upon the promises of the Bible, but are now dependent upon practitioners and practices that attempt to mediate God's blessings through emotional experiences and periodic catharsis created by guided imagery.

13

Self-Idolatry

Let him who boasts, boast in the Lord.... For no
man can lay a foundation other than the one which
is laid, which is Jesus Christ.
1 Corinthians 1:31; 3:11

The seduction of Christianity is definitely not confined to fringe
elements. The Freudian/Jungian myths of psychic determinism
and the unconscious have been so universally accepted that these
unfounded assumptions now exert a major influence upon
Christian thinking throughout the church. The practice of
shamanic visualization runs the spectrum from inner healing to
self-improvement techniques, and the latter involves various forms
of self-hypnosis, from Positive Affirmations and Positive Confession to subliminal-persuasion tapes. This seduction now
touches every aspect of Christian life, and infects the church from
charismatics to anticharismatics, from liberals to evangelicals,
from Catholics to Protestants, from clergy to laymen. As a
major vehicle of the seduction that unites most of its elements,
psychology is a Trojan horse par excellence that has slipped past
every barrier.

In 1973 Jay Adams, author of many books on Christian
counseling, gave a series of lectures at a leading evangelical
seminary emphasizing the necessity to stick strictly to the Bible
and avoid psychological influences. Adams told the students and
faculty: "I do not think I need to labor this point.... I am sure
that the reason why I was invited to deliver these lectures in the

first place was because of our common conviction about this vital imperative.''[1]

Adams has made his conviction crystal clear: "In my opinion, advocating, allowing and practicing psychiatric and psycho-analytical dogmas within the church is every bit as pagan and heretical (and therefore perilous) as propagating the teachings of some of the most bizarre cults. The only vital difference is that the cults are less dangerous because their errors are more identifiable.''[2] He warned that group of future pastors:

> Members of your congregation, elders, deacons, and fellow ministers (not to speak of Christians who are psychiatrists and psychologists) may turn on the pressure and try to dissuade you from any resolute determination to make your counseling wholly scriptural.
>
> They may insist that you cannot use the Bible as a textbook for counseling, try to shame you into thinking that seminary has inadequately trained you for the work, tempt you to buy all sorts of shiny psychological wares to use as adjuncts to the Bible, and generally demand that you abandon what they may imply or openly state to be an arrogant, insular, and hopelessly inadequate basis for counseling.
>
> They may even warn and threaten, as they caricature the biblical method: "Think of the harm that you may do by simply handing out Bible verses like prescriptions and pills.''[3]

This seminary has remained a bastion of biblical truth, one of the very few seminaries without a psychology department. In spite of this fact, however, psychology has managed to make increasing inroads. Twelve years after Adam's lecture series, what is still known as "Pastoral Counseling" is taught by two psychiatrists and a psychologist. They espouse the commonly held misconception that psychology is scientific.[4] In fact, it is a pseudo-science riddled with contradiction and confusion. The textbook used at the seminary, jointly written by the "Pastoral Counseling" staff, presents the very antithesis of what Jay Adams perceived to be the orientation of that school in 1973: "A basic concept underlying this book is that all truth is God's truth, no matter where one finds it...the authors hope that this book will help to reduce any antagonism Christians may have experienced toward psychology."[5]

Psychological Seduction

The basic problem with the "all truth is God's truth" approach lies in the fact that psychology pretends to offer answers which, even if it were a science, it could never give. We have no quarrel with chemistry, medicine, or physics, but with psychology's pretense to scientifically understand and deal with the heart of man, who is a spiritual being made in the image of God. To attempt to deal with human behavior "scientifically" denies man's free will and spiritual nature. If consciousness, personality, and human reactions can be scientifically or psychologically explained, then to say "I love you!" would be no more meaningful than to say, "I have a gastrointestinal pain." Love and joy, as well as a sense of justice, beauty, and meaning, would all be the product of natural processes governed by scientifically explicable laws, and thus meaningless.

Psychology, in contrast to biblical counseling by very definition, can neither explain nor adequately deal with man as God created him, much less as the redeemed man is intended to be through Christ living in him. Science can deal with such things as nutritional deficiencies or chemical imbalances in the *brain,* but it has nothing to say about *mind,* which is nonphysical. Moreover, psychology not only pretends to bring "science" to bear on problems which it cannot even define, much less solve, but it claims to meet needs that the Bible says it alone can provide. Thus psychology is in the fullest sense a rival religion that can never be wedded to Christianity. Furthermore, psychotherapy involves the danger that is implicit in all false religions: Those who practice it open themselves to all manner of demonic delusion. If the Bible is true, then psychology pretends to offer what we do not need:

His divine power has given to us all things that
pertain to life and godliness (2 Peter 1:3 KJV).... I

came that they might have life, and might have it abundantly (John 10:10).... Which things we also speak, not in words taught by human wisdom, but in those taught by the Spirit (1 Corinthians 2:13).

G. Campbell Morgan described the Christian life in these terms:

Christ must be formed within by the communication of Himself.... Here we have reached the realm of mystery....

None can perfectly understand the act of the Spirit of God in which He communicates to the individual soul the very Christ life itself....

In that moment when the soul submits to the claim of Christ, Christ is formed within by the Holy Spirit. Directly there is submission to Him as the absolute Lord of life, and trust reposed in Him for the putting away of sin, and for the communication of life, then, by a process utterly beyond the explanation of men, the Spirit communicates Christ's life, and Christ begins to live and reign and work in the soul of the submitted and trusting one.

There can be no simulation of this life of Christ. It must be Christ in us. Holiness is not *it*...[but] *Him*![6]

Evangelical Humanism

The idea of man's innate goodness—of the innocent child that still resides within us all—is the cornerstone of psychology. Under that sponsorship, evangelical tradition is being replaced by a new humanistic view of man, which ridicules as "worm theology" the former emphasis upon conviction of sin, repentance, and humanity's unworthiness.

The new gospel of self-esteem has even been embraced by earnest Christian leaders with effective ministries. One of the most highly regarded writes:

In a real sense, the health of an entire society depends on the ease with which the individual members gain personal acceptance. *Thus, whenever the keys to self-esteem are seemingly out of reach for a large percentage of the people, as in twentieth-century America, then widespread "mental illness," neuroticism, hatred, alcoholism, drug abuse, violence, and social disorder will certainly occur....* [emphasis in original].[7]

This idea that low self-esteem is rampant and the root of almost all problems is confidently stated as though it were proven fact. Yet many other psychologists would strongly disagree. Although the author sincerely desires to be biblical, he has based his ministry upon a belief that was not derived from Scripture, but is only one of many conflicting psychological theories. Selfism is also at the heart of the entire success/motivation world. One of the best-known Christian leaders in that field writes:

> As you accept yourself, you will see yourself as a person who truly deserves "the good things in life".... Shakespeare said it, "This above all, to thine own self be true".... Once you accept yourself for your true worth, then the symptoms of vulgarity, profanity, sloppiness, promiscuity, etc. disappear. There, my friend, goes your problem.[8]

This seductive gospel of selfism is now preached by prominent pastors and proclaimed by well-known conference speakers. This selfist psychology dressed up in Christian terminology would be easily recognized for the obvious fraud it is, were it not for the fact that what is allegedly "God's truth" in psychology has been granted authority at least equal to the Bible.

The Scriptures differ with the current assessment that many of mankind's problems arise from a deficiency of self-esteem or self-love. In contrast, the apostle Paul warns that self-love in the end times will be at the root of such problems. Are we seeing this prophecy fulfilled in our day?

> But realize this, that in the last days difficult times will come. For men will be lovers of self, lovers of money, boastful, arrogant, revilers, disobedient to

> parents, ungrateful, unholy, unloving, irreconcilable,
> malicious gossips, without self-control, brutal, haters
> of good, treacherous, reckless, conceited, lovers of
> pleasure rather than lovers of God (2 Timothy 3:1-4).

Some of the most sincere servants of the Lord are accepting ideas completely at odds with what evangelicals stood for only a few years ago. What makes this problem so difficult to unmask is the fact that psychologists and psychiatrists are usually sincerely devoted to helping other people. Moreover, psychiatrists are medical doctors (as were Freud and Jung), the medical profession stands behind psychiatry, and no one has the trust of society like the family physician (unless it is the pastor). Increasing numbers of pastors are getting advanced degrees in psychology in order to better help those who come to them for counseling, and those without such degrees feel compelled to accept the seemingly insightful pronouncements of the professionals.

But far from being supported by the Bible, this new "self-esteem" theology/psychology is opposed by Scripture. God chose Moses, who was "very humble, more than any man who was on the face of the earth" (Numbers 12:3), to confront the mightiest emperor on earth and to deliver Israel, so that God and not man would get the glory. Moses shrank from this call, considering himself incapable. Instead of giving him months of psychological counseling to bolster his poor self-image and build up his self-esteem, God promised to be with Moses and to work through him miraculously (Exodus 3). Today we are being robbed of the presence and power of God (that Moses and others like him knew) by being told that the lack of joy and power in our lives is due to a poor self-image.

The only correct self-image comes from viewing God, not ourselves, and it isn't flattering—but it changes lives and turns us from self to Him. It was when Isaiah "saw the Lord sitting on a throne, lofty and exalted" that he cried, "Woe is me...I am a man of unclean lips" (Isaiah 6:1-5). This glimpse of God's glory, and his own unworthiness in comparison, changed Isaiah's life. The turning point in Job's life came when he said, "...now mine eye seeth thee. Wherefore I abhor myself and repent in dust and ashes...So the Lord blessed the latter end of Job more than his beginning..." (Job 42:5,6,12 KJV). So it has been with all men and women of God in the past, but today such an experience would be considered psychologically damaging to one's self-esteem.

Old and New Principles

Once psychology is presumed to contain parts of God's truth that are missing from the Bible, its pronouncements must be accepted as equally authoritative. The practical effect is to give psychology the final word, for those who understand only the Bible but not psychology are unqualified to judge this new truth. Those who have degrees in psychology can therefore make pronouncements that cannot be challenged on any other basis inside or outside the church. This secular priesthood claims the authority to dictate new "scientific" standards of everything from our thought life to our sex life to raising our children. These "sound psychological principles" become the new grid through which the Bible is interpreted.

One thing is certain, however: The Bible never urges self-acceptance, self-love, self-assertion, self-confidence, self-esteem, self-forgiveness, nor any of the other selfisms that are so popular today. The answer to depression is not to accept self, but to turn from self to Christ.

A preoccupation with self is the very antithesis of what the Bible teaches, and would be unknown in the church today were it not for the seductive influence of selfist psychologies. God made man in His own image. One thinks immediately of a mirror, which has *one purpose only*: to reflect a reality *other than its own*. It would be absurd for a mirror to try to develop a "good self-image." It is equally absurd and certainly unbiblical, for humans to attempt to do so. If there is something wrong with the image in the mirror, then the only solution is for the mirror to get back in a right relationship with the one whose image it was designed to reflect. So it is with man who is designed to reflect the image of God. And to whatever extent we focus upon a self-image, no matter how sincerely, we are robbing ourselves and God of that relationship we must have with Him if we are rightly to reflect His image.

There seems to be no stopping the proliferation of these unbiblical, illogical, and unsupportable theories. It should be clear that none of today's popular selfisms delivers from self, which is our real enemy; but, on the contrary, self is being strengthened with greater esteem, confidence, assertion, etc. to reign over its kingdom. The only thing the Bible tells us to do with self is to deny it through accepting Christ's death as our very own. That used to be sufficient for the apostles and early church. It is implied that it doesn't work anymore. To deny ourselves will shatter our fragile self-esteem and thereby destroy our sense of "authentic personhood." The following suggestions from a Christian author are representative of much that is popular today:

> To build your self-image, make a list of your positive qualities on a card and keep it for handy reference. . . . Brag on yourself from time to time. Get in your own corner. . . .
>
> You should also set aside a few minutes each day for the sole purpose of deliberately looking yourself in the eye [in a mirror]. As you do this, repeat some positive affirmations of things you have done (use your victory list from step ten).
>
> Then repeat many of the things other people have said to you or about you that were positive. . . .
>
> There are also cases where plastic surgery can be quite helpful in building a self-image. This is especially true in cases of an unusually large or long nose, protruding ears. . . grossly oversized or undersized breasts, etc.[9]

Strangely enough, too few within church leadership seem uncomfortable with the fact that Christianity is beginning to sound much like humanistic psychology. Compare what Christian leaders are saying with the following by Los Angeles psychotherapist Nathaniel Branden, author of *The Psychology of Self* and *Honoring the Self*. Sin, even criminal violence is viewed as a "psychological problem." No one is willfully doing evil; we are all innocent victims of a *disease* for which we cannot be held accountable. A plague of "poor self-concept" is sweeping our world and *that* is the cause of all that has gone wrong. Explains Branden:

> I cannot think of a single psychological problem—from depression to fear of intimacy to criminal violence—that is not traceable to poor self-concept. . . .
>
> Until we are willing to honor the self and proudly proclaim our right to do so, we cannot fight for self-esteem—and we cannot achieve it.[10]

In contrast to the new ideas that have been borrowed from selfist psychology, William Law reveals the view that the church held for centuries:

> Men are dead to God because they are living to Self. Self-love, self-esteem and self-seeking are the essence and the life of pride; and the Devil, the father of pride, is never absent from these passions, nor without an influence in them. Without a death to self, there is no escape from Satan's power over us. . . .
>
> To discover the deepest root and iron strength of pride and self-exaltation, one must enter into the secret chamber of man's soul, where the Spirit of God, who alone gives humility and meek submission, was denied through Adam's sin. . . .
>
> Here in man's innermost being, self had its awful birth, and established its throne, reigning over a kingdom of secret pride, of which all outward pomp and vanities are but its childish, transitory playthings. . . .
>
> Imagination, as the last and truest support of self, lays unseen worlds at his feet, and crowns him with secret revenges and fancied honors. This is that satanic, natural self that must be denied and crucified, or there can be no disciple of Christ. There is no plainer interpretation than this that can be put upon the words of Jesus, "Except a man deny self, and take up the cross and follow me, he cannot be my disciple."[11]

An Epidemic of Humility?

Not only is it the clear teaching of the Bible, but even non-Christians know in their hearts that the besetting sin of humanity is pride. We all tend by nature to think too highly of ourselves. That long-established biblical truth, however, has lately been discovered to be in error. Enlightened by psychology, pastors and Christian leaders are now proclaiming that the besetting sin of the human race is not pride after all, but humility. We don't think too highly of ourselves, but too poorly. We all have a bad self-image, or low self-esteem, from which nothing but psycho-therapeutic rituals, which have been Christianized for the church, can rescue us.

But this advice from psychology is in direct conflict with Philippians 2:3: "In lowliness of mind let each esteem others better than himself" (KJV). Paul's clear warning in Romans 12:3 not to think more highly of ourselves than we ought to is somehow turned around to mean that the greatest danger we face is not to think highly enough of ourselves.

Under this new inspiration that has come to us through the apostles of psychology, Christian leaders are devoting sermons, seminars, and even entire books to the gospel of self-esteem. If it exists, such an "epidemic of inferiority" would be a first in the history of humanity and no doubt was caused by the flood of lectures, sermons, and books warning about it. Instead of being salt and light, the church has bought the world's philosophy of success and honored its stereotype of the self-assured and self-assertive man or woman exuding self-acceptance and a good self-image. Craig W. Ellison edited *Self Esteem*, a compilation of the writings of leading Christian psychologists on this subject, published by the Christian Association for Psychological Studies. Ironically enough, the modern idea that these men have accepted and preached not only opposes the truth of God, but is contradicted by the findings of psychology itself. In *The Inflated Self*, psychologist David G. Myers points out:

> Jean-Paul Codol conducted twenty experiments with French people ranging from twelve-year-old school-children to adult professionals. Regardless of those

involved and the experimental methods, the people's self-perceived superiority was present consistently....

[American] students typically rate themselves in the top of the class.... Judging from their responses...[to self-rating tests], it appears that America's high school students are not racked with inferiority feelings. In "leadership ability," 70 percent rated themselves above average, two percent below average.... In "ability to get along with others," *zero* percent of the 829,000 students who responded rated themselves below average, 60 percent rated themselves in the top 10 percent, and 25 percent saw themselves among the top 1 percent!...

Note how radically at odds this conclusion is with the popular wisdom that most of us suffer from low self-esteem.... Preachers who deliver ego-boosting pep talks to audiences who are supposedly plagued with miserable self-images are preaching to a problem that seldom exists.[12]

The Myth of Self-Hate

Jesus summed up the law and the prophets in what has become known as the Golden Rule: "Just as you want people to treat you, treat them in the same way" (Luke 6:31). Without complete confidence that every human already loves himself, Jesus could never have made such a statement. Certainly if we all innately hate ourselves, then we would wish upon others the same evil that we wish for ourselves. But who wishes evil upon himself? No one, except the very insane. Ephesians 5:29 states the universal truth that we all recognize: "For no one ever hated his own flesh, but nourishes and cherishes it...." Yet in the face of this, a deluge of Christian radio and TV talk shows, tapes, magazines, and books has been pouring forth the idea that we innately hate ourselves and must *learn* to love ourselves before we can love other people and even God.

Of course, there are many who express varying degrees of self-hatred. That they don't actually hate themselves can easily be seen. The person who says, "I'm so ugly, I hate myself!"

doesn't hate himself at all, or he would be *glad* that he was ugly. It is because he loves himself that he is upset with his appearance and the way people respond to him. The person who grovels in depression and says he hates himself for having wasted his life would actually be glad that he had wasted his life if he really hated himself. In fact, he is unhappy about having wasted his life because he loves himself. The apparently remorseful criminal, who says he hates himself because of the crimes he has committed, should then be glad to see himself suffer in prison. Yet he hopes to escape that fate, which proves he loves himself in spite of his protestations of self-loathing. So it is with the person who takes his own life. Most of these tragic people consider suicide to be an escape; but who helps someone he hates to escape? It is the ultimate act of self attempting to escape circumstances without considering anyone else.

The person who is always putting himself down doesn't really hate himself or have a bad self-image; he is simply letting others know that his performance is not up to the standard he has set for himself. This is not a symptom of low self-esteem, but the flip side of pride. A. W. Tozer explained it well:

> Self-derogation is bad for the reason that self must be there to derogate. Self, whether swaggering or groveling, can never be anything but hateful to God....
>
> Boasting is an evidence that we are pleased with self; belittling, that we are disappointed in it. Either way we reveal that we have a high opinion of ourselves....[13]

It was Freidrich Nietzsche, the father of "God is dead" philosophy, and the great inspirer of Hitler, who laid the foundation for the modern interpretation of Christ's Golden Rule. Nietzsche wrote: "Your neighbor love is your bad love of yourselves. Ye flee unto your neighbor from yourselves and would feign make a virtue thereof! But I fathom your 'unselfishness.' You cannot stand yourselves, and you do not love yourselves sufficiently."[14] Nietzsche is saying that we fail to really love our neighbor as ourselves because we don't love ourselves enough.

He was among the first to complain of this "epidemic" of self-loathing which evangelical leaders are bemoaning today.

For 1900 years the church has taught that we are innately self-centered beings who do not need to *learn* to love ourselves. What we are urged to do is to love God and others. (For an excellent treatment of this subject, see Paul Brownback, *The Danger of Self-Love*, Moody Press, Chicago, 1982.) Yet through the influence of Fromm and other psychologists, the church has now accepted the idea that when Jesus said, "Love your neighbor as yourself," He was teaching that we must "learn to love ourselves first of all" before we can love God or our neighbor. Robert Schuller was among the first church leaders to pick up and promote this radical re-interpretation in his book *Self-Love, The Dynamic Force of Success*. Many others followed suit, until today this is the generally accepted interpretation, heard from many evangelical pulpits.

Psychotherapeutic errors, no matter how sincerely held, inevitably corrupt one's view of Scripture. The statement by Jesus that we are to love our neighbor as ourselves is not limited to those who have a so-called "healthy self-love." Such a distinction, which Christian psychologists try to make, cannot be derived from the Bible. This command is to *all of us*, and there is not even a hint that certain people may not love themselves in a correct or sufficient manner to understand and obey what Jesus said.

Biblical exhortations not to think too *highly* of self, when interpreted in light of modern psychology, are understood actually to be admonitions against esteeming ourselves too *lowly*. And those who fail to accept this new gospel "just don't know their psychology," even though they may be very mature in their understanding of Scripture. To encourage selfism in creatures whose besetting sins are all centered in self is like pouring gasoline on a fire that is already raging out of control. A. W. Tozer puts it all in perspective:

> Self is one of the toughest plants that grows in the garden of life. It is, in fact, indestructible by any human means. Just when we are sure it is dead it turns up somewhere as robust as ever to trouble our peace and poison the fruit of our lives....

The victorious Christian neither exalts nor down-
grades himself. His interests have shifted from self to
Christ. What he is or is not no longer concerns him.
He believes that he has been crucified with Christ and
he is not willing either to praise or deprecate such a
man.[15]

Disillusioned Psychotherapists

By now it should be more than clear to the reader that psychology is playing a major role in an ongoing and staggering seduction
of Christianity. The high respect and indisputable authority
granted to this pagan emperor within the church is all the more
astonishing in view of the fact that its nakedness has been so
thoroughly exposed by secular psychologists and psychiatrists
themselves. Yet at the same time that its own crew is so desperately
trying to plug the many leaks in this obviously sinking ship,
Christians continue to climb aboard with ever-increasing enthusiasm. This is all the more incredible when one considers that
they are selling their biblical birthright in order not just to buy
a mess of pottage, but to purchase passage aboard a doomed
vessel.

The disillusionment of those who once believed in psychotherapy, and the reason why psychotherapists (and he himself)
are turning to Eastern religions, are expressed poignantly by Jacob
Needleman:

Modern psychiatry arose out of the vision that man
must change himself and not depend for help upon an
imaginary God. Over half a century ago. . .the human
psyche was wrested from the faltering hands of organized religion and was situated in the world of nature
as a subject for scientific study. . . .

The era of psychology was born. By the end of the
Second World War many of the best minds of the new
generation were magnetized by a belief in this new
science of the psyche. Under the conviction that a way
was now open to assuage the confusion and suffering

of mankind, the study of the mind became a standard course of work in American universities....

Against this juggernaut of new hope, organized religion was helpless. The concept of human nature which had guided the Judeo-Christian tradition for two thousand years had now to be altered....

But although psychiatry in its many forms pervades our present culture, the hope it once contained has slowly ebbed away....

The once magical promise of a transformation of the mind through psychiatry has quietly disappeared.... The psychiatrists themselves...despair over their inability to help other human beings....

A large and growing number of psychotherapists are now convinced that the Eastern religions offer an understanding of the mind far more complete than anything yet envisaged by Western science. At the same time...the numerous gurus...are reformulating and adapting the traditional systems according to the language and atmosphere of modern psychology.[16]

Numerous studies have shown that the amount of "psychological" problems in society increases in direct proportion to the growing number of psychologists and psychiatrists. Jerome Frank, professor emeritus at Johns Hopkins University School of Medicine, and himself a psychiatrist, has said:

The greater the number of treatment facilities and the more widely they are known, the larger the number of persons seeking their services.

Psychotherapy is the only form of treatment which, at least to some extent, appears to create the illness it treats.[17]

Sagging Under the Weight

Although this profession, as Dorothy Tennov says in *Psychotherapy: The Hazardous Cure*, is "sagging under the weight of its own ineffectiveness" and making a "desperate last-ditch effort to find a rationale for its survival,"[18] nevertheless a gullible public and self-serving government agencies continue to support its exponential growth. No one has more gullibly believed its ideas than church leaders themselves, who have not only adapted their theology to its "truths" but passed them on to a trusting flock. The psychology departments in Christian colleges and seminaries, are now so large and well-established and the numbers of pastors and pastoral staff counselors with degrees in psychology are so great that it almost seems too late to turn the tide. In an article titled "Psychology Goes Insane, Botches Role as Science," psychologist Roger Mills writes:

> The field of psychology today is literally a mess. There are as many techniques, methods and theories around as there are researchers and therapists.
>
> I have personally seen therapists convince their clients that all of their problems come from their mothers, the stars, their bio-chemical make-up, their diet, their life-style and even the "kharma" from their past lives.[19]

"In the psychotherapeutic marketplace there are about 200 different therapeutic approaches and over 10,000 specific techniques available to the consumer."[20] Most of them contradict each other. Moreover, far from being an aid to Christian living, as is so often claimed, psychology is in fact a rival religion that competes with Christianity. Jerome Frank has said that psychotherapy "resembles a religion."[21] Admitting this fact, Jolan Jacobi, one of Jung's best-known students, declared that "Jungian psychotherapy is...a way of healing and a way of salvation ...lead[ing] the individual to his salvation...and spiritual guidance."[22] Lance Lee calls psychoanalysis "a religion hidden beneath scientific verbiage," and a "substitute religion for both practitioner and patient"[23] New York University psychology professor Paul C. Vitz says of Jung's final goal of "self-realization" and Abraham Maslow's goal of "self-actualization" that they are each a "secular form of salvation."[24] William Kirk Kilpatrick, who finally realized that his devotion to psychology was leading him far from biblical Christianity, writes:

Despite the creation of a virtual army of psychiatrists, psychologists, psychometrists, counselors and social workers, there has been no letup in the rate of mental illness, suicide, alcoholism, drug addiction, child abuse, divorce, murder and general mayhem. Contrary to what one might expect in a society so carefully analyzed and attended to by mental health experts, there has been an increase in all of these categories.

It sometimes seems there is a direct ratio between the increasing number of helpers and the increasing number of those who need help. . . . We are forced to entertain the possibility that psychology and related professions are proposing to solve problems that they themselves have helped to create.[25]

Building Upon a Foundation of Sand

It is inexplicable that in face of the devastating evidence that psychotherapy is a pseudo-science riddled with contradiction and confusion, the great dream of most Christian psychologists is to integrate it with Christianity. Organizations such as the Christian Association for Psychological Studies and periodicals such as the *Journal of Psychology and Theology* as well as numerous books promote this possibility. Not only have Freud's successors modified his original theory many times, as Freud himself did during his lifetime, but his ideas have been "under consistent criticism from almost all quarters for a number of years"[26] and psychoanalysis of whatever brand has been largely discredited.[27] Nobel prize winner Richard Feynman says that "psychoanalysis is not a science."[28] New York University associate professor of psychology Paul Vitz—

has criticized Christians' tendency to "buy high and sell low" in regard to the social sciences—to adopt popular trends of thought at the time that secular professionals are beginning to subject the trends to serious criticism.

It's a matter of climbing on the bandwagon just about the time it's slowing down.[29]

Karl Popper, who is considered by many to be the greatest living philosopher of science, has said that Freud's theories, "though posing as science, had in fact more in common with primitive myths than with science; that they resembled astrology rather than astronomy."[30] As one of the world's top research psychiatrists, E. Fuller Torrey declares: "The techniques used by Western psychiatrists are, with few exceptions, on exactly the same scientific plane as the techniques used by witchdoctors."[31] Mount Sinai School of Medicine clinical professor of psychiatry Arthur Shapiro, who calls psychoanalysis "a concoction of the mind," has said:

> Just as bloodletting was perhaps the massive placebo technique of the past, so psychoanalysis—and its dozens of psychotherapy offshoots—is the most used placebo [a pill that has no value in itself, but often produces the effect that the user believes it will] of our time.[32]

An Orwellian Nightmare?

It is staggering to realize that the discredited theories upon which psychotherapies rest not only form the basis for the burgeoning practice of inner healing and Christian psychology, but also for a new gospel of selfism that is seducing the church more effectively than anything in its history. This naked emperor before whom the church now bows is not a vulnerable old fool as in the story of *The Emperor's New Clothes*, but a vicious and calculating tyrant. It now seems that without miraculous intervention the consequences both to the world and the church will be frightening beyond anyone's present comprehension. The influence of psychology within the church has been established upon the same false basis as in the secular world: that it deserves dictatorial authority by virtue of being the science of human behavior. As a result of having accepted its false credentials, society can now place no limit upon its powers. The trend has already been established. In his book *The Powers of Psychiatry*, Jonas Robitscher, who is both a psychiatrist and a lawyer, reminds us:

> Our culture is permeated with psychiatric thought. Psychiatry, which had its beginnings in the care of the sick, has expanded its net to include everyone, and it exercises its authority over this total population by methods that range from enforced therapy and coerced control to the advancement of ideas and the promulgation of values.[33]

It is true that many voices are being raised to protest the sham and shame of psychotherapy; but still the dangerous delusion increases. It is indeed worse than the story of the emperor's clothes. There are now so many millions of psychologists, psychiatrists, sociologists, psychiatric social workers, university professors, and government agencies ad infinitum whose livelihood depends upon keeping up the pretense that it is no longer realistic to hope that this trend could be reversed.

Stanford University's Alumni Association published an interesting collection of papers by experts examining the question of whether we had arrived at the year 1984 ahead of or behind George Orwell's scenario. The conclusions of some of the writers were devastating. Reference was made to the abuse of psychiatry in the Soviet Union; and it was pointed out that equally frightening possibilities exist even in a so-called free society. Remarking that "Orwell deserves credit for seeing the potential power of professionals whom society sanctions to intervene into the lives of its citizens 'for their own good,' " Philip G. Zimbardo pointed out that Orwell had nevertheless "barely hinted at the extent and depth of that power which is so evident in our 1984." Zimbardo continued:

> [In] the new ideology of intervention...instead of punishment, torture, exile, and other tricks of the tyrant trade, we are seeing such tricks of the treatment trade: intervention as therapy, education, social service, reform, retraining, and rehabilitation.

In a critical attack on the role of the mental health establishment as the new Party of our 1984, investigative journalist Peter Schrag warns us of the insidious danger inherent in the unquestioning acceptance of its seemingly benign ideology.[34]

What Zimbardo and Schrag did not point out, however, is the fact that psychology has moved heavily into the realm of "spirit" and is promoting shamanic techniques. This increases immeasurably both the power and danger of the seduction and control. Zimbardo does, however, recognize the part that psycho-spiritual mind techniques could play in establishing control over millions by "mortal messiahs."[35] Such gurus are merely the forerunners for the big guru, Antichrist himself. The seduction continues to follow the prophesied pattern. And there are growing similarities developing between what is happening out there in the world and within the church.

How can we get everyone to take another, but this time objective and critical, look? The emperor has no clothes. He is stark naked! But so many respected and sincere leaders are extolling the beauty of his regal attire that those who do not see the fabled fabrics are convinced that their vision is defective, and are encouraged to use their imagination. That loss of objectivity opens the door to the full power of the seduction.

Biblical Salvation

The Bible clearly declares that "Christ died for our sins" (1 Corinthians 15:3) and that those who receive Him as Savior and Lord are new creations, for whom old things have passed away and all things have become new (2 Corinthians 5:17). The past is taken care of on the basis of our faith in God and the finished work of Christ on the cross—not on the basis of some psychotherapeutic process that must be engaged in to make God's promises effective (which the Bible neither teaches nor the early disciples practiced). In contrast, psychotherapy is based upon the premise that the past is still attached to us, buried deep within the unconscious, from where it determines our attitudes and actions. This secular form of salvation offers psychospiritual rituals for digging up the past and wiping the slate clean. It is at best an unbiblical addition that detracts from the power of the cross and at worst a secular substitute for the gospel that destroys true faith in God.

We are not denying the value of professional counsel for those areas of daily function that are not covered in the Bible and do not find resolution solely through our relationship with God in Christ. In seeking counsel, however, it should always be biblical to the extent that the Bible covers the situation. God's Word offers the best of counsel in every area of human behavior and human relationships. While Proverbs and Ecclesiastes deal primarily with such matters, example and instruction sufficient to guide us in every situation is found throughout all of Scripture, which is another reason why the entire Bible must be studied as a unit. There is sound ethical instruction and even some valuable counsel on diet and hygiene.

The Bible does not, however, pretend to be a book of instruction in chemistry, physics, medicine, nutrition, law, accounting, economics, etc. This leaves the door open for help not only from doctors, lawyers, accountants, etc., but from qualified psychologists who deal with things such as learning problems and the probable conduct of a psychotic or alcoholic husband or wife. The psychologist is rare, however, whose counsel even in these limited areas is free of contamination from the fallacious assumptions and practices that pervade psychology as a whole. There are some Christian "psychologists" who have determined to counsel only from Scripture; however, it is not easy for even those who desire to be strictly biblical to be completely free from the influence of years of studying and honoring erroneous ideas, which may color their interpretation of the Bible in ways that they themselves may not recognize.

What we really need is to turn from any preoccupation with self to Christ. God redeemed us because of who He is, not because of who we are or even what He could make us become. God loves us because He is love, not because we are lovable or lovely. Here is a solid basis for deep confidence. The new teaching that God valued me so highly that Christ died for me may make me initially feel more secure, but that feeling will last only so long as

I can continue to have this sense of self-worth. In turning from the One who loves to myself as the object of His love, I am being robbed of the true joy and freedom that is found in Him alone. To know that God loves me not because of who I am but because of who He is, really sets me free and gives me a security that the gospel of self-esteem can never produce.

14

Tomorrow the World!

You turned to God from idols to serve the living and
true God, and to wait for His Son from heaven.
1 Thessalonians 1:9b,10a

The writing of this book has not been motivated by a desire
to be critical or divisive, but to meet a very real need evidenced
by a growing flood of phone calls and letters from around the
world, sometimes angry, almost always bewildered, begging for
help. We pray that this book will serve as a response to the many
appeals for counsel that it has not been physically possible to
answer in sufficient depth (and too often not at all). There are
the many questions from confused Christians who have been
taught occult mind techniques in the business world and even after
becoming affiliated with what they thought were Christian-
oriented organizations. Mind-science and PMA techniques (from
visualization to positive self-talk and other forms of self-hypnosis
and self-image psychology) and similar methods promoted in sales
and recruiting training make many people feel uncomfortable,
but they don't know why and want an explanation.

A Growing Problem

After becoming Christians, many who have been involved in
the New Age movement and know it from the inside inquire why
they find much of the same occultism in the church and on Christian TV, and why very few pastors seem willing or able to

confront this issue. There is a growing grass-roots concern that most Christian television is controlled by a handful of people who have the final say on all programming. They wield great power and influence, yet are insulated from any correction from the financially supporting body of Christ and are accountable to no one but themselves. The same thing applies to the spreading Christian satellite networks. Typical is the following from a woman who expressed by letter and phone conversation her concern for teaching coming into her church by satellite:

> I used to be into karate, levitating physical objects by projecting "energy" through my hands, reading auras and such, and at one time this "power" almost killed me, I was so possessed by it.
>
> I don't see much difference in what they [she names several charismatic leaders and one of the top Christian success/motivation speakers] are teaching. Will this open up the people in our church to something they shouldn't be involved in? . . .
>
> There's a lot said about signs and wonders, but I know for a fact that some of the people who have supposedly been healed haven't been healed at all.
>
> I don't want to leave our church, but I feel that it is wrong.[1]

The tools for understanding and avoiding this growing seduction ought to be supplied by the local church. Unfortunately, the local church often promotes shamanism. The following excerpts are from a letter written by a Christian bookstore owner whose husband is a practicing surgeon:

> Honestly, when I first read *Peace, Prosperity, and the Coming Holocaust* I thought it was interesting but far removed from me. . . . [Then] our United Methodist pastor led the congregation in an imaging exercise ("Close your eyes. . . see Jesus coming through the door. . . .") I recognized it and did not participate. . . .
>
> Recently he attended a seminar in California and is teaching it during Sunday school. . . a visualization technique that helped his son control pain after surgery.

He asked me what I thought ꝺbout it and I told him
it sounded like New Age...he said that Jesus used
guided imagery in the Bible in the parables....

My husband found a copy of the *New Age Journal*
in the Doctors' Library at the local hospital...placed
there unauthorized...the course that our pastor took
is listed in the *Journal*.[2]

There can be little doubt that we are in the midst of an unprecedented revival of sorcery worldwide that is deeply affecting not only
every level and sector of modern society, but the church as well.
Known as the New Age, Holistic, Human Potential, or Consciousness movements, at its heart is what anthropologists now call
shamanism, which is simply the old occultism made to sound
native, natural, earthy, and thus wholesome. It is also made to
sound Christian. We have attempted to present an understanding
of the various ways under which the same delusion that is preparing the world for the Antichrist is now seducing Christianity
itself.

It has been our concern to document the fact that the seduction
is already upon us, and that not only in the secular world,
but within the church as well, what is happening seems to
fit the very pattern prophesied for the period of time just
before the return of Christ for His own. It should be clear
that what we are facing is not merely a pocket of questionable teaching here and there, but a rapidly spreading acceptance of ideas within the church that represent a revival of
ancient occultism and can be traced back to the lie of the
Serpent in the Garden of Eden.

We are by no means condemning everyone who gets involved in selfist psychologies, visualization, success/motiva-
tion and self-improvement techniques, or other questionable
practices we have dealt with. Nor are we suggesting that the
Christian leaders who promote these ideas are knowingly cooperating with the spirit of Antichrist. Our concern has been
to show that there is a growing pattern of seduction pointing in a particular direction prophesied in the Scriptures, and
that none of us is immune from being deceived and deceiving
others.

Missionaries of Another Gospel

In a recent development, some of America's largest and most powerful corporations, with branches in many countries, have begun to sponsor an unprecedented worldwide missionary effort. It is not Christianity that these management-experts-turned-missionaries take to the world, but Eastern mysticism incorporated into and now redefined as the latest techniques for successful personal and business performance. The Ascended Masters from the Temple of Wisdom who came across the astral plane to commit to their "ambassador" Napoleon Hill the secret success formula must be pleased with the progress being made by his many disciples.

The sophistication, advanced degrees, affluence, and respectability of these new jet-set missionaries lend a credibility that makes their already seductive gospel almost irresistible: how to become the person you want to be, how to enjoy life, and above all how to be *successful* at everything you do. These are a new breed of business leaders who talk about planetary unity, brotherhood, caring for our ecology, and the necessity of sharing our know-how with developing nations. They especially want to share the psychospiritual technologies of the mind, which they hope will help all of us to realize our full humanness and thereby turn this suffering world into paradise at last. This all sounds so right; yet these are the very goals that Antichrist will promise to fulfill. How can one work for a new world without falling into his camp? The answer to that question could be very important if we are indeed in the last days.

An Emerging Eschatology

The influence of selfist psychology has increasing numbers of Christians preaching a new gospel. Rather than bringing conviction of sin, it presents Jesus as a means to fulfilling the ambition of the Human Potential movement to turn this world into a paradise through the restoration of everyone's self-esteem. The heavy concern to rescue our world from ecological disaster and nuclear destruction is a legitimate one. However, the manner in which this rescue is to be effected must be biblical. If not, Christians could find themselves promoting humanistic salvation and possibly even cooperating with the forces of Antichrist. If we are indeed in the end times, then interpretations of eschatology—the Bible's prophetic depictions of the future—will become increasingly important and controversial in the days ahead.

There are many groups representing seemingly widely divergent points of view about whether the world can be saved, and if so, how. There is one point, however, upon which even those who seem to be opposed to each other find agreement. This otherwise-surprising unity is expressed in the growing opposition from many quarters to the traditional fundamentalist view that the *only* hope for this world to be saved from destruction is miraculous intervention by Jesus Christ. Increasing numbers of Christian leaders and their followers are rejecting this view, and at the same time they are also rejecting the idea that Christians are really citizens of heaven, not of this world, and that Christ is going to "rapture" His church out of this world. The whole idea of the rise of Antichrist to rule the world during a tribulation period, and the rapture of the church, whether pre-, mid-, or post-trib is falling into disfavor. The views of many Christians concerning the future of the world are beginning to have more and more in common with the humanistic hope that mankind can really "find itself" and on the basis of a common brotherhood begin to love one another and live up to our potential of humanness and authentic personhood.

Two factions are now emerging within the church. One side adheres to the belief that an apostasy is coming for the church in the last days, and with it a great tribulation and God's judgment for the world. We are to rescue as many as we can before it is too late, calling them to citizenship in heaven. On the other side are those, equally sincere, who see the primary call of the church as solving social, economic, and political problems. Although they are also concerned to see souls saved, the conversion of the masses provides the means for taking over the world for Christ, taking dominion back from Satan, and thereby establishing the kingdom in order that Christ might return as king to reign at last.

Within the latter group are two divergent factions whose goals are beginning to sound more and more alike. Christian socialists hope for a redistribution that will share what the wealthy have with the poor, while the success-oriented Christians of the Positive Confession or Faith Movement hope to make everyone wealthy. From their increasingly isolated corner, the fundamentalists warn that neither will succeed because the world is heading for a great tribulation climaxing in the Battle of Armageddon, which will involve the return of Christ to rescue Israel, to stop the destruction, and to set up His kingdom. There is a growing rejection within the church of this fundamentalist scenario as negative, "gloom-and-doom" eschatology.

Can We Prevent Armageddon by Ignoring It?

Some Christians mistakenly assume that anyone who takes Armageddon seriously must therefore be a fatalist resigned to coming worldwide destruction, and even happy to see signs that it is near at hand. This is not necessarily so. If the world would take these warnings seriously and repent, God might withhold His judgment. He has done so in the past, as in the case of Nineveh, which repented when Jonah warned of coming destruction. However, if the prophecies of pending judgment, which are numerous and very clear, are swept under the rug by the church, there is no reason why the world should take them seriously, much less repent. Dare we ignore entire sections of the Bible because we find them disturbingly "negative"? Armageddon isn't going to go away just because we all determine to think positively.

Whether it appeals to our generation or not, the fact remains that the Bible does predict in unequivocal language great judgment from God coming upon planet Earth, and gives us the reasons for this judgment. As we have already seen, Satan will be worshiped by the *whole world* (except for the elect), and his man the Antichrist will be worshiped as God. Those living upon earth, united under a new world government and all espousing a new world religion, will defy the true God and bring His righteous judgment upon themselves. At the same time, their own evil will manifest itself as they seek to destroy Israel and one another at Armageddon. Jesus Himself declared that He would have to intervene, not only to save Israel, but to save mankind itself, "or no flesh would be spared." Honestly facing what the Bible itself says about coming judgment ought to cause us to work all the more diligently to win the lost to Christ before it is too late.

Success•N•Life: A "Christian" Human Potential Movement

Two parallel developments over the last 20 years have set the stage for an astonishing partnership that is just now emerging. On the one hand there has been the exponential growth of the Positive Mental Attitude movement in the secular world. At the same time the fastest-growing movement within the church has involved two distinct but closely related factions: the Peale/ Schuller Positive Possibility thinkers, with their roots in New Thought, and the Hagin/Copeland Positive Confession and Word of Faith groups, which have their roots in E. W. Kenyon, William Branham, and the Manifested Sons of God/Latter Rain movement. Peale and Schuller have long been popular speakers on the PMA circuit, and there has been little difference in what they presented either to Christian or secular audiences. This accommodation of the church to the world is growing at an alarming rate, and has received unprecedented evangelical support from the formation of Success•N•Life Clubs, under the inspiration of Robert Tilton, the innovative pastor of Word of Faith World Outreach Center in Dallas, Texas. An ad in the December 1984 *Saturday Evening Post* declared:

FOR MEN & WOMEN WHO WANT TO ACHIEVE THEIR MAXIMUM POTENTIAL

Success•N•Life Chapters are blossoming all over America, where business and community leaders are planning exciting events for local men and women who want to achieve their maximum potential in life.

Top keynote speakers...along with major performing artists are being broadcast live via satellite on giant screens to Dinner/Program events in locations across the nation. These events will help you capture and conquer your most fervent dreams for you and your family.[3]

The monthly club meetings and other activities and benefits are designed to raise up an army of successful and wealthy Christians who can finance and otherwise help in a takeover of the world for Christ. Within six months of the first meeting, in November 1984, about 800 clubs were set up across the country, and that number is growing. Guest speakers during that time, beamed live from Dallas, included Denis Waitley, Og Mandino, and Zig Ziglar. It is no longer possible to deny the connection between secular Positive Mental Attitude success/motivation teaching, Positive/Possibility thinking, and the Positive Confession movement. They are just slightly different variations of the same theme, now for the first time being sold under one new label.

The "God-Men"

Robert Tilton is emerging as one of America's most influential pastors. About 1400 other churches across the country (that number also is growing) are connected by satellite to his church in Dallas, from which they may pick up live special events, speakers, conferences, and teaching seminars. In keeping with the basic theology underlying the Positive Confession movement, as we have already seen, Tilton believes that man was created to be the god of this earth, that he lost this dominion to Satan, who became the god of this world, and that it is up to us to take that dominion back from Satan and begin functioning as the gods of this world once again. In order for this to happen, we Christians must begin, as E. W. Kenyon taught, to "walk as Jesus walked, without any consciousness of inferiority to God... have[ing] faith that will stagger the world...."[4] Echoing this teaching, Kenneth Copeland declares:

> And you impart humanity into a child that's born of you..... Because you are a human, you have imparted the nature of humanity into that born child.

> God is God. He is a Spirit.... And He imparted
> in you when you were born again—Peter said it just
> as plain, he said, "We are partakers of the Divine
> Nature." That Nature is alive eternal in absolute
> perfection, and that was imparted, injected into your
> spirit man, and you have that imparted into you by
> God just the same as you imparted into your child the
> nature of humanity.
> That child wasn't born a whale. It was born a
> human.... Well, now, you don't *have* a human, do
> you? No, you *are* one. You don't *have* a God in you.
> You *are* one.[5]

As we have already documented, this is not a slip of the tongue
or some new doctrine. This is at the heart of the Positive Confession movement today, and can be traced back to numerous
groups of earlier eras, such as the Manifested Sons of God and
Latter Rain movements. It is in the writings of leaders in these
earlier movements, such as Kenyon, Branham, and John G. Lake
that we first find the major teachings of Hagin, Copeland, Capps,
etc. Lake wrote: "Man is not a separate creation detached from
God, he is part of God Himself.... God intends us to be
gods.... He is calling forth a soul-awakening to the realization
that the man within is the real man. The inner man is the real
governor, the true man that Jesus said was a god."[6] Lake's
sermons (The God-Men, etc.) are still being published today by
Christ for the Nations. Pastor/author Earl Paulk is one of today's
leaders in this growing movement. Says Paulk:

> Just as dogs have puppies and cats have kittens, so
> God has little gods....
> Until we comprehend that we are little gods and we
> begin to act like little gods, we cannot manifest the
> Kingdom of God.[7]

The Logical Consequence

This is the lie that Satan deceived Eve with and which Paul
declared the entire world would embrace under Antichrist. Its

growing acceptance within both the church and the world could be an indication that we are nearing the time when Antichrist will be revealed. The origin of the lie at the mouth of the Serpent in the Garden of Eden is so clearly stated, and the warnings about its revival in the last days so unequivocal, that it is incomprehensible that anyone who has read the Bible at all, much less Christian leaders, could be taken in by it. Yet this is happening.

It is staggering that what the Bible so clearly presents as the ancient lie of the ages is now being taught and accepted within the church as a great new truth. In the same manner that this lie brought about man's original fall, so it has a special part to play in the deception of the last days. If we are the gods of this world, in God's class, created to exercise dominion over this earth, and can have what we say by claiming our "divine right," then the logical conclusion is that we ought to exercise this power in ridding this world of sickness, poverty, and sin itself. That was the message presented during a "Satellite Network Seminar" dealing with the future held December 9-12, 1984 at Robert Tilton's Word of Faith World Outreach Center in Dallas, Texas. Summing up the first evening's message, Pastor Tilton said:

> I sat there and I was just making my spirit man soak this up so that I won't be blinded by my natural eyes....
>
> I saw it just as clear as I'm looking at this congregation, and I didn't see it during the Millennium, I saw it now....
>
> We're a powerful group, and we're not going to go limping in [to the Kingdom] barely making it.... When God delivered the children of Israel they were laden down with silver and gold....
>
> He's given us power to create wealth and we're already seeing this thing happen, and I believe that in these last days the believer is not going to be at the back of the bus taking a back seat any longer! We're the righteousness of God!
>
> I tell you, we're in the greatest hour the church has ever had.... I tell you we're going to take this city, this nation and the world with this good news...of Jesus Christ![8]

It is confusing if not disturbing that the Church of Laodicea, of whom Christ said, "I will spit you out of my mouth," described itself in similar terms: "I am rich, have become wealthy, and have need of nothing" (Revelation 3:17).

This enthusiasm for the belief that Christians are going to take over the world is spreading widely. For many in the Positive Confession Movement, to imagine that Jesus would have to return to rescue this earth from destruction would be to admit that we have failed in our assigned task. And to suggest that Christ will rapture the church in the traditional sense is an escape theory unworthy of those who expect to be the overcomers and to establish the kingdom of God on earth. Earl Paulk declares:

> When we first began to point out that the Church was...[foolishly] standing gazing into the heavens waiting for some dramatic escape from this earth, some began to scream "heresy"!
>
> But...the Word proves that the earth is the Lord's and dominion over it is the first task the Church must accomplish....
>
> Cast aside traditions and hear what the Spirit of God is trying to say to the Church.... Don't expect the "rapture" to rescue you!... If you want to bring Christ back to earth, you can do it...WE CAN DO IT!... Take the time to contact us. God is mobilizing His army.[9]

Although their basic beliefs differ, those who expect to establish a perfect kingdom on earth prior to the return of Christ have a goal that bears much resemblance to humanistic plans for uniting the world in love, peace, and brotherhood. The call to realize our full potential, to act out our destiny, to rise to new heights in the face of threatened ecological collapse and nuclear destruction and save our world and our race by setting up a new world government of love and equality has a universal appeal. It caters to our pride to tell ourselves that after all *we can do it*. And if in the doing we thereby demonstrate that we are really gods, that humanness and godness are one, what could be more noble?

So it seemed to M. Scott Peck, a psychiatrist who purportedly became a Christian in the process of writing two recent best-selling books, *People Of The Lie* and *The Road Less Traveled*, which have brought Christians and non-Christians together in a new sense of taking responsibility for our mutual fate. Both of these books appeared on a leading evangelical magazine's Book of the Year list, finishing seventh and sixth, respectively. (Book selections are determined by the votes of a group of evangelical writers, leaders, and theologians....)[10] Both books contain the new psychologized spirituality that we have already addressed and which is being so widely accepted in the church. As one reviewer observed, Peck "lets what he deems to be psychological necessity dictate theological truth."[11] It is clear how this all fits in with the delusion. Peck writes:

> For no matter how much we may like to pussyfoot around it, all of us who postulate a loving God and really think about it eventually come to a single terrifying idea: God wants us to become Himself (or Herself or Itself).
>
> We are growing toward godhood. God is the goal of evolution. It is God who is the source of the evolutionary force and God who is the destination....
>
> Were we to believe it possible for man to become God, this belief by its very nature would place upon us an obligation to attempt to attain the possible. But we do not want...God's responsibility....
>
> As long as we can believe that godhood is an impossible attainment for ourselves, we don't have to worry about our spiritual growth, we don't have to push ourselves to higher and higher levels of consciousness and loving activity....[12]

Once again it all sounds familiar. In admitting our innate godhood, we supposedly at last face up to our responsibility to clean up our lives and this planet. After all, we are worth it, we are in God's class, and we can do it. The humanists have been saying this for years, but now they are being joined by a number of evangelical Christian leaders who are saying much the same thing and are working toward the same goal of creating a new world of peace, love, and brotherhood. While the goal is commendable, how it is reached is critically important. That is where the pitfalls lie.

If the real Jesus is in fact going to "rapture" His own out of the world (whether before, during, or after the Great Tribulation), then those who are still standing on planet Earth when they meet their "Christ" will obviously have been deceived. Those who visualize their own Jesus as they imagine Him to be are setting themselves up for a delusion. So are those who follow their own imaginings rather than the Bible in looking for a "Christ" who will come to earth to take over a beautiful kingdom they have built for His return.

It would be well to remember that in the Germany of the 1930s even the evangelical Christians were taken in by Hitler for a long time. He only seemed like a candidate for Antichrist when it was too late to escape the consequences. His publicly stated goals included a restoration of "Positive Christianity" to Germany. He brought law and order, took a strong stand against homosexuality, pornography, prostitution, encouraged prayer in the schools, and brought peace and prosperity to a nation that had been trembling on the brink of disaster.

The Simplicity of Christ

Whatever one's particular eschatological view, it can hardly be correct if it does not take seriously the biblical warnings both of God's judgment coming upon the world and concerning deception and apostasy for the last days. If it is "negative" to think in these terms, then Jesus and Paul and the others who warned of delusion and destruction in the end times set the example. They also spoke a great deal about the coming kingdom.

Paul declared that "flesh and blood cannot inherit the kingdom of God" (1 Corinthians 15:50), so the kingdom cannot be the millennium, with its flesh-and-blood humans multiplying across the earth, much less the world of today taken over by Christians exercising dominion. We are told many times in the Bible that God's kingdom "is an everlasting kingdom."[13] Of the coming

Messiah, Isaiah prophesied that there would be no end both to His kingdom and to the peace it established (Isaiah 9:6,7). On this count also the kingdom cannot be the millennium, for that wonderful time of peace on earth as Christ reigns from Jerusalem not only ends, but with a great war (Revelation 20:7-9). Jesus clearly said, "My kingdom is not of this world" (John 18:36). Although the kingdom begins in the hearts of all who obey Christ as King, the outward manifestation of this kingdom will not come in its fullness until God has destroyed this present universe and created a new one into which sin will never enter (2 Peter 3:10-13; Revelation 21:1; etc.).

The Bible calls us to *that* kingdom, which cannot be established by our programs or efforts, but which we can enter through repentance of our attempts to play at being gods. Eternal life is what God offers to a race deserving of eternal judgment, and it can only be received as a free gift of His grace by those willing to receive Christ as their only Savior and Lord, the One who died for their sins and rose again to live His life in them. This may sound too elementary to those who confront a world of chaos and hopelessness and who imagine that modern methods and therapies lately developed by this or that school of psychology are needed in this advanced age. Yet this is the simple prescription given by God in His Word, and since the basic disease hasn't changed, we don't need a modern version of the remedy.

What we desperately need is to get back to the simplicity that is in Christ and earnestly begin to follow the Good Shepherd rather than the many who claim to speak for Him. Do not take our word, but test everything yourselves. Be like the Bereans, who didn't accept what Paul said just because he was the great apostle to the Gentiles, but "searched the Scriptures daily [to see] whether these things were so" (Acts 17:11 KJV). We must each come to the firm conviction of what we believe and why we believe it on the basis of the Bible itself, not on the basis of someone else's interpretation.

There are many pertinent Scriptures, but these two are especially appropriate:

> The grace of God has appeared, bringing salvation
> to all men, instructing us to deny ungodliness and

worldly desires and to live sensibly, righteously and godly in the present age, looking for the blessed hope and the appearing of the glory of our great God and Savior, Christ Jesus (Titus 2:11-13).

We know that the son of God has come and has given us understanding in order that we might know Him who is true; and we are in Him who is true, in His Son Jesus Christ. This is the true God and eternal life. Little children, guard yourselves from idols (1 John 5:20,21).

NOTES

CHAPTER ONE

1. Charles Colson, *The Struggle For Men's Hearts and Minds* (Prison Fellowship, 1983), p. 16.
2. *Brain/Mind Bulletin*, Dec. 10, 1984, "New Story of Science: including mind in the world," p. 1.
3. Ibid.
4. *Human Potential*, Dec. 1984, Marta Vogel, "Superlearning: Making the Most of What We've Got," p. 4.
5. Manly P. Hall, *Masonic, Hermetic, Qabbalistic and Rosicrucian Symbolical Philosophy* (Los Angeles, 1969, Sixteenth Edition), pp. CI, CII.
6. Robert Schuller, *Living Positively One Day at a Time* (Revell, 1981), p. 201; and *Self-Esteem, The New Reformation* (Word Books, 1982), p. 115.
7. Robert H. Schuller, *Self-Esteem, The New Reformation* (Word Books, 1982), pp. 14-15.
8. *Eternity*, Nov. 1983, Lloyd Billingsley, "The Gospel According to Schuller," p. 23.
9. *Time*, Mar. 18, 1985, p. 70.; *Los Angeles Times*, May 29, 1983, p. 1.
10. *Christianity Today*, August 10, 1984, pp. 23-24.
11. Ibid.
12. *Christianity Today*, Oct. 5, 1984, p. 12
13. Paul Yonggi Cho, *The Fourth Dimension* (Logos, 1979), Foreword.
14. Success Motivation Cassette Tapes (Waco, TX), "Think and Grow Rich," Side 1.
15. Og Mandino, *The Greatest Secret in the World*, p. 276.
16. Stephen B. Douglass and Lee Roddy, *Making the Most of Your Mind* (Here's Life Publishers, 1983), pp. 18-19, 169.
17. Ibid., p. 263.
18. Napoleon Hill, *Grow Rich With Peace of Mind* (Ballantine Books, 1967), pp. 158-60.
19. Ibid., p. 176.
20. Ibid.
21. Ibid.
22. Napoleon Hill and W. Clement Stone, *Success Through A Positive Mental Attitude* (Pocket Books, 1977), p. 55.
23. Ibid., p. 72.
24. Ibid., pp. 16, 18, 78.
25. *Christianity Today*, Mar. 1, 1985, "Is God a Psychotherapist?" by Ben Patterson, pp. 22-23.
26. Charles Capps, *The Tongue—A Creative Force* (Harrison House, 1976), pp. 24, 131, 132.
27. Paul Yonggi Cho, *Solving Life's Problems* (Logos, 1980), p. 51.
28. Paul Yonggi Cho, *The Fourth Dimension* (Logos, 1979), p. 83.
29. H. A. Ironside, "Exposing Error: Is It Worth While?" Tract.

30. David Wilkerson, "A Prophecy Wall of Fire," available from World Challenge, Inc., P.O. Box 260, Lindale, TX 75771.

CHAPTER TWO

1. James Reid, *Ernest Holmes: The First Religious Scientist* (Science of Mind Publications, Los Angeles), p. 14.
2. Ibid.
3. "The Viewpoint in the Science of Mind Concerning Certain Traditional Beliefs" (Science of Mind Publications).
4. Ernest Holmes, *The Science of Mind* (textbook), p. 30, cited in *Science of Mind*, September 1983, p. 47.
5. Norman Vincent Peale, *Positive Imaging* (Fawcett Crest, 1982), p. 77.
6. Robert Schuller, *Tough Times Never Last, But Tough People Do* (Bantam Books, 1984), p. 161.
7. Mack R. Douglas, *Success Can Be Yours* (Zondervan, 1977), p. 37.
8. Cho, *Fourth*, p. 44.
9. Robert Schuller, "Possibility Thinking: Goals," Amway Corporation tape.
10. Tape of the First Annual Leadership Conference, Prestonwood Baptist Church, North Dallas, Mar. 18, 1985, Mary Kay Ash.
11. Hill, *Grow Rich*, pp. 215-20.
12. Ibid., p. 117.
13. Ibid., pp. 213-14.
14. Ibid.
15. Hill, *Think and Grow Rich* (Fawcett, 1979), p. 137.
16. Hill, *Grow Rich*, op. cit. p. 166.
17. Douglass and Roddy, *Most*, op. cit. pp. 50-51.
18. Ibid.
19. Hill and Stone, *Success*, op. cit. p. 44.
20. Ibid., p. 13.
21. Ibid., p. 14.
22. *Life*, Jan. 7, 1957.
23. E. Brooks Holifield, *A History of Pastoral Care in America: From Salvation to Self-Realization* (Abingdon Press, 1983), pp. 270-71.
24. Paul Clayton Vitz, *Psychology As Religion: The Cult of Self-worship* (Eerdmans, 1977), p. 10.
25. Holifield, *History*, op. cit. p. 264.
26. Martin L. Gross, *The Psychological Society* (Random House, 1978), pp. 3-5.
27. *Journal of Humanistic Psychology*, Fall 1981, Vol. 21, No. 4, Beverly-Colleene Galyean, "Guided Imagery in Education," pp. 58, 61.
28. From the brochure.
29. *Saturday Review of Literature*, Mar. 1973.
30. *The Tarrytown Letter,* June/July 1983, "Jean Houston: The New World Religion," p. 4.
31. *Whole Life Times,* Oct./Nov. 1984, pp. 5, 26.
32. Robert Masters and Jean Houston, *Mind Games: The Guide To Inner Space* (Dell Publishing, 1972), pp. 198-206.
33. Hill, *Think*, op. cit. pp. 215-19.
34. Cho, *Fourth*, op. cit. pp. 39-44.

35. Norman Vincent Peale, *Positive Imaging* (Fawcett Crest, 1982), Introduction, p.1.
36. Ibid., p. 1.
37. Ibid., Introduction, p.1.

CHAPTER THREE

1. Louisa Rhine, *Hidden Channels of the Mind* (Sloane Associates, 1961).
2. Russell Targ and Harold Puthoff, *Mind-Reach* (Dell Publishing, 1977), pp. 111-19.
3. Undated letter on Institute of Noetic Sciences letterhead signed by Edgar Mitchell, Founder.
4. Ibid.
5. From tape No. 1 of a 1984 talk by Andrija Puharich to the Colorado Psychotronics Association.
6. Shirley MacLaine, *Out On A Limb* (Bantam, 1983).
7. Martin & Deidre Bobgan, *Hypnosis and the Christian* (Bethany House Publishers, 1984), p. 23.
8. Helen Wambach, *Reliving Past Lives: The Evidence Under Hypnosis* (Harper & Row, 1984).
9. Marilyn Ferguson, *The Aquarian Conspiracy* (J.P. Tarcher, 1980), p. 175.

CHAPTER FOUR

1. *Los Angeles Times,* Oct. 28, 1984, Part VI, p. 4.
2. James P. Warburg, *The West In Crisis* (Doubleday, 1959), p. 30.
3. *The Economic and Social Consequences of Disarmament: U.S. Reply to the Inquiry of the Secretary-General of the United Nations* (Washington, D.C.: USGPO, June 1964), pp. 8-9.
4. *Washington Post,* Jan. 16, 1977.
5. Anthony Sutton and Patrick M. Wood, *Trilaterals Over Washington, II* (Scottsdale, AZ, 1981), p. 173.
6. *Whole Life Times,* Oct./Nov. 1984, Cover Story, p. 24.
7. Ibid., p. 5.
8. *The Tarrytown Letter,* June/July 1983, "Jean Houston: The New World Religion" (an interview), p. 5.
9. *Spectrum*, Nov.-Dec. 1984, Buckminster Fuller, "Human Integrity," p. 7.
10. *India-West,* Jan. 14, 1983, p. 22.
11. Ibid.; *The Movement Newspaper,* Jan. 1983.
12. Samuel H. Sandweiss, M.D., *Sai Baba, The Holy Man ...and the Psychiatrist* (San Diego, 1975), pp. 79-82.
13. David Spangler, *Reflections on The Christ* (Findhorn, 1978), pp. 36-37.
14. Werner Erhard, *If God Had Meant Man to Fly, He Would Have Given Him Wings,* p. 11.
15. Benjamin Creme, *The Reappearance of the Christ and the Masters of Wisdom* (London: The Tara Press, 1980), Message No. 81, Sept. 12, 1979, p. 246.
16. *Meditations of Maharishi Mahesh Yogi,* p. 178.
17. Sun Myung Moon, *Christianity In Crisis,* p. 5.
18. Ernest Holmes, *What Religious Science Teaches,* p. 21.
19. Hill, *Grow Rich,* op. cit. p. 164.

20. Alan Watts, *This Is It,* p. 90.
21. *Newsweek,* Dec. 20, 1976, p. 66.
22. Ibid., p. 68.
23. Shirley MacLaine, *Out On A Limb* (Bantam Books, 1983), Introduction inside front cover.
24. From *Teach Only Love,* as quoted in *Orange County Resources,* "Interview with Gerald Jampolsky, M.D.," by Phil Friedman, Ph.D., p. 3.
25. Spangler, *Reflections,* op. cit. p. 41.
26. Ibid., pp. 40-41.
27. Ibid., pp. 44-45.

CHAPTER FIVE

1. Milton R. Hunter, *The Gospel Through the Ages* (Salt Lake City, 1958), p. 110.
2. *Deseret News*, Church Section, June 18, 1873, p. 308, as cited in Ed Decker and Dave Hunt, *The God Makers* (Harvest House, 1984), p. 30.
3. *Journal of Discourses,* Vol. 6, p. 176.
4. Ibid., p. 167.
5. Ibid., Vol. 5, p. 331.
6. Letter by Edgar Mitchell, undated promotional material from The Institute of Noetic Services, Sausalito, CA 94965; *The Tarrytown Letter,* February 1983, p. 3.
7. *The Movement,* Dec. 1984, Roberts C. Taylor, "Brian O'Leary, The Threshold of Outer-Inner Space," p. 10.
8. Ibid., pp. 12-13.
9. Rodney R. Romney, *Journey to Inner Space: Finding God-in-Us* (Abingdon, 1980).
10. Ibid., p. 26.
11. Ibid., p. 30.
12. Ibid., p. 28.
13. Ibid., p. 29.
14. Ibid., p. 14.
15. Ibid., p. 82.
16. Ibid., p. 83.
17. Ibid., p. 85.
18. Ibid., p. 84.
19. Ibid., p. 31.
20. Desmond Doig, *Mother Teresa: Her People and Her Work* (Harper & Row, 1976), p. 156.
21. *The Tarrytown Letter,* November 1984, "Building the Earth at St. John the Divine: A Gothic Cathedral Shapes a New Worldview and a Wider Vision of Humanity," p. 5.

CHAPTER SIX

1. William Kroger and William Fezler, *Hypnosis and Behavior Modification: Imagery Conditioning* (Lippincott, 1976), p. 412.
2. *California Law Review,* Mar. 1980, Bernard L. Diamond, "Inherent Problems in the Use of Pretrial Hypnosis on a Prospective Witness," pp. 333-37.

3. Martin and Deidre Bobgan, *Hypnosis and the Christian* (Bethany House, 1984), p. 23.
4. *Whole Life Times,* Oct./mid-Nov. 1984, No. 38, Shepherd Bliss, "Jean Houston: Prophet of the Possible," pp. 24-25.
5. Ibid., p. 26.
6. Ibid.
7. *Los Angeles Times,* Oct. 11, 1981, p. 1, Section I-B.
8. Ibid., pp. I-B, 2; Marilyn Ferguson, *The Aquarian Conspiracy* (J.P. Tarcher, 1980), p. 420.
9. *The Tarrytown Letter,* June/July 1983, "Science and Soul in the Twentieth Century," p. 3.
10. *Los Angeles Times,* op. cit., pp. I-B, 1.
11. *Holistic Life Magazine,* Fall 1983, Robert Muller, op. cit., pp. 15-16.
12. Ibid.
13. Agnes Sanford, *The Healing Gifts of the Spirit* (Fleming H. Revell, 1966), pp. 10-14.
14. Ibid., p. 22.
15. Ibid., p. 27.
16. Ibid., pp. 25-26.
17. Bruce Larson, *There's A Lot More To Health Than Not Being Sick* (Word Books, 1984), p. 124.
18. Bruce Larson, *The Whole Christian* (Word Books, 1978), p. 180.
19. Ibid., p. 23.
20. Ibid., p. 27.
21. Ibid., p. 153.
22. Ibid., p. 132.
23. Ibid., pp. 16, 120.
24. *New Age Dawning* (General Assembly Special Committee on Evangelism and Church Growth, Presbyterian Church USA), 1984.
25. Ibid., p. 12.
26. Larson, *The Whole Christian*, op. cit. pp. 16, 176.
27. Norman Grubb, *Union Life Magazine,* June 1978, pp. 1, 3; Ibid., Dec. 1976, p. 2.
28. Bill Volkman, *The Wink of Faith: Living "As Gods" Without Denying Our Humanity* (Union Life, 1983), pp. 79-85.
29. *Cornerstone,* Oct. 23, 1980, interview with Bill Volkman.
30. Casey Treat, "Believing in Yourself," tape 2 in a four-tape series.
31. Volkman, *Wink,* op. cit. pp. 83-84.
32. Personal letter dated Aug. 25, 1982.
33. Personal letter dated June 4, 1982.
34. Kenneth Copeland, "The Force of Love," Tape BCC-56.
35. Robert Tilton, *God's Laws of Success* (Word of Faith, 1983), pp. 170-71.
36. Herbert Schlossberg, *Idols for Destruction* (Thomas Nelson, 1983), p. 40.

CHAPTER SEVEN

1. Robert Jastrow, "The Case for UFO's," in *Science Digest,* Nov./Dec. 1980, pp. 83-85.
2. Schlossberg, *Idols,* op. cit. p. 143.
3. Ibid., p. 144.

4. Ibid., p. 145.
5. Aldous Huxley, *Brave New World Revisited* (Harper Colophon, 1960), p. 80.
6. C. S. Lewis, *They Asked for a Paper* (London, 1962), p. 163.
7. From an Institute for Conscious Evolution brochure, San Francisco, CA 94121.
8. *Harper's,* Feb. 1985, p. 45.
9. *Self-Help Update,* Jan. 1985 (Scottsdale: Valley of the Sun books and tapes), pp. 6-9.
10. *Harper's,* Feb. 1985, pp. 49-50.
11. Ibid.
12. Douglas Dewar and L. M. Davies, "Science and the BBC," *The Nineteenth Century and After,* Apr. 1943, p. 167.
13. *Radix,* July/Aug. 1979, Paul Arveson and Walter Hearn, "God and the Scientists: Reflections on the Big Bang," pp. 9-14.
14. *Los Angeles Times,* June 25, 1978, Part VI, pp. 1, 6.
15. Charles Capps, *The Tongue—A Creative Force* (Harrison House, 1976), pp. 8-9, 17, 130-36.
16. Capps, *Tongue,* pp. 7, 109, 129-41.
17. *Seikyo Times,* Mar. 1983, p. 58.
18. E.C. Prophet quotes re: science, spoken word, etc.
19. Capps, *Tongue,* pp. 146-47.
20. Ibid.
21. Hall, *Philosophy,* op. cit. p. CI.
22. Gloria Copeland, *God's Will Is Prosperity* (Harrison House, 1978), pp. 48-49.
23. Cho, *Fourth,* op. cit. p. 50.
24. Ibid., p. 64.
25. Cho, *Fourth,* op. cit. pp. 36-43.
26. Ibid., p. 64.
27. Ibid.
28. Frank Goines, *Best of Prophecy & Economics Newsletter,* p. 53.

CHAPTER EIGHT

1. Norman Vincent Peale, *The Power of Positive Thinking* (Fawcett Crest, 1983), pp. 52-53.
2. Mortimer J. Adler, *The Difference of Man and the Difference it Makes* (New York, 1967), p. 294.
3. Schlossberg, *Idols,* p. 161.
4. *Science Digest,* July 1982, John Gliedman, "Scientists in Search of the Soul," p. 78.
5. Ibid.
6. Schlossberg, *Idols,* pp. 147-48.
7. William Tiller "Creating a New Functional Model of Body Healing Energies," *Journal of Holistic Health* (San Diego: The Word Shop, 1978), p. 73.
8. Ibid.
9. *Science Digest,* John Gliedman, op. cit.
10. Cho, *Fourth,* op. cit. pp. 38-40.
11. Cho, *The Fourth Dimension, Volume Two* (Bridge Publishing, 1983), p. 38.

12. Cho, *Fourth*, p. 43.
13. Cho, *Fourth, Volume Two*, pp. 26-27.
14. Martin L. Gross, *The Psychological Society* (Random House, 1978), pp. 43-44.
15. *Personal Christianity* newsletter, Aug. 1979, C. S. Lovett, "The Medicine of Your Mind."
16. Ralph Wilkerson, *ESP or HSP?—Exploring Your Latent Seventh Sense* (Melodyland Publishers, 1978), pp. 258-59.
17. *Association for Humanistic Psychology Newsletter*, Feb. 1984.
18. Ibid.
19. Thomas Szasz, *The Myth of Psychotherapy* (Doubleday, 1978), pp. 27-28.
20. Walter Bromberg, *From Shaman to Psychotherapist* (Chicago, 1975), p. 336.
21. *The Journal of Holistic Health,* 1977, Jack Gibb, "Psycho-Sociological Aspects of Holistic Health," p. 44.
22. Michael Harner, *The Way of the Shaman* (Harper & Row, 1980), p. 136.
23. Ibid., p. 20.

CHAPTER NINE

1. John and Paula Sandford, *The Transformation of the Inner Man* (Logos, 1982), pp. vi, 4.
2. Agnes Sanford, *The Healing Light* (Macalester, 1947), pp. 125-26, 165; Sanford, *The Healing Gifts of the Spirit* (Revell, 1982), pp. 140-41.
3. Sanford, *Gifts,* p. 48.
4. Sanford, *Light,* p. 146.
5. Ibid., pp. 10, 34-35.
6. Ibid, p. 30.
7. Ibid., p. 74.
8. Ibid., pp. 60, 65-67.
9. Ibid., pp. 28, 37, 94-95, 137-47.
10. Ibid., pp. 63-64, 68, 112.
11. Agnes Sanford, *The Healing Gifts of the Spirit* (Fleming H. Revell, 1966), p. 48.
12. Ibid., pp. 49, 131.
13. Sanford, *Light,* pp. 143-44.
14. Richard Foster, *Celebration of Discipline* (Harper & Row, 1978), p. 36.
15. William L. Vaswig, *I Prayed, He Answered* (Augsburg, 1977), pp. 59, 88-89.
16. Foster, *Celebration,* pp. 16, 22-27, 36, 136, 169-70.
17. Ibid., p. 136.
18. Sanford, *Light,* op. cit. pp. 98-113, 142-43.
19. Ibid., inside front cover.
20. Sanford, *Gifts*, op. cit. p. 49.
21. Ibid., p. 45.
22. Ibid., p. 49.
23. Ibid., p. 119.
24. Ibid., p. 152.
25. Ibid., p. 101.
26. Ibid., pp. 102-18, etc.

27. Robert L. Wise, *Healing of the Past* (Presbyterian and Reformed Renewal Ministries International, 1984), p. 9.
28. Ibid., p. 23.
29. Ibid., p. 24.
30. Ibid., p. 22.
31. Ibid., p. 30.
32. Morton T. Kelsey, *Christo-Psychology* (Crossroad, 1982), pp. 136-37; Kelsey, *Discernment: A Study in Ecstasy and Evil* (Paulist Press, 1978), pp. 54-55, 76-77, etc.
33. Morton T. Kelsey, *The Christian and The Supernatural* (Augsburg, 1976), pp. 113-23.
34. Ibid., pp. 93, 109, 113, 142.
35. Kelsey, *Christo,* p. 39, 148-49; see also Kelsey, *Afterlife: The Other Side of Dying.*
36. Ibid., p. 28.
37. Kelsey, *Supernatural,* pp. 120-43.
38. Ibid., p. 102.
39. Ibid., p. 149.
40. Ibid., p. 111.
41. Ibid., p. 93.
42. Ibid.
43. Ibid., pp. 100-43, etc.
44. Robert Schuller, *Peace of Mind Through Possibility Thinking* (Fleming H. Revell, 1977), pp. 131-32.
45. Kelsey, *Dreams: A Way to Listen To God* (Paulist Press, 1978), pp. 6, 29, 30.
46. Ibid.
47. Ibid.
48. Ibid.
49. Ibid.
50. Ibid., p. 29.
51. Morton Kelsey, *Healing and Christianity* (Harper & Row, 1976), p. 51.
52. Harner, *Shaman,* op. cit. p. 136.
53. Ibid., p. 20.
54. Ibid., pp. 20, 50.
55. William Fezler, Ph.D., *Just Imagine: A Guide to Materialization Using Imagery* (Laurida Books, 1980), Introduction.
56. Carl Rogers, *A Way of Becoming* (Houghton Mifflin, 1980), p. 352.
57. Kelsey, *Christo,* pp. 153-54.
58. Barbara Hannah, *Encounters With The Soul: Active Imagination as Developed by C. G. Jung,* back cover.
59. *Brain/Mind Bulletin,* Apr. 16, 1984, p. 3.

CHAPTER TEN

1. Fezler, *Imagine,* Introduction.
2. Adelaide Bry and Marjorie Bair, *Visualization* (Barnes and Noble, 1979).
3. *New Age Source,* Sept. 1982, Laurie Warner, M.A., "New Age Energies," p. 13.

4. Psychosynthesis Institute, *Synthesis Two: The Realization of the Self,* pp. 119-20.
5. Fezler, *Imagine,* p. 16.
6. Sanford, *Light,* p. 145.
7. Cho, *Fourth,* pp. 39-44.
8. *The Journal of Transpersonal Psychology,* 1984, Vol. 16, No. 1, pp. 108, 21-23.
9. Mike Samuels and Nancy Samuels, *Seeing With The Mind's Eye* (Random House, 1975), pp. 30-33.
10. Amy Wallace and Bill Henkin, *The Psychic Healing Book: How to Develop Your Psychic Potential,* (Wingbow Press, 1982) p. 43.
11. Steller, *Psi Healing,* p. 41.
12. Shakti Gawain, *Creative Visualization* (Whatever Publishing, 1978), pp. 13, 20.
13. Ibid., Acknowledgements.
14. David Conway, *Magic: An Occult Primer,* p. 59.
15. Bry, *Visualization,* p. 40.
16. Document on file.
17. Document on file.
18. Psychosynthesis Institute, *Synthesis Two,* op. cit. pp. 119-20.
19. Dane Rudhyar, *Occult Preparations For A New Age* (The Theosophical Publishing House, 1975), pp. 8-11.
20. Cho, *Fourth,* p. 48.
21. Foster, *Celebration,* pp. 27.
22. Ibid., p. 26.
23. Cho, *Fourth,* Volume Two, pp. 25-28, 68; *Fourth,* p. 44.
24. Fezler, *Imagine,* pp. 15, 16.
25. Norman Vincent Peale, *Positive Imaging* (Revell, 1982), p. 1.
26. Bunny Marks, Tape of inspirational talk.
27. Sanford, *Light,* p. 65.
28. Sanford, *Gifts,* p. 49.
29. Sanford, *Light,* p. 66.
30. Ibid., p. 69.
31. Ibid., p. 68.
32. Norman Vincent Peale, *Positive Imaging* (Fleming H. Revell, 1982), p. 20.
33. Ibid. pp. 16, 17.
34. Ibid., Introduction.

CHAPTER ELEVEN

1. *The Wall Street Journal,* May 12, 1983, pp. 1-2.
2. Harner, *Shaman,* pp. xi, 41.
3. Glenn Clark, *The Soul's Desire,* p. 13.
4. Charles Braden, *Spirits In Rebellion* (Southern Methodist University Press), pp. 392, 396.
5. Ibid., p. 390.
6. Ibid., p. 387.
7. Ibid., p. 391.
8. *Family Weekly,* Ventura Free Press, April 15, 1984, Cover Story.
9. From a transcript of the Phil Donahue Show, October 23, 1984.

10. Robert Schuller, address at Unity Village, Unity tape.
11. Ibid.
12. *The Word of Faith*, November 1984, p. 3.
13. Dave Hunt, *Peace, Prosperity, and the Coming Holocaust* (Harvest House, 1983), pp. 117-20.
14. David Stoop, *Self-Talk: Key to Personal Growth* (Revell, 1982), p. 135.
15. Sanford, *Light*, p. 32.
16. Denis Waitley, *The Winner's Edge*, p. 80.
17. Denis Waitley, *Seeds of Greatness*, pp. 60-61.
18. *New Thought*, Autumn 1983, Ann B. Martin, "The Great American Educational Blackout," p. 6.
19. Vaswig, *I Prayed*, pp. 55-56.
20. Ibid., pp. 51-52.
21. Waitley, *Seeds,* p. 61.
22. Waitley, *Winner's,* p. 61.
23. C. S. Lovett, *Longing To Be Loved* (Personal Christianity, 1982), p. 85.
24. Capps, *Tongue,* p. 129.
25. Ibid., p. 130.
26. Ibid., pp. 132, 135.
27. Alain Danielou, *Hindu Polytheism* (Pantheon Books), p. 28.
28. Sir John Woodroffe, *The Garland of Letters: Studies in the Mantra-Shastra,* (Ganesh & Co.), p. 261.
29. *The Coming Revolution,* Spring 1981, Elizabeth Clare Prophet, "The Control of the Human Aura Through the Service of the Spoken Word," p. 36.
30. Irving Dardik and Denis Waitley, *Quantum Fitness*, p. 37.
31. Jose Silva and Philip Miele, *The Silva Mind Control Method* (Pocket Books, 1977), pp. 32, 36.
32. Annie Besant and C. W. Leadbeater, *Thought Forms* (The Theosophical Publishing House, 1971), pp. 3, 15.
33. Harner, *Shaman,* p. 20.
34. Ibid., p. 137.
35. Mike Samuels, *Spirit Guides: Access to Inner Worlds.*
36. C. S. Lovett, *Longing,* pp. 13-16, 87-90.
37. Calvin Miller, *The Table of Inwardness* (Inter-Varsity Press, 1984), pp. 93-94.
38. Lovett, *Longing,* p. 68.
39. Rita Bennett, *You Can Be Emotionally Free* (Fleming H. Revell, 1982), p. 85.
40. Miller, op. cit. p. 94.
41. Dennis Linn, Matthew Linn, and Sheila Fabricant, *Praying With Another For Healing* (Paulist Press, 1984), p. 30.
42. Foster, *Celebration,* p. 26.
43. Ruth Carter Stapleton, *The Experience of Inner Healing* (Word Books, 1977), p. 17.
44. Foster, *Celebration,* p. 27.
45. Bennett, *Free,* p. 118.
46. A. W. Tozer, *That Incredible Christian* (Christian Publications, 1964), p. 68.
47. Ibid., pp. 68-69.

48. Frank Laubach, *Practicing His Presence: Brother Lawrence, Frank Laubach* (Christian Books, 1973), ed. Gene Edwards, pp. 10-11.
49. John Calvin, *Institutes of the Christian Religion,* Book I, p. 46.
50. Lovett, *Longing,* p. 89.
51. J. I. Packer, *Knowing God* (Inter-Varsity Press, 1973), pp. 38, 39, 41, 42.
52. C. S. Lewis, *The Screwtape Letters* (Spire, 1976), pp. 34-35.

CHAPTER TWELVE

1. Christian Life Magazine, July 1984, Robert L. Wise, "Healing of the Memories: A Prayer Therapy For You?" pp. 63-64.
2. Ibid.
3. Bennett, *Free,* p. 116.
4. Ibid., p. 122.
5. Ibid., p. 138.
6. Lovett, *Longing,* pp. 88, 103, 113.
7. Foster, *Celebration,* p. 22.
8. C. G. Jung, *Memories, Dreams, Reflections* (Pantheon, 1963), p. 176.
9. Kelsey, *Christo,* p. 13.
10. John Wimber, *Signs and Wonders and Church Growth* (Vineyard Ministries International, 1985), Introduction.
11. Dennis Linn, Matthew Linn, *Healing Life's Hurts* (Paulist Press, 1978), p. 98.
12. Vaswig, *I Prayed,* pp. 59, 72.
13. Kelsey, *Christo,* p. 149.
14. Francis MacNutt, *Healing* (Ave Maria Press, 1974), p. 188.
15. Linns and Fabricant, *Praying,* pp. 13,16-18.
16. Wimber, op. cit. pp. 8-9.
17. *The Ojai Foundation,* 1985 Schedule of Retreats, pp. 5-6.
18. Bobgans, *Psychological Way,* pp. 85-89.
19. *The Tarrytown Letter,* December 1983, p. 3.
20. Ibid.
21. Ibid.
22. Rita Bennett, *How To Pray For Inner Healing For Yourself and Others* (Fleming H. Revell, 1984), p. 99.
23. Ibid., p. 99; Bennett, *Free*, pp. 79-107.
24. Bennett, *How To,* p. 89.
25. Francis MacNutt, *Healing* (Ave Maria Press, 1974), p. 186.
26. Stapleton, *Experience,* pp. 22-23.
27. MacNutt, *Healing,* p. 183.
28. From a tape of her Feb. 26, 1978, talk at Christ Universal Temple, Chicago, IL.
29. Lyle E. Bourne, Jr. and Bruce R. Eckstrand, *Psychology, Its Principles and Meanings,* Second Edition (Holt, Rinehart and Winston, 1976), p. 326.
30. Ibid., p. 23.
31. *The Seduction of Christianity Seminar*, Nov. 1984, from Tape No. 3 by Martin Bobgan, available from Spread The Good News Ministries, 3093 Rawlins, Ave., Salem, OR 97303.

32. Camille B. Wortman and Elizabeth F. Loftus, *Psychology* (Alfred A. Knopf, 1981), p. 408.
33. Morton T. Kelsey, *Healing and Christianity* (Harper & Row, 1977), p. 286.
34. B. R. Hergenbahn, *An Introduction To Theories of Personality* (Prentice-Hall, 1980), p. 19.
35. Ibid., p. 33.
36. Ibid., p. 41.
37. Kelsey, *Healing,* pp. 282, 285.
38. Bobgan, *Seduction.*
39. John and Paula Sandford, *The Transformation of the Inner Man* (Bridge Publishing, 1982), Front Cover.
40. Ibid., p. 102.
41. Ibid., pp. 256-57.
42. *Prime Time,* October 1980, Carol Tavris, "The Freedom To Change," p. 28.
43. Martin L. Gross, *The Psychological Society* (Random House, 1978), pp. 197-98.

CHAPTER THIRTEEN

1. Jay E. Adams, *The Use of the Scriptures in Counseling* (Baker Book House, 1975), p. 1.
2. Jay E. Adams, *More Than Redemption* (Baker Book House, 1979), pp. xi-xii.
3. Adams, *Use of Scriptures,* p. 3.
4. Paul D. Meier, M.D., Frank B. Minirth, M.D., Frank Wichern, Ph.D., *Introduction to Psychology and Counseling* (Baker Book House, 1982), pp. 15-18.
5. Ibid., p. 16.
6. G. Campbell Morgan, *The Life of The Christian* (Baker Book House, 1976), pp. 22-23.
7. James Dobson, *Hide or Seek* (Revell, 1974), pp. 12-13.
8. Zig Ziglar, *See You At the Top* (Pelican, 1975), pp. 90-91.
9. Ibid. pp. 84,88.
10. *Brain/Mind Bulletin,* September 10, 1984, "Nathaniel Branden Rises to the Defense of Self," p. 3.
11. William Law, *The Power of the Spirit* (Christian Literature Crusade, 1971), ed. Dave Hunt, pp. 141-44.
12. David G. Meyers, *The Inflated Self* (The Seabury Press, 1980), pp. 23-24.
13. A. W. Tozer, *Man the Dwelling Place of God* (Christian Publications, 1976), p. 71.
14. Freidrich Nietzsche, *Thus Spake Zarathustra* (Modern Library), p. 75.
15. Tozer, op. cit. p. 72.
16. *Consciousness: Brain States of Awareness, and Mysticism,* ed. Daniel Goleman, Richard Davidson, "Psychiatry and the Sacred," Jacob Needleman, p. 209.
17. Gross, op cit. p. 16.
18. Dorothy Tennov, *Psychiatry: The Hazardous Cure* (Abelard-Schuman, 1975), p. 83.

19. *The National Educator,* July 1980, Roger Mills, "Psychology Goes Insane, Botches Role As Science," p. 14.
20. Martin and Deidre Bobgans, *The Psychological Way/The Spiritual Way* (Bethany House Fellowship, 1979), p. 23.
21. Jerome Frank, "Mental Health In a Fragmented Society," *American Journal of Orthopsychiatry,* July 1979, p. 404.
22. Jolan Jacobi, *The Psychology of C.G. Jung* (Yale University Press, 1973).
23. *Los Angeles Times,* March 23, 1980, Lance Lee, "American Psychoanalysis: Looking Beyond the Ethical Disease," Part VI, p. 3.
24. *The Christian Vision: Man In Society* ed. Lynne Morris, Paul C. Vitz, "A Covenant Theory of Personality: A Theoretical Introduction," p. 77.
25. William Kirk Kilpatrick, *Psychological Seduction* (Thomas Nelson, 1983), p. 31.
26. Paul Vitz, *Psychology As Religion: The Cult of Self- Worship* (Eerdmans, 1977), p. 13.
27. Gross, op. cit., pp. 195-231.
28. Richard Feynman et al, *The Feynman Lectures on Physics* (Reading, 1963), Vol. 1, pp. 3-8.
29. *Pastoral Renewal,* March 1983, "The Kohlberg Phenomenon, Part I: An Interview With Paul Vitz," p. 63.
30. Karl Popper, "Scientific Theory and Falsifiability," *Perspectives In Philosophy,* Ed. Robert N. Beck (Holt, Rinehart, Winston, 1975), p. 342.
31. E. Fuller Torrey, *The Mind Games: Witchdoctors and Psychiatrists* (Emerson Hall, 1972), p. 8.
32. From an interview with Dr. Shapiro reported by Martin L. Gross, op. cit. p. 230.
33. Jonas Robitscher, *The Powers of Psychiatry* (Houghton, Mifflin, 1980), p. 9.
34. *On 1984* (Stanford Alumni Association, 1984), Ed. Peter Stansky, pp. 209-210.
35. Ibid., p. 211.

CHAPTER FOURTEEN

1. Letter on file.
2. Letter on file.
3. *Saturday Evening Post,* Dec. 1984, as cited in *Times Arrow,* Apr. 1985, p. 8.
4. E. W. Kenyon, *The Blood Covenant* (Kenyon Gospel Publishing), p. 53.
5. Kenneth Copeland, "The Force of Love," Tape BCC-56.
6. Ed. Gordon Lindsay, *Spiritual Hunger, The God-Men and Other Sermons by Dr. John G. Lake* (Christ For the Nations, Inc., 1976), pp. 20-21.
7. Earl Paulk, *Satan Unmasked* (K Dimension Publishing, 1984), pp. 96-97.
8. "Pat Robertson, Richard Roberts, Rex Humbard, Dr. Robert Schuller, Seminar by Word of Faith Satellite Network," Tape No. 1 of a four-tape series, Robert Tilton Ministries, P.O. Box 819000, Dallas, TX 75381.
9. *Harvest Time,* June 1984, p. 2.
10. *Christianity Today,* Mar. 1, 1985, "Is God A Psychotherapist?" p. 21.
11. Ibid., p. 22.
12. M. Scott Peck, *The Road Less Traveled* (Simon and Schuster, 1978), pp. 269-70.
13. Psalm 145:13; Daniel 4:3,34; 7:14,27; 2 Peter 1:11.

DAVE HUNT is an internationally known author and lecturer. His extensive research has taken him to more than 40 countries of the world. Dave's research/consulting expertise has contributed to three powerful films including the Billy Graham film *Time to Run*.

Other Books by Dave Hunt:

Beyond Seduction (newly released sequel to *The Seduction of Christianity*)—a strong call back to the Word of God and a true biblical foundation with dependence upon God alone.

Secret Invasion—the suspense-filled true story of Hans Kristian's journey from pastor to "spy, thief, and robber" as he smuggles Bibles to persecuted Christians in Russia and Eastern Europe.

The God Makers—a unique, carefully researched exposé of Mormonism that brings staggering new insights.

The Death of a Guru—Yogi Rabindranath Maharaj's story of his difficult search for meaning and his struggle to choose between Hinduism and Christ.

The Cult Explosion—must reading for anyone wanting to understand the subtle ways cults prey upon people's fears and needs.

Peace, Prosperity, and the Coming Holocaust (sequel to *The Cult Explosion*)—a startling account of the rapidly growing New Age Movement and its relation to the return of Jesus Christ.

T.A. McMAHON holds a master's degree in communications and has researched and written numerous Christian documentaries. He and his wife and four children live in southern California.

For a catalog of audio and video tapes and other information, questions, or comments concerning the subject matter of this book, please write to:

> Christian Information Bureau
> P.O. Box 3120
> Camarillo, CA 93011

Please enclose a self-addressed stamped envelope.